Creative Marketing Communications

Creative Marketing Communications

3rd edition

A PRACTICAL GUIDE TO PLANNING, SKILLS AND TECHNIQUES

DANIEL YADIN

IN ASSOCIATION WITH
Marketing

KOGAN PAGE

First published in 1994
Second edition 1998
Third edition 2001

Kogan Page Limited
120 Pentonville Road
London
N1 9JN
UK

Kogan Page Limited
163 Central Avenue, Suite 2
Dover
NH 03820
USA

British Library Cataloguing in Publication Data

A CIP record for this book is available from the British Library.

ISBN 0 7494 3458 9

Typeset by Jean Cussons Typesetting, Diss, Norfolk
Printed and bound in Great Britain by Clays Ltd, St Ives plc

Contents

Introduction: A Practical Book for Practical Marketers

Advertising is the most fun you can have with your clothes on
– Jerry Della Femina

You've seen it done many times. You have probably admired the technique. You may have wondered how it was done, and how you could perfect the technique for yourself. I am, of course, talking about sales-winning marketing communications. Probably first-class advertisements or editorial features that really motivated you or changed your mind about something important.

The first edition of this book was conceived while lecturing to management executives at the Chartered Institute of Marketing and other training organisations. Many delegates confided that creative tasks, especially copywriting, had been landed on them at short notice. The problem was always that they had few of the skills necessary to handle the challenge. Naturally, this was not their fault, but the problem remained to be solved. This change now seems a permanent feature of marketing life; and growing in other business areas.

This third edition, like the first two, is a practical answer. There is also much more of it. There are new chapters on branding and positioning, the Internet, the law and the effective use of words and printing techniques. There is an excellent new one on what's what in marketing communications, and how it works. It is your personal, practical companion to creating sales-winning marketing communications.

THEORY INTO PRACTICE

I am a pragmatic, professional marketing communicator, and turn theory into practice every working day. Now that you have this book, I hope you will treat it as a personal guide to successful marketing communications for your own organisation. Using it as I have prescribed, you will be well-equipped to put into action, day by day, the thinking and techniques I have outlined.

There are many hundreds of ambitious CIM students in full-time employment, working towards the Certificate and Diploma. The Central London Branch of CIM alone has nearly 2,000. It's a tough programme, and the exams are even tougher. If you are potential DipM or MCIM, and this book helps you, I shall be well pleased. You have my best wishes for success.

I also commend this book to a generation of bright, enthusiastic CAM students. Because of changes in the CAM syllabus, many will have lost a chance to glimpse the intriguing creative side of marketing communications. I hope they will pick up a flavour of it here.

Finally, because you can gain so much from this book, I trust you will regard it as an excellent return on your investment.

HOW YOU BENEFIT FROM THIS BOOK

It offers you practical advice on creating successful marketing communications. It is about applying the art of good salesmanship to the craft of advertising, public relations and sales promotion.

Above all, it's about motivation, persuasion and seduction. Think of it as the art of enticing and seducing your customer into changing his or her attitude, and making a decision in favour of your brand, product, service or ideas.

These are proven communication techniques. In the publicity mix, you select different technique combinations for different marketing situations and target audiences. Selecting which will work for your current marketing plans is up to your good judgement. The creative ammunition is in these pages.

WHO WILL BENEFIT

Creative Marketing Communications is for experienced marketers striving for greater impact from their efforts, and better value for their budgets. It also benefits those aiming for a higher order of professionalism.

It is particularly for directors, managers and executives responsible for:

- advertising
- brand management
- corporate communications
- direct mail
- exporting
- importing
- marketing
- marketing communications
- marketing training
- marketing services
- merchandising
- product management
- public relations
- sales
- sales management
- sales promotion.

Plus ...

- owners and managers of small businesses
- directors and managers of charities and non-profit organisations with modest promotional budgets
- advertising agency marketing and creative departments
- everyone using marketing communications to generate greater response and more sales.

Even if you are a copywriter, print buyer, art director, designer, press or print production specialist, it is worth your while having this book for consultation whenever the need arises.

HOW TO USE THIS BOOK

◼ Most chapters start with a checklist Guideline, the main points of a particular technique. This is a reference to use as an *aide mémoire*.

It is followed by:

◼ A tutorial, point by point, based on the Guidelines.

This format gives you the opportunity to study in detail a technique you want to use. Later, when you need to refer quickly, just consult the Guidelines.

THANKS

My thanks to Ruth Yadin for checking the typescript; and to Martyn Davis, for reading the proofs and making many helpful comments and suggestions.

NOTES

◼ Throughout this book, for the sake of brevity and simplicity, man embraces woman, so to speak; 'he' is used to include 'she'.
◼ In the text, you will discover repetition of certain ideas, sentences and phrases. This is quite deliberate. It allows Guidelines and other material to be presented in different places complete and self-contained.
◼ Certain brand and personal names, addresses, telephone and fax numbers in advertisement and script examples have been created especially for this book. They are solely for illustration purposes.

Part 1

Practical Planning Techniques

1

Creative Planning Techniques

Every time you fail to plan, you plan to fail.
— *Anonymous but prudent marketer*

The problem with creative planning is that you always need it, but hardly ever have time to do it.

Inspiration sometimes does indeed come to marketing creatives, but is unreliable. Anyone who tells you that great campaigns are conceived in the bath is probably lying. To meet deadlines, you need something more professional, more structured and systematic.

Creative planning starts with the marketing plan. This is a comprehensive working document, detailing the marketing team's total approach for the forthcoming campaign. Examine it; familiarise yourself with its contents. Much of what is regarded as inspiration can be found within. With a bit of study, great creative ideas can drop straight into your lap.

If the marketing team has done its job well – and they usually do – creative planning can save you time, as well as organise your thinking and creativity.

Brand management is in the ideal position to analyse the marketing plan. A good brand manager will digest the plan, and abstract the elements needed for preparing integrated creative proposals. Agency account managers usually do this for their creative teams.

If you are in a marketing department and assigned a creative task, you should be able to lift out the creative elements from the marketing plan for yourself.

GUIDELINES

- At whom is the communication aimed?
- What are the media and delivery methods?
- What is the specific objective of the communication?
- What information is to be conveyed?
- What is the lead benefit?
- What satisfactions must be targeted?
- What are my recipient's expectations from this communication?
- How will I meet them?
- What response do I want from this communication?
- My communication objective will be achieved if my customer thinks, believes, or is convinced that ...

EXPLOITING THESE TECHNIQUES

This is a *practical checklist*. It helps to organise your thinking for creative marketing communications, and acts as a model for evaluating the results.

It is not a substitute for thought. It is an essential aid to better organised planning, and faster, more accurate fulfilment of your communications objectives.

At whom is the communication aimed?
You need to know and understand your target audience. For example: are your targets new users, existing users, or brand-switchers? See Figure 1.1.

However, there may be a complex pass-along route for your proposition: initiators, specifiers, influencers, decision-takers, buyers, end-users. Each may need different treatment and motiva-

TARGET AUDIENCES

When identifying target audiences, you must also identify what individual messages you need to deliver. It is not as straightforward as it seems. Different targets need different approaches. For example, existing users of your product will not respond to a message aimed at potential users. It is difficult, if not sometimes impossible, to aim a single message at all your target audiences, and make it work. But this is what some advertisers do. To help you decide which messages to create for your markets, consider the four main categories of target audience, and their sub-categories.

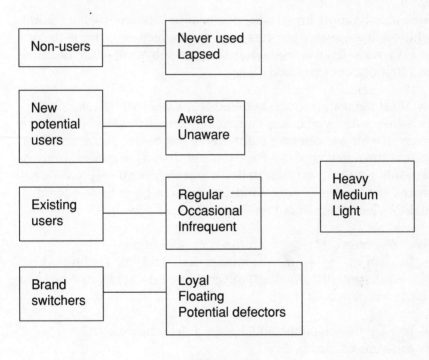

Figure 1.1

tions to push them over the edge; they may all have to agree, separately and together, on your proposition.

What are the media and delivery methods?
The same thinking applies here. You also need to consider whether your communication is delivered via printed or broadcast media, by mail; or delivered by a salesman and left with a customer for further study and decision-making.

What is the specific objective of the communication?
Is it, for example, to generate enquiries or sales leads, or to elicit
money off the page? Decide here.

What information is to be conveyed?
You need to list all the information needed for this communication,
and arrange it in order of priority.

What is the lead benefit?
Seek out the most important, practical or attractive selling point,
which will motivate your customer most effectively. This is the one
to lead with. Consider making this the subject of your headline
and first paragraph of body copy.

What satisfactions must be targeted? How will I meet them?
Consider what your target audience actually wants to hear or
learn. If you are offering solutions to problems, make sure you
feature them in your copy. For example: doctors in general practice
certainly want to cure their patients, but they want empty waiting-
rooms even more. If your product can help them to achieve this,
make it clear; think about making it the lead benefit.

What response do I want from this communication?
Is the appeal of your communication, and its leading ideas,
powerful enough to make your customer do what you need to
fulfil your objective:

▓ pick up the telephone and ask for a demonstration?
▓ call a credit-card hotline?
▓ fill in a coupon? visit a store or office?
▓ visit an exhibition?
▓ change his fixed ideas?
▓ take a decision in favour of your brand?

*My communication objective will be achieved if my customer thinks,
believes or is convinced that ...*
This is the toughest of all the tasks in the chapter, but essential if
you are to arrive at the correct message.

The easiest way is to write the answer out in full, using your
customer's thoughts as your guide.

If you find it difficult to resolve right away, go back to your brief. Then handcuff yourself to your desk until you have completed the answer completely and honestly.

A tiny consolation: you are not alone here. I and many of my most experienced colleagues often find this task difficult. It does get a little easier with practice, however.

CREATIVE PLANNING CHECKLIST

One of the most important things you need to do at the planning stage is to understand what markets you are in. You need to know what your position is within these markets. You must also understand the marketing conditions you are working in. Needless to say, you need to get to know your product intimately.

The checklist below is a framework of what you need to know. You will, of course, develop and add to it as your experience and commitment to structured planning grows.

1. **Product name and description.**
2. **Product background:**
   a. Where are we now?
      product age
      market share and position
      how long we have been there
      competition profile and activity
      other factors
   b. How did we get here?
      Marketing & advertising activities
      track record
      competitors' activities
      their track record
   c. Where could we be:
      market share
      sales
      distribution
   d. How do we get there?
      marketing objectives
      define problems
      outline solution
      promotion objectives
3. **Target audience:**
   detailed profile
   socio-economics
   demographics
   psychographics
   buyer psychology
   media delivery
   product use
   ability to respond
   attitude to product now
   secondary targets
4. **Positioning mode:**
   See your marketing plan
5. **Desired brand image:**
   See your marketing plan
6. **The product:**

features
associated consumer
   benefits
which do we use in this
   campaign?
in which order?
product information:
   technical
   literature to be
   studied
background research
people to be interviewed
see, handle and try
   product

7. **Desired response:**
precisely what must this
   campaign achieve?
what responses do we
   want from:
   the distributors
   the consumers
precisely what do we want
   from each advertisement
   from each commercial
   from each brochure and
   leaflet
   from each page
outline the follow-up
   procedure

8. **Offer and promise:**
exactly what is on offer?
what are we selling?
what is the consumer
   buying?
what promises must we
   make?

9. **Single-minded
proposition:**
what is the key consumer
   proposition?

what is the most
   motivating and
   differentiating thing we
   can say to launch the
   proposition?

10. **Substantiation:**
what is the substantiation
   for propositions we are
   using?
can we substantiate
   everything we say in
   copy?

11. **Communication goals:**
communication
   objectives
creative platform
demonstration and
   illustration
rational: selling points
           what priority?
emotional: triggers
          consumer
          psychology
tone of voice

12. **Media delivery:**
media schedule
mechanical data
database

13. **Visual considerations:**
can we frame this
   proposition visually?
illustrations to be used
references and sources
advertiser information for
   visual

14. **Mandatory inclusions:**
technical
creative
legal
logos, slogans, straplines

corporate mandatories,
   including colours
all address, 'phone and fax
   data to be verified
15. **Deadlines:**
copy
visuals

artwork
approvals
copy dates
production schedule
print schedule
16. **Have we forgotten anything?**

2

Creative Briefings

When I write an advertisement, I don't want you to tell me you find it creative. I want you to find it so interesting that you buy the product.

– David Ogilvy

CREATIVE BRIEF

- Job no: Date: Brand name:
- Background: *See attached background statement.*
- Consumers' attitude: *See attached research.*
- Target audience: *See consumer profile attached.*
    - New users
    - Existing users
    - Brand-switch
- The objective.
- Key proposition.
- Headline promise and benefit.
- Features and benefits. *NB: They are not the same!*
- Associated and secondary benefits.
- Other messages, motivations, offers and propositions to be considered.
- Branding devices to be used.
- Why should the consumer try or buy *this* brand?
- Tone of voice: *eg warm and friendly, conservative and formal.*
- Consumer action required.

■ Action/reply elements.
■ Mandatory inclusions.
■ Desired response. *My creative objective will be fulfilled if, having read this copy, my target audience is convinced that ...*
■ Media: *See attached media briefing and schedule.*
■ Timings: *Copy, visuals, presentations, revisions, artwork, copy dates.*

This is a practical briefing checklist; we use it every working day in our own business. It is not a substitute for thought, but an aid to better organised creative thinking. An essential discipline for briefing your colleagues, it also helps to discipline those briefing *you.*

It helps you to arrive at the *correct* messages, which you can hone to perfection, and avoid wasting time on incorrect ones.

This is just about the minimum you need for getting started on your next creative assignment. You will certainly be adding practical elements of your own – using your professional experience to guide you. In other words, the hard way.

Date, job number and brand
If you have several jobs running at the same time, you must have a clear system of identification. If you haven't, set one up now.

Background
There should always be a background statement available. This can range from the complete history of the brand to a simple statement of intent. If you are launching a brand, you need to see the marketing and promotion briefs in their entirety. A good account manager usually produces a digest for creative purposes, and simplifies things for you.

Consumers' attitude
The same applies. The way your consumers feel or use the brand may have changed since the previous campaign; the research keeps you up to date.

Target audience
Because you want specific results from different target audiences, the messages you aim at them should also be specific.

New users: you want them to start using your product, to try your brand for the first time.

Existing users: you want them to use more of the brand, or use it more frequently.

Brand-switch: you want them to come over to your brand.

Bear in mind that there may be considerable overlap among these categories.

The objective
1. The objective of the campaign, clearly stated in terms you can use.
2. Answer these questions:
   – What precisely does this advertisement, mailer or brochure have to achieve?
   – What response must the copy produce?

Key proposition
Decide on the *lead benefit*: the single, strongest most important sales point in the whole brief which will best motivate your reader, viewer or listener.

Headline promise and benefit
The major sales point you have decided on now needs to be written as a persuasive headline. You may need to consider using a sub-headline as well. Remember to link your first line, sentence and paragraph of body copy to it.

Features and benefits
The features and facts you are promoting are what your product does; the benefits are what your product does *for your customer*!

In copy, features and benefits should always be locked together. Sometimes it is best to show only the benefits. This applies especially when space and time are restricted. Whatever you decide, every consumer benefit must have a feature behind it. And every product feature shown as a consumer benefit.

Associated and secondary benefits
Guarantees, warranties and other benefits which do not form part of your main persuasion, but nevertheless reward the reader for deciding on your brand.

Branding devices to be used
If your product has a strong branding device, strive to build it in to your headline copy. Look at Boots, The Halifax, Daewoo, IBM, Microsoft, and other strong branders in today's media.

Why should the consumer try or buy this brand?
In copywriting, intellectual honesty is greater than absolute truth. Examine what you have written and designed. If you can see the answer to this question in it, you have succeeded. If you cannot, start again.

Tone of voice
Tailor the technique to the target. Decide which effect you want to achieve, relative to the target audience and its needs.

Consumer action required
Decide exactly what you want your reader, viewer and listener to do after absorbing your message.

Action/reply elements
Choose the elements which maximise it most efficiently. Consider coupon, Freepost, telephone, free-phone, 0800, 0345, fax – and other reply tools at your disposal.

Mandatory inclusions
Space and airtime are always limited, so you need to reserve room for mandatories in your copy. Financial, tobacco and medical products have specific mandatories. Don't forget logos, straplines and campaign slogans.

Desired response
This is the final test of your ability to drive the message home and get the response you want. Complete the sentence; be honest about it.

Media

The media schedule will give you a great deal of information about your target audience. Insist on seeing the schedule, and the research data that goes with it.

Timings

Time is not elastic. Make sure you have enough time to complete your assignment. If not, you may have to work at night. Don't we all?

GETTING AND GIVING A CREATIVE BRIEFING

Creatives are specialists. Like you, they are professionals; they deserve to be treated in a professional way.

- Always give a clear brief.
- Before every briefing, make up your mind what you want.
- Don't mess them about. Don't keep on changing your mind.
- Be prepared to take advice. Creatives know their jobs as well as you do yours. They should be *encouraged* to make a contribution.
- Insist on work of the highest quality; make it clear that this is what you are buying.
- Get a reputation for paying promptly. It's amazing how the most skilled creatives tend to gravitate to your office.

When you are receiving a briefing from your boss, colleagues or other non-creatives, make sure you get these guidelines working for you.

3

Branding and Positioning

Try to give each advertiser a becoming style. To create the right individuality is a supreme accomplishment.

– *Claude Hopkins*

BRANDING

This is the use of techniques by which a company, organisation or product distinguishes itself from others. This is how it expresses its identity and function in its markets.

In modern marketing thinking, branding is the process of identifying and differentiating a product or service, and establishing its uniqueness. In practice, of course, we know it's much more than that.

Rosser Reeves and David Ogilvy are the two gurus primarily responsible for the modern concept of branding. Reeves seeks to establish the branding of a product by means of facts and reason. Ogilvy seeks to make a product famous in its market by the impact of emotion.

In reality, branding is a mixture of both these concepts. It is the process of presenting your product to your customers, with strong reasons for trying or buying it; seducing them into it.

In proposing this, I am not quarrelling either with Reeves or Ogilvy. I am simply trying to make branding more tangible as a technique, because we have to use it in our daily work.

Branding is part of the job of being sensitive to how customers perceive your product or company. You use branding to send signals to customers at whom you have aimed the product, and who will benefit from possessing or using it.

Consider some advantages of branding:

■ The product is more easily remembered and identified.
■ It provides strong links between advertising and other forms of promotion. For example, public relations, sales promotion, sponsorship and packaging.
■ It provides a bridge between the different media you are using, such as press, television, radio and created media; and between campaigns.
■ A brand has *promotional value*. Customer benefits can be associated with it.
■ New products can be introduced more easily under a well-established, respected brand name. This applies equally to existing markets as to new ones. Take Heinz, Coke, Cadbury and Canon as examples.

Heinz don't have to start from the beginning and introduce themselves when launching a new packaged product.

Canon operate in several different markets, such as televisions and video recorders, cameras and office copiers. The brand name helps to bridge the gap.
■ A manufacturer in one sector of the market can enter another sector with a different brand. Virgin, for example, now operates an airline, a railway and a pensions and investment company.
■ Branding and positioning affect the messages we aim at existing and potential customers.
■ Supermarket chains such as Sainsbury, Safeway and Tesco offer their own labels at lower prices. This is in direct competition with the established brands they stock. The aim is to divert customer attention from the major brands into the retailers' own, without seriously affecting sales of the established brands.

The essential elements of successful branding

■ identity
■ differentiation
■ uniqueness.

Figure 3.1 *The ultimate in branding achievement*

A global brand, Coke is promoted as a lifestyle, rather than as a product. To the consumer, its appeal is visual. It is this, rather than the taste alone, that successfully crosses international borders. After all, you cannot distinguish Coke from its major competitor unless you recognise the pack on the shelf, and reach for it. In promoting the brand through advertising, the marketing team need to take into account cultural, political and geographical differences. Its identity must be clear even when the market is not English-speaking; as in this illustration, where the language is written right to left.

Identity
You need to establish, firmly and unambiguously, the identity of your product, service or company, and its distinct personality.

Differentiation
You need to make absolutely clear the distinction between your
own product and all others.

Uniqueness
In your advertising, public relations, sales promotion and packaging, you must take a strong position with:

■ statements only *you* can make about your product, service or
  company
■ statements no competitor can say, or dare say, or bothers to say,
  about theirs.

The modern notion of branding started with the branding of live-
stock. In films about the American West, for example, you may
have observed how cowboys mark ownership of their cattle. They
catch a steer, wrestle it to the ground, tie its legs and plunge a hot
branding iron into its flesh. The iron carries the trademark of the
ranch that raised the steer.

Clear, unambiguous branding like this gives you a number of
advantages:

It establishes your identity
Good branding helps you gain recognition of your brand at the
points of sale and consumption.

A buyer might say: 'That's a Twin Forks steer. No mistaking it.
See the brand?'

It establishes your reputation for high quality
'That's a great-looking steer. They're all from that same ranch. You
can rely on the quality of the meat from that spread!'

It establishes your responsible attitude towards your market
'They sure care about what they sell to us. Look at the way they're
improving the quality of their beef, year after year. They're sure
keen for us to enjoy good steaks.'

It encourages memorability
Good branding is based on the criteria by which you judge your
product's memorability in the marketplace.

POSITIONING

A technique for placing in the customer's mind the unique, most distinguishing idea you want him to remember when considering your brand.

What a mouthful. What does it actually mean?

You have attracted your potential customer's attention in a commercial or advertisement. You have appealed to his needs, wants and self-interest. You strive to get a decision in favour of your brand, above all the others competing for his custom. Only then can you ask him to take the action you want.

But what is he actually buying? A product? The after-sales service behind it? The company that made it? Reliability? Guaranteed performance? A gimmick? Perhaps all of these.

The essence of successful positioning

■ You need to decide in advance exactly what you want your customer to think or feel, both before taking the decision, and while he is actually making the purchase.

■ In promotional terms, you must use ideas, images and motivations which differentiate your brand from all others.

■ You must give the customer the most compelling reasons for considering it as a purchase. These reasons must be based on the customer's needs, wants and self-interest. They can be rational or emotional, or both.

■ In other words, you must *position* it.

Try this exercise: Go to a supermarket and buy 10 different brands of margarine or spread. Bring them home, remove all the packaging and burn it. What do you have left?

You have in front of you 10 slabs of yellowish, greasy, semi-solid goo. Can you now tell the brands apart? It is well-nigh impossible.

Most of what you know about each brand is what the advertiser has told you. For example: in his advertising, one margarine manufacturer tells you that his product is high in polyunsaturates and low in saturates. No more information is given. You probably don't know a polyunsaturate from Adam. Ninety-nine customers out of a hundred don't either. So why does the advertiser give these two facts, and little else, in his promotion?

The technical nature of these two facts seems to have no promotional significance. But they do have importance when a customer is thinking about buying healthy products for the family. The advertiser plans to ensure that this idea remains in the customer's mind at the point of sale. He has *positioned* the product. The bulk of the market is housewives with husbands and young children. The *positioning* mode is *health*. Call this product A. Can you identify it?

Here's another. The advertiser claims that you can spread his margarine on to your bread straight from the fridge. The television commercial shows a young career-person rushing home from the office, having a quick snack, and rushing out again. The advertiser's market is identified in the commercial. He too has positioned his product. The positioning mode is *convenience*. Call this product B. Can you identify it?

A better end-result

A third example. The commercial shows a picnic, with a child eating a piece of cake. As he takes the first bite, he rises slowly off the ground. Here, the market for the product is not specifically identified on screen, but strongly implied: housewives with children. This advertiser has adopted yet another positioning mode: lighter baking and pastry, and therefore *a better end-result in the kitchen*. Call this product C.

A fourth: the advertiser's copy states that his product, a spread, is low in fat, with half the calorie content of butter or margarine. This approach is designed to appeal to those with calories on their minds. The positioning mode for this brand is therefore slimming. This is product D.

A final example. A margarine packed in golden foil. The launch advertising claimed that research revealed this product to be 'closer to butter than other margarines'. What therefore was the positioning mode? Customers were encouraged to go *up-market with a butter-replacement product*, away from margarines and butters they were using. This is product E, an international brand.

Summarising: here you have five similar-looking products, without their packaging virtually indistinguishable from each other. But they have five different positioning modes:

Product	Positioning
A	Health
B	Convenience
C	Better end-result
D	Slimming
E	Up-market butter replacement

This is the essence of successful positioning. Your customer's view of your product is what you say it is.

A CASE STUDY IN SUCCESSFUL BRANDING: GILLETTE

One excellent example of branding – or rather, rebranding – is Gillette. Four unsuccessful hostile takeover bids and a declining global market share could spell disaster for many organisations. At Gillette, these competitive pressures prompted a rethinking of the company's business strategy, and a successful re-emergence as a world leader.

Gillette set out to become 'raider-proof', and regain market share. Its commitment was a bold one: to be the number one player in the blade and razor category.

This tough challenge was given to identity consultants Anspach Grossman Enterprise, the New York arm of the Enterprise Identity Group.

Their first task was the identity and branding of a new product, the Gillette Sensor razor. Rather than introduce this revolutionary new shaving system as an individual product, they saw it as the starting point for global Masterbranding.

Combining Gillette's name equity with this innovative product was a win-win situation. Using the leverage of the Gillette name gave Sensor instant credibility. The product's innovative technology and design resulted in leading edge image spillover across the company's entire blade and razor product line.

The Masterbranding strategy was brought to life with a dynamic new Gillette logo. This was represented by a proprietary typeface, plus a new branding system for use on all Gillette's blade and razor products.

The look of the brand was more than an attractive product

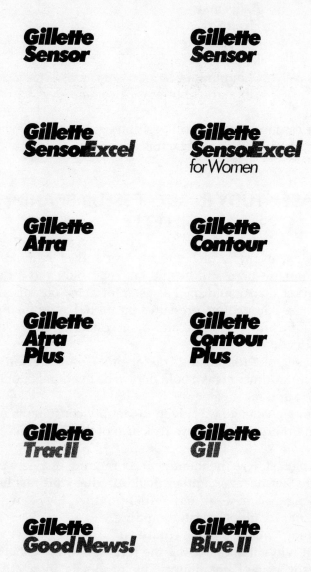

Careful typography and consistency give this range almost unlimited scope for extension. At the same time, it enables consumers to identify with the company as well as the products. The company's objective is to ensure that every impression is a Gillette impression.

Figure 3.2　*Unlimited branding potential*

design. The design was the foundation of Gillette's branding system. Equally important was the change in relationship between the Gillette Masterbrand and individual marketing brands. This applied especially to product packaging.

In the past, the individual product names were two to three times as dominant as the Gillette name. Consumers were buying individual product brands, not the Gillette brand. The Masterbrand gave Gillette and individual products equal exposure. Now every consumer product impression is also a Gillette impression.

The strengthened and consistent relationship of Gillette to its respective marketing brands resulted in greater product awareness. It also enhanced shelf impact, and the ability to introduce new product brands under the Gillette name.

What happened with the Sensor

The Sensor represented the first major launch of a new shaving product under the 'Number One Player' business strategy. Because Gillette committed to it the necessary marketing, identity and positioning resources, it was in every sense a global victory.

Twenty-one million Sensors were produced in the first six months, making it the most successful razor in history.

Once the Sensor programme was in place, other Gillette brands adopted the Masterbranding system. These included Atra, Trac II, Daisy and Good News. A totally new product line reflected the Masterbrand and its distinctive appearance, communications clarity and leadership tone.

As new products were introduced, market acceptability was immediate. These included Gillette Sensor for Women, Gillette SensorExcel and Gillette SensorExcel for Women.

The bottom line

The positive, cumulative effect of Gillette Masterbranding across all product lines was also immediate. Through heightened awareness, its brands began to regain market dominance. Once again, Gillette owned the sales environment.

A fading brand name had been transformed to a vital growth brand. Financial markets noticed. In the months following the introduction, Gillette shares rose from $46 per share to $69. Both its stock value and its market share continue to grow, based upon its global marketing strategy. This is a fine example of a successful business strategy that recognises the importance of branding.

TEN PRINCIPLES OF GOOD BRAND ADVERTISING

Some years ago, a conference was held in New York, sponsored by Unilever. The main subject for discussion was the principles of creative advertising. The participants included some of the biggest names in the business.

Then, as now, members of the business community were anxious to maximise the performance of their marketing tools. The 1960s and 1970s were boom times in many areas of business. But, as history demonstrates, booms always come to an end, and bust is often the fate of many prosperous companies.

It may have been at the back of the conference's mind that, in boom times, those who operate the engines of prosperity drift into complacency. Like most individuals, organisations need stimulus.

After a great deal of debate, undoubtedly of a high professional order, a number of principles were formulated. The most powerful and far-reaching of these concerned the quality of brand advertising.

Today, they are relevant not only to consumer advertising and sales promotion. They apply equally to business-to-business, industrial, technical and retail promotion; to press, print and broadcast media.

These were the main conclusions:

It is consumer-oriented
It is based on fundamental consumer needs, attitudes and interests. It reflects the consumer's point of view, rather than the manufacturer's or dealer's preference or selfish interests.

It concentrates on one selling idea
It does not scatter its efforts or diffuse its impact. It focuses on one single selling idea that can establish a penetrating, memorable reason for trial.

It concentrates on the most important and persuasive idea available
Since effective advertising implants a single concept about the
brand, the selection of that concept is of the most critical importance. Effective advertising presents and registers the most
powerful and persuasive selling idea available … the true key to
the consumer's mind.

It presents a unique and competitive benefit
It contains the promise of a unique competitive advantage. It
creates a distinctive quality and brand identity. It is highly competitive in its impression and effect.

It involves the customer
Effective advertising recognises that the consumer's motivation to
buy comes both from the head and the heart; that the consumer
wants rational justification for his selection of a brand, even
though his primary reasons may be emotional ones.

Effective advertising is personal. It appeals to the consumer's
self-interest. It solves human problems. It persuades the consumer
by interesting and involving him through reason and emotion.

It is credible, sincere and true
It is credible, even though the consumer may not always believe it
implicitly. Where possible, it documents, demonstrates or otherwise proves its claims. It provides assurance. It is straightforward,
honest in concept and presentation. It talks the consumer's
language, avoids nonsense, sham and insult. It recognises that the
consumer is not a moron.

It is simple, clear, complete
It says what it has to say clearly, simply and unmistakably. There is
no alternative meaning, no possibility of confusion or misunder-
standing. It is uncomplicated, completely understandable.

It clearly associates the selling idea with the brand
It tells or shows the consumer what the brand is used for. It clearly
registers the brand name and links it with the selling idea.

It takes full advantage of the medium
Certain selling ideas are better fitted to one medium than another.

Even where there is no such compelling difference, effective advertising varies its presentation of the selling idea to capitalise on the physical characteristics, and the audience mood provided, by the medium.

It demands action that will lead to the sale

Since the objective of packaged-goods advertising is to persuade the consumer to buy the brand, effective advertising transforms passive acceptance or interest into action. It demands immediate response – not merely a change in long-term attitude. It implants in the consumer's mind the urge to buy, or take some action now that moves him towards the sale. A truly persuasive advertisement produces immediate action.

Part 2
Improving Your Creative Skills

4

The Right Word in the Right Place

Any fool can write. But it takes a hungry fool to write for money.
— *Dr Samuel Johnson*

TRIGGER WORDS

Trigger words are those that you use in copywriting calculated to influence your target audience. You use them to attract attention, generate and hold interest, and encourage action. You also use them to push your reader over the edge of an argument or proposal, so that he thinks what you want him to think and takes the action you have planned for.

Trigger words are of at least three kinds: motivating, friendly, encouraging words; and the demotivating kind. You can demotivate a reader, viewer or listener simply by using a word he does not understand. Mostly, you use demotivating words to drive your reader away from an idea; a competitor's sales pitch, for example. The third category comprises words which discourage your reader from taking action, if that is what you want, or to remain neutral.

The question is, which words are which? The answer lies in the context in which you are using them. Words that are friendly and motivating in one context may be just the opposite in another. You will, of course, have planned it to work this way. Never use a word just because you like it. Every word you use must be used in the light of how your target audience understands it and will react to it. You will never get better advice than this.

In the two lists below, some words appear in both. It follows that you should use these lists with the same care and prudence you use elsewhere in marketing communications.

Friendly, motivating triggers

ability	effective
abundant	efficient
achieve	energy
active	enhance
admirable	enthusiasm
advance	equality
advantage	excellence
agree	exceptional
ambition	free
appreciate	good
approval	great
aspire	guarantee
attainment	handsome
authoritative	harmony
benefit	helpful
capable	honest
cheer	honour
comfort	humour
commendable	imagination
cost-effective	improvement
course	industry
courtesy	inexpensive
definite	ingenuity
dependable	initiative
deserve	integrity
desirable	intelligent
determined	investment
distinction	judgement
diversity	justice
easy	more
economical	motivate

new
notable
now
opportunity
perfect
permanent
please
popular
practical
praise
prestige
progress
prominent
promote
reasonable
recognition
recommend
reliable
reputable
seduce

simple
subtle
success
superior
supreme
thorough
thrifty
today
truth
try
useful
utility
value
vigour
vital
vivid
wise
wisdom
you
yours

Hostile, confusing triggers

abandon
abuse
affected
alibi
allege
apology
bankrupt
beware
biased
blame
buy
calamity
cheap
collapse
collusion
commonplace
complaint

contract
crisis
crooked
deadlock
decline
desert
difficulty
disaster
discredit
dispute
entice
evict
exaggerate
expedite
extravagant
failure
fault

fear
flagrant
flat
flimsy
fraud
gloss over
gratuitous
hardship
harp on
hazy
ignorant
illiterate
imitation
immature
implicate
impossible
improvident
ingenuity
insolvent
in vain
liable
long-winded
meagre
misfortune
middle
negligence
now
obstinate
opinionated
oversight
pay
perseverance
plausible
precipitate
prejudiced
premature
pretentious

proficient
propriety
punctual
retrench
rude
ruin
salient
seduce
sell
shirk
shrink
sketchy
slack
smattering
split hairs
squander
stagnant
standstill
straggling
stunted
subtle
superficial
tamper
tardy
timid
tolerable
truth
unfair
unfortunate
unstinted
unsuccessful
untimely
verbiage
waste
weak
worry
wrong

QUEEN'S ENGLISH, AMERICAN ENGLISH

Every language has its problems. English is no exception, partly because it is used throughout the world. It is the language of science, of the airlines and the Internet. Bernard Shaw wasn't the first to think it, but dared to say that England and America were two nations divided by a single language.

If you are preparing campaigns for the United States, and areas under American influence, be careful. There are at least 155 differences between Queen's English and the American version. There are many major differences in meaning, as well as in spelling. There are differences in pronunciation too. In New York, for example, Houston is pronounced 'howston', not 'hewston'.

As far as pronunciation is concerned, remember that the British see more American films on television than the Americans do British ones. The British are therefore familiar with how American English sounds. Americans, on the other hand, regard Queen's English as something of a curiosity; perhaps even slightly alien.

I have been misunderstood in upper-crust New Jersey, when I thought I was speaking impeccable Queen's English.

Here I have compiled some of the major differences in meaning and spelling between the two languages.

Queen's English	American English
admitted to hospital	hospitalised
aerial	antenna
analyse	analyze
angry	mad
anywhere	anyplace
autumn	fall
banknote	bill
barrister, solicitor	attorney
bill (restaurant)	check
biscuit	cookie
bonnet (car)	hood
boot (car)	trunk
braces	suspenders
car	automobile
caravan	trailer
caretaker	janitor

centre	center
chemist	drugstore
cheque	check
cinema	the movies
colour	color
condom	rubber
constable (police)	patrolman
cooker	stove
corn, wheat	wheat
cot	crib
cotton (sewing)	thread
crash (vehicle)	wreck
crisps	potato chips
crossroads	intersection
cupboard	closet
curtains	drapes
defence	defense
diversion	detour
draughts	checkers
drawing pin	thumbtack
dual carriageway	divided highway
dummy (baby)	pacifier
dustbin, rubbish bin	trashcan, garbage can
dustman	garbage collector
dynamo (car)	generator
engine	motor
engine driver	engineer
estate agent	realtor
fag (slang, cigarette)	homosexual (offensive)
film	movie
flat	apartment
flyover	overpass
gaol, jail	jail
garden	yard
gear-lever	shift, gear shift
got	gotten
graduate	alumnus
grill	broiler
ground floor	first floor
guard (train)	conductor

handbag	purse, pocketbook
hoarding	billboard
holiday	vacation
honour	honor
ill	sick
interval (theatre)	intermission
jewellery	jewelry
jug	pitcher
ladder (tights)	run
lift	elevator
lorry, van	truck
luggage	baggage
macintosh, raincoat	raincoat
mad	crazy
main road	highway
maize	corn
maths	math
mean (not generous)	stingy
motorway	freeway, expressway, parkway
nappy	diaper
nasty, vicious	mean
nowhere	noplace
nursing home	private hospital
offence	offense
offender (criminal)	perpetrator
off-licence	liquor store
optician, oculist	optometrist
paraffin	kerosene
pavement	sidewalk
peep	peek
petrol	gas, gasolene
plough	plow
post	mail
postbox	mailbox
postcode	zip code
postman	mailman, mail carrier
practise (verb)	practice
pram	baby-carriage
pretence	pretense
programme	program

pub	bar
public toilet	rest room
pudding	dessert
pullover, jersey	sweater
puncture (flat tyre)	flat, blow-out
purse	coin-purse
pushchair	stroller
pyjamas	pajamas
queue	stand in line
railway	railroad
railway carriage	railcar
reel of cotton	spool of thread
return (ticket, journey)	round-trip
reverse charges	call collect
rise (salary)	raise
road surface	pavement
roundabout	traffic circle
rubber	eraser
rubbish	trash
saloon (car)	sedan
sceptic	skeptic
schedule (pronounced shedule)	schedule (pronounced skedule)
school, college, university	school
sellotape	scotch tape
shop	store
silencer	muffler
single (ticket, journey)	one-way
somewhere	someplace
spanner	wrench
speciality	specialty
staff (university)	faculty
sump	oil-pan
sweet	dessert
sweets	candy
tap (water, indoors)	faucet
tap (water, outdoors)	spigot
taxi	cab
tea-towel	dish-towel
tennis shoes, gym shoes	sneakers
term (university, school)	semester

tights	pantyhose
timetable	schedule
tin	can
titbit	tidbit
toll road, toll motorway	turnpike
torch	flashlight
tramp	hobo
trousers	pants
turn-ups (trousers)	cuffs
tyre (car)	tire
underground, tube (transport)	subway
underpants	shorts
verge, hard shoulder (highway)	shoulder
vest	undershirt
waistcoat	vest
wallet	billfold
wash hands	wash up
wash up	wash dishes
wellington boots	rubbers
windscreen	windshield
wing (car)	fender
zip	zipper

5

Sales-winning Copywriting Techniques

Promise, large promise, is the soul of an advertisement.
— *Dr Samuel Johnson*

By this time, you should have looked at the promotional plan for the campaign you are going to create. You will also have acquired all the information you need.

You will have set your communications objectives using the checklist in Chapter 1, and gone through the creative briefing session, using the checklist in Chapter 2.

You will have identified your target audience, and decided on your copy platform – what you need to say.

What you need now is to start writing and designing. For that, you use another essential tool: a creative discipline.

There are several well-known techniques. One we use very successfully is AIDA. If you have ever been a sales rep, you will recognise this as a discipline of *progressive* steps in the process of making a sale.

AIDA is a communication discipline, an intellectual tool which helps you to achieve:

■ the levels of understanding *you* need for writing effective copy
■ the level of understanding you want *your target audience* to achieve, to give you the response you want.

AIDA is an acronym for:

Attention
Interest
Desire
Action.

This is a logical progression, and applies to all marketing communications.

■ You must first grab your reader's attention.
■ Tell him something that appeals to his self-interest.
■ Arouse a strong desire to try, buy or examine your product, to send for your literature or to ask for a sales call.
■ Urge your reader into taking the action you want.

You may feel that this technique is too basic. However, if you want to enjoy caviare and champagne, you should start with meat and boiled potatoes. If you really want to sharpen your creative skills, and do it quickly and reliably, you need to practise basics that are both proven and reliable.

GRABBING ATTENTION

Your attention-grabber must do the job in a single glance, otherwise you lose your reader. You must therefore make a promise strong enough to reach off the page and grab your reader by the eyeballs.

In writing a press advertisement, your objective should be to entice your reader to *read on*.

For TV and radio commercials, you must get your viewer to pay attention, and *continue looking or listening*. Given the transient nature of these media, this is a tough task.

Writing a brochure, your primary objective is to get the reader to *open the first page*, and discover what the proposition is going to do for him.

For sales-winning videos that grab your customers by the eyeballs

Need something special for sales presentations? Call us now.
We'll make you outstanding videos that really win sales and influence buyers.

Telephone Creative Director Martin Jones for a discussion and a showreel:
082 090 0550, or fax 082 090 0506

VIDEO DYNAMICS
Dynamics House, Alban Street, London NW1 4VD

Does the visual attract attention? Is there a promise in the headline?
Is the copy benefit-led? Are the contact numbers bold enough?

AROUSING INTEREST

When producing advertisements and print, your creative work must fulfil three important criteria:

■ It must *be interesting* to the reader.
■ It must *look interesting*.
■ It must be *easy to read and understand*.

To be interesting, your copy must appeal to your reader's self-interest – the magic ingredient.

■ Copy must be specific, full of interesting benefits, facts and features, preferably linked together. Avoid generalisations – they turn your reader off.
■ Make your copy lively. Your reader won't take boring copy, however short it is. He may read quite long copy if it is interesting enough.
■ When editing your copy, purge the generalisations and leave the benefits and facts intact.
■ Use personal words like 'you' and 'yours'. It's a way of assuring your reader that you understand him, his needs, problems and aspirations.

MAKING COPY LOOK INTERESTING

How to make your copy look interesting

■ Break your copy into short, easy-to-understand paragraphs. Don't make them too short; it looks messy.
■ Vary the length.
■ Limit each paragraph to two or three related ideas.
■ Punctuate your copy with sub-heads and cross-heads. They encourage the customer to read on. It makes it easier to get into the copy at any point that offers immediate appeal. Don't think your reader will go through your copy from end to end – he won't.
■ Use typographical devices; they help to make copy readable and encourage the customer to read on. For more, see Chapter 16.

MAKING COPY EASY TO UNDERSTAND

How to make your copy easy to understand

- Short sentences are usually easier to assimilate than long ones.
- Don't put more than one idea into a sentence.
- Be reasonable about the length of sentences; don't tax your reader's concentration. As a general rule, if there are more than two commas in the sentence, you have just written, it's too long. Vary the length.
- Use simple words and phrases. Ordinary consumers and professionals can be swayed by strong, well-reasoned arguments, simply expressed.
- Paragraph length: similar principles apply. If you find other writers' long paragraphs tedious and off-putting, so will readers of your copy. To be read, be reasonable about length.

AROUSING THE READER'S DESIRE

You need to do more than just create a desire for your brand.

- Before action comes decision. You must aim to get your reader to make *a decision in favour of your brand*.
- Your aim should be to arouse an avid desire, an eagerness, an impatience to possess it, examine it, get a demonstration.
- To do this, you should implant the idea of using your product and *benefiting* from it. Generate the euphoria of owning it – remembering, of course, to avoid mentioning the pain of paying for it.
- Make sure it's *your* brand the reader desires. Create a preference for it above all others. Don't sell other brands by implication, or by using generalisations.

To get a preference for your brand:

- distinguish it from all others
- show your customer why it's so good for him
- get him to agree it's the only one that's good for him.

GETTING THE ACTION YOU WANT

This, of course, is what you have been working towards all along. It follows that you should strive to make the utmost of the space you have for the reply element.

You should have your reader on a 'high' at this point. Now you are ready to study the Guidelines.

GUIDELINES

- Put a promise in the headline.
- Make it a benefit; offer a solution.
- Appeal to your customer's self-interest.
- Write visually. Arouse visual images in your reader's mind.
- Use strong branding. Bolt your idea and the brand name firmly together.
- The first sentence of your body copy should link straight into your headline.
- Begin with a fact, not a generalisation; go for the jugular.
- Use benefits, not facts alone.
- Remember: what you are selling may not be what your customer is buying.
- Be persuasive.
- Get your customer involved. Use 'you' frequently.
- Keep copy terse. Make paragraphs and sentences short but readable.
- Use sub-heads to guide your reader through the copy.
- Avoid long words where short ones do the same job.
- Talk your customer's everyday language.
- 'The more you tell, the more you sell.' Who wrote that?
- Urge your customer to take the action you want.
- Use as much persuasion in the reply element as in the rest of the advertisement.
- Show your customer it's *in his interest* to respond to your proposition.
- Demonstrate *the benefits* that come from responding.
- Make it *worthwhile* to respond – offer an incentive.
- Show clearly *how* to respond.
- Make it as *easy as possible* to take action.
- Tell him *to do it*, and to take the action now.

EXPLOITING THESE TECHNIQUES

Put a promise in the headline
The question you have to address is the one going through the customer's mind when he sees your headline:

'What's in it for me? If nothing, why should I bother to read on?'

This thought may not be expressed in words, but in the abstract. Either way, if your reader can't see immediately what the promise is, there's nothing to hold his attention. After that, nothing will encourage him to read the rest of your copy.

Most people are exposed to over 1500 promotional messages every day. You see how vital it is to get your headline and its promise noticed and understood. The rest of your copy depends on it.

Make it a benefit; offer a solution
Because life is full of problems, everybody is looking for solutions. People want solutions to their domestic, personal, physical, medical, business and financial problems.

If you can offer solutions to your readers' problems, you're in business! When your headline shows that your product or service promises such solutions, you can rely on their rapt attention and sustained interest.

Appeal to your customer's self-interest
Most people act in their own self-interest, either instinctively, out of habit, or after careful consideration. You can rely on it, so write your copy to appeal to it.

Write visually
Writing abstract copy is sometimes unavoidable.

Next time you write an abstract line, think about how your art director will handle it. His job is getting your copy on to a layout pad or computer screen, in support of what you have written. I'm sure you've seen art directors struggling with abstractions; have you felt their desperation?

Use strong branding
Research suggests that sometimes people see an advertising

message and unconsciously substitute their favourite brand name for the one in the message. It seems they do this even when the message content appeals to them very much.

Aim to avoid this. Make your branding work persuasively with the creative idea you are using.

Link the body copy with your headline
If your headline is doing its job, and arousing your reader's expectations, he will look for them to be fulfilled at once. Don't keep him hanging about for fulfilment. Put it in the first sentence of the body copy.

Get your customer involved
Every customer, every reader, viewer and listener, is an individual. Each has individual needs, so make sure your copy helps to fulfil them. By using personal words, you can get your customer more involved in understanding your offer and its personal value.

Keep copy terse
'Terse' doesn't mean 'short'; it means 'tight'.

Redundant words and phrases can slow down your message, and also give an amateurish feel to your copy. If that's what you want, fine. Otherwise purge redundant words carefully but ruthlessly. Effective, creative copy depends as much on efficient editing as on careful planning.

Use sub-heads
Plan to write paragraphs that contain related ideas which group together logically. Sub-heads signal what is coming, and should be both logical and informative. They help both to guide the reader through the copy, and encourage those who like to skim before reading everything.

Avoid long words
Where a short word does the same job as a long one, use it. This makes your text easier to read and understand.

Use everyday language
The language you use in copywriting should be your customer's, not your own. Think about the language of his geographical

area, occupation, age, social group. Think about his needs and problems.

What you are selling – and what your customer is buying
You may be selling electric irons – electro-mechanical hardware. But your customer will be buying the ability to impress an employer, a supplier, or a member of the opposite sex. Think about his *motives*.

Use benefits, not facts alone
You can make facts and product features work more persuasively when you bolt them together with the benefits they bring to your customer. In copy, always harness them together.

'The more you tell, the more you sell'
Hardly anybody today remembers Claude Hopkins. He invented test marketing, copy testing and brand research. David Ogilvy says that nobody should be allowed to go near advertising until he has read Claude Hopkins' book seven times. I agree. And the same applies to this book too.

Urge your customer to take the action you want
Be specific. Feature the response element boldly and visibly – even dramatically. It could increase your response level.

This decision is based on the most efficient method of getting the response, how easy it is for your customer to respond, and how fast and efficiently your company can handle the response you generate.

You can get action off the page, off the screen or off air by using:

- coupons
- telephone numbers
- order forms
- credit card hotlines
- outlet addresses
- reply cards
- e-mail addresses.

Use as much persuasion in the reply element as in the rest of the advertisement
Every coupon and reply card you write should be a mini-ad in itself: a persuasive headline, short, benefit-led copy, campaign slogan, strong branding.

Show your customer it's in his interest to respond
Tempt your customer into action – offer an incentive wherever possible. Use facts and benefits persuasively, and your customer will be seduced into listening – and responding – to your propositions.

Make it worthwhile to respond – offer an incentive.
A discount, a free gift, a special pack, three for the price of two – the incentive can be quite modest. Be sure to highlight it.

Demonstrate the benefits that come from responding
Your customer will take your proposition seriously when you show how he benefits from responding. Use images as well as words.

For sales-winning videos to knock your customers' socks off ... call
VIDEO DYNAMICS

Need something really *special* for sales presentations? Get Video Dynamics to make your videos.

With our experience and creative expertise behind you, you'll make a great deal more than just a good impression on your customers. You'll make an outstanding one that wins sales and influences buyers!

We analyse your objectives, research your needs, find the solutions, stick to your budget and deliver on time.

Want to know more? Telephone our Creative Director Martin Jones now for advice (no obligation), and our dynamic showreel, on

082 090 0505, or fax him on **082 090 0506**

VIDEO DYNAMICS
Dynamics House, Alban Street, London NW1 4VD

Is there a promise in the headline? Does it go through AIDA? Is the copy benefit-led? Is the writing terse, active? Is the response element visible?

Show clearly how to respond
Design and write coupons with the reader in mind. Allow adequate space for the information you want. Put it in words. For example: 'Fill in your initials, surname, job title and company address.' This also helps you build viable databases. If you are featuring a telephone number, *really* feature it – make it big and bold and visible.

Make it as easy as possible to take action
You can make it easy to respond by using:

- Freepost
- reply-paid envelopes
- Free-phone

- 0800 numbers
- 0345 numbers
- e-mail addresses.

Give the customer a name to ask for when he telephones for information. This can prevent a breakdown of the enquiry at the switchboard, and channels your customer direct to the right person without delay.

Tell him to do it, and to take the action now
Put a time limit on your offer. Add an extra benefit if the customer responds within the limit, and you have a powerful incentive for action.

A word of warning: if a prospective customer puts your coupon under the mantelpiece clock, for attention after tea, you may never see it again. Likewise, the 'pending' or 'action' tray is a graveyard.

6

How to Write Sales-winning Headlines

On average, five times as many people read headlines as read body copy. It follows that unless your headline sells your product, you have wasted 90 per cent of your money.

– David Ogilvy

What makes a headline effective? It depends who you are.

If you are a product manager, it is a promotion device that helps to sell your brand. If you are a marketing director, an effective headline is something that helps to move crates of product out of your factory at high speed. As a company accountant, you may regard a headline as something that helps to swell your bottom line.

On the other hand, when you are a copywriter, an effective headline is a piece of well-crafted, motivating text. It sits on top of your advertisement, reaches off the page and grabs readers by the eyeballs. It helps to drive your prospective customers into making decisions in favour of your brand.

If you are a prospective customer, is it something you see in a magazine that prompts you to think, 'I like that; I'll try it?'

There is more controversy over headlines than almost any other aspect of marketing communications. For example, I have had marketing managers on copywriting courses waver over really excellent headlines, on the grounds of length or of brevity.

Having a birthday?
Bring out the Sunshine!

Sunshine Margarine brings out the very best in your baking. Gives heavenly texture and taste to everything you touch. For cakes with child-appeal. Brilliant biscuits. Perfect pies.

Put golden Sunshine on your shopping list now. Even if it's not your birthday, you'll love the taste. And so will your guests.

That heavenly taste

Peckish?
Bring out the Sunshine!

Reach for the Sunshine Margarine, everybody's favourite taste. Spreads like a dream – straight from the fridge, so there's no waiting for a snack to relieve the pangs.

Put golden Sunshine on your shopping list now. Even if you're not absolutely ravenous, that heavenly taste will keep you going till dinner-time.

That heavenly taste

Same brand, different target audiences. Are these advertisements aimed at new users, existing users or brand-switchers?

I have had really motivating headlines rejected by clients because of full-stops at the ends.

Some people, David Ogilvy among them, feel that headlines should not print reversed white out of black. Others, that headlines should not be set in caps, since this impedes readability.

Whatever your own problems with headlines, this chapter will give you practical guidelines on resolving them.

GUIDELINES

- ▓ Put a promise into your headline. Make it an important consumer benefit.
- ▓ Use strong branding.
- ▓ Differentiate your brand. Show its uniqueness.
- ▓ Use positive propositions. Offer solutions.
- ▓ Appeal to your reader's self-interest. Talk his language.
- ▓ Make your headlines relevant.
- ▓ Never use wit for its own sake.
- ▓ Don't exaggerate. Avoid superlatives, unless they do a real job.
- ▓ Write visually. Arouse visual images in your reader's mind.
- ▓ Use trigger-words, emotive words, interesting words, motivating words.
- ▓ Avoid long words where short ones do the same job.
- ▓ Keep headlines terse.
- ▓ Entice. Seduce. Aim to urge the customer to read on. Use 'you' frequently.
- ▓ Get your reader involved.

EXPLOITING THESE TECHNIQUES

Put a promise into your headline
David Ogilvy, one of the world's most successful copywriters, has some illuminating things to say about headlines.*

On average, he claims, five times as many people read headlines as read body copy. It follows that, when you have created your

---

*Ogilvy, D (1962) *Confessions of an Advertising Man*, Atheneum, New York.

FRESHAIR
air purifiers

For greater comfort, protection and productivity at work

Installing 👍Freshair air purifiers does much more than improve the atmosphere in your office, boardroom, meeting rooms and canteen.

RESTORES AIR FRESHNESS
👍Improves your working environment by constantly restoring air freshness all over your office. 👍Helps your staff to work more comfortably; helps raise their productivity and morale.

CUTS DOWN TOBACCO SMOKE, DUST AND POLLEN
👍Helps to prolong the working life of your equipment by protecting against dust build-up and nicotine corrosion. 👍Helps all your staff to work more comfortably and productively – especially non-smokers and hay-fever sufferers.

REDUCES STATIC BUILD-UP
👍Helps to protect your sensitive equipment and magnetic media from irreversible damage.

Get a demonstration of 👍Freshair air purifiers in your own office. For a demo, a discussion or an information pack, please telephone Derek Smyth on 082 090 0505, or fax him on 090 0506.

👍 FRESHAIR
Freshair House, Alban Row, London NW1 4FR

There is a promise in the headline; features and user-benefits march together. Using Derek Smyth's name in the action line directs enquiries to someone who knows about the product and the solutions it offers.

headline, you have committed eighty pence of your promotional pound. If you haven't fired your best selling shot in your headline, you have probably wasted 80 per cent of your money.

Read again what I have said about this in Chapter 5.

Use strong branding
Lock the creative idea in the headline with your brand name or other brand property. Make them work together, and your reader will identify them as one, and the benefit you are offering as well.

Differentiate your brand
If your brand faces competition, make sure your reader knows the difference, clearly expressed in the main benefit. See the chapter on branding and positioning, Chapter 3.

Use positive propositions
If you really need to highlight a problem your reader has, offer the solution at the same time, and base it on your brand.

Appeal to your reader's self-interest
If you don't, why should he bother to read it? See what I have said in Chapter 3 about this.

Make your headlines relevant
Relevant to what? To your reader's self-interest. And, of course, to what you are selling – to your brand.

Never use wit for its own sake
Humour is a minefield. But a joke is hard to ignore – you either love or hate it. Its practical use is getting your reader involved with your proposition.

Don't exaggerate
Be careful with words like 'amazing', 'fantastic' and 'incredible'. They won't do a proper job unless they are part of a thoroughly believable proposition.

Write visually
Especially if your headline is abstract. You need to plant strong images in your reader's mind. Give your art director a fair chance to get your idea on paper. Consult before you write!

Use trigger-words

What's a trigger-word? One which propels your reader into your proposition, towards the action you want. Examples: *free, new, opportunity, guarantee, service, love, save, value, extra.* Be careful: your words must be relevant to your target.

Avoid long words where short ones do the same job

Talk your reader's everyday language. Where you must use jargon, try to use common language for persuasion.

Keep headlines terse

Terse does not mean short. It means tight. Purge redundant words and phrases. A headline can be any length, provided that every word pays its way.

Entice, seduce

You cannot *make* your reader do anything. But you can attract, entice and persuade. Again, tailor the technique to the target.

Get your reader involved

Don't write a headline as though it were aimed at an anonymous third party. If you want to influence your reader, talk direct to that reader. Use words like *you, yours, yourself, your company, your home.*

7

How to Write Successful Body Copy

The way we sell is to get read first.

– Raymond Rubicam

GUIDELINES

- Your first sentence and paragraph should link into your headline.
- If your headline asks a question, supply the answer immediately.
- Appeal to your customer's self-interest.
- Use benefits as well as facts and features.
- Maintain the strength of the branding theme.
- Make ideas and sentences flow logically into each other.
- Use your reader's language.
- Write with clarity; aim to persuade.
- Keep copy terse. Don't waste words.
- Avoid repetition, except for emphasis.
- Use short words, unless long ones achieve more impact and authority.
- Use sub-heads, cross-heads, italics, bold, small caps and other typographical devices.

> ■ Use sentences to separate ideas; use paragraphing to keep similar ideas together.
> ■ Urge the customer to respond actively.

EXPLOITING THESE TECHNIQUES

Link into your headline
Your reader will not wait to make the connection; therefore, get straight into it.

If your headline asks a question, supply the answer immediately
The same applies. What's more, if you don't supply an answer, in whatever form, your reader may feel cheated, and could turn to another brand in revenge. The answer, therefore, *must* be a consumer or business benefit.

Appeal to your customer's self-interest
Again, the magic ingredient. You cannot expect him to read what you have written unless you continue the relevance you have created.

Use benefits as well as facts
Lock them together – side by side, if you can, especially if your research tells you that the customer likes substantiation. In any case, you should not create a benefit without having a fact to support it. And vice versa.

Maintain the strength of the branding theme
You can actually build up the impact of your branding in body copy. Aim to leave your reader even better disposed towards your brand than when he started reading.

Make ideas and sentences flow logically
If your copy jumps around, your reader gets confused. What do readers tend to do when confused? Nothing. And that's definitely not what you want.

Use your reader's language
Your readers or viewers may not talk the way you do. Study how *they* speak, what style they most easily absorb and understand. The way to do this is to study the media they are exposed to. If you can't spare the time to go to Aberdeen and listen to the way people speak there, read their local paper.

Write with clarity; aim to persuade
Use the benefits and facts at your disposal and use them persuasively. Be direct about it. You have to make a conscious decision to do this before you begin writing. It's not easy, but you must do it.

Keep copy terse. Don't waste words
Terse does not mean 'short'. It means tight, concise and smooth-flowing. Purge all redundant words and phrases from your copy.

Avoid repetition
Some arguments and copywriting styles benefit from repetition. It helps to convey emphasis, credibility and authority. However, try not to use exactly the same words the second time round. And don't overdo it.

Use short words
I am *not* saying that short words are best under all circumstances. But that's the way most people speak. Tailor the technique to the target; as always, use your judgement.

Use sub-heads, cross-heads, italics, bold, small caps and other typographical devices
Use them to separate major ideas from one another; it makes your copy easier to read and understand. Equally important, they enhance the visual impact of your body copy – make it *look* more interesting, which encourages your customer *to start reading*.

For specific techniques that help you, see Chapter 16.

Using sentences and paragraphs
They have specific uses in copywriting. Read Chapter 16 for specific techniques.

Urge the customer to respond actively

Show the customer that it is *worthwhile* to respond; demonstrate all the benefits that come from responding. Then tell him to do it, to act *right* away: pick up the phone and ask for information, a brochure or a sales call; phone your credit-card hotline; send a fax or e-mail; fill in and post the coupon. If the action you want is physical, ask for it.

Remember the rep's dictum: *Never leave without asking for the order!*

8

Writing Successful Direct Mail

I have made this letter longer than usual, because I lack the time to make it short.

– Blaise Pascal

DIRECT MAIL AS A MEANS OF PERSONAL COMMUNICATION

Because direct mail is so selective, you can use it as a method of *personal communication*. In this way, you take full advantage of the directness and intimacy the medium offers.

You are able to control almost everything involved in a mail-shot. For example:

colour	envelope	size
content	frequency	stamping
contents	mailing list	timing
copy	production technique	typography
creativity	reply element	volume
design	samples	weight

There are few creative limitations. There are no limits to copy length, no restrictions on design, beyond those relating to legality, honesty and decency.

BASIC PRINCIPLES OF CREATING DIRECT MAIL

In creating sales letters, leaflets and brochures, the same basic principles apply as for press advertisements.

■ Grab your reader's attention.
■ Get him to turn the first page.
■ Show how your brand is of benefit to him.
■ Arouse a desire to try it, buy it or own it.
■ Get action.

If a brochure you are creating is going to be sent out cold, that is almost certainly the reaction you will get: the cold shoulder. Wastebins all over Britain are full of unsolicited mail!

A powerful and positive influence

On the other hand, sending a skilfully written letter with your brochure tempts your recipient with a personal message. It could exert a powerful, positive influence on the response you get.

GUIDELINES
Effective sales letters

■ Start with a headline. Put a promise or benefit into it.
■ Make the promise personal.
■ Address your reader by name in the salutation, and in the body copy.
■ In a business mailing, use the recipient's job title.
■ Try not to use 'Dear Sir or Madam'.
■ Your first paragraph of body copy should link into the headline.
■ If your headline is a question, make sure you supply the answer immediately in the body copy.
■ Ensure your questions are open-ended.
■ Make your copy easy to read – use typographical devices and colour.
■ Keep copy terse.
■ Body copy should be just long enough to cover facts, benefits and persuasion.

- Urge your reader to take action.
- Sign it.
- Use a PS as a clincher.
- Make it easy for your reader to reply.
- Put a persuasive sales message into the reply element.

EXPLOITING THESE TECHNIQUES

Start with a headline. Put a promise or benefit into it
Make sure your reader knows, without a shadow of doubt, what's on offer. Put your key benefit here. Be persuasive. Use AIDA. To see how to do this, see Chapter 3.

Make the promise personal
Your letter is a personal communication. Make your promise a direct, personal benefit. Tailor the copy to the target.

Address your reader by name in the salutation, and in the body copy
Make sure your mailing house gets it right. Ensure your in-house lists do.

In a business mailing, use the recipient's job title
Again, your mailing house should be up-to-date enough to ensure accuracy; otherwise it can prejudice the response.

Try not to use 'Dear Sir or Madam'
I am not needlessly condemning this salutation, of course. Some companies with extensive mail-order lists get a good response with it; others have no choice but to use it. One delegate on a recent CIM Print course had no alternative, and was getting worthwhile results from a huge consumer list. However, where there are alternatives, use and test them systematically.

However, it is *not* compulsory to use a salutation in a sales letter. Try a couple of hundred copies of your next letter without one, and compare the results. It is much more important to have a benefit-led headline than a salutation.

Your first paragraph of body copy should link into the headline
Don't waste your reader's time easing yourself into the copy. As
with press ads, gets straight to the point.

*If your headline is a question, make sure you supply the answer
immediately in the body copy*
If you bury the answer in the body of your letter, your reader
won't wait to get to it. Your letter will be binned.

Ensure your questions are open-ended
Make sure the answer you are seeking is not a straight 'no'. If it is,
the communication with your reader could end right there. Then
where do you go?

Make your copy easy to read – use typographical devices and colour
Use cross-heads, bold type, underlining, colour. Add visual variety
to your copy. See Chapter 16.

Keep copy terse
Terse does not mean 'short'; it means 'tight'. As with press ads,
purge unnecessary words and phrases, avoid clichés and generalisations. Make every word pay its way. Your aim should be easier
reading and better comprehension. Don't overdo the purging;
copy can look eccentric, and also be difficult to read.

*Body copy should be just long enough to cover facts, benefits and
persuasion*
When you have grabbed your reader's attention and aroused his
interest, hold that interest with important benefits and facts. Show
how they give the satisfactions and solutions he is seeking.

If your sales letter turns out shorter than you expected, do not
be tempted into padding it for the sake of length. If you use
repetition, do so deliberately and with a specific objective;
repeating an important offer, for example, could increase awareness of a particular benefit at the end of a four-page letter.

If you can't get your sales pitch across in four or five paragraphs,
consider creating a leaflet that tells the complete story. You can use
the letter as temperature-raiser.

Urge your reader to take action

Try putting action copy in more than one place in the letter – in the second paragraph, for example, as well as at the end. The reason: if you can get your reader to agree to take action even *before* he has read the whole text, you have him on your side at the end too.

Sign it

Even though you may not have begun with a salutation, a signature at the foot of a sales letter is a friendly way to end. It is also a convention, which most people are used to. Not all signatures are legible, so have the writer's name typed beneath it.

Use a PS as a clincher

The postscript achieves high readership, while taking little space, so don't waste this opportunity to persuade.

There are several ways a PS can be useful:

▨ reinforcing a major offer
▨ bringing out a minor point already made in body copy
▨ introducing a new benefit, which might have been overlooked in body copy
▨ introducing the closing date of an offer.

If you are repeating a point here, write it in a different way; don't make it a straight repeat.

Make it easy for your reader to reply

Highlight the reply element; give it as much space as possible. If it is a telephone number, make it large enough to be really visible. If your reply element is a coupon, don't hide it away on a back page; if it is a reply card, feature it within the body copy.

Design every coupon and card with the reader in mind – make everything clear, with adequate space for first name, initials, surname, job title, company name, address. Include tick-boxes for information options.

Put a persuasive sales message into the reply element

Write every coupon and reply card as a persuasive advertisement; make it pay its way! Give it a benefit-led headline and a line of body copy; illustrate the offer, sample or information pack. Do everything you can to *maximise* the response.

9

Improving Your Brochures and Leaflets

It is not uncommon for a change of headlines to multiply returns from five to ten times over.

– Claude Hopkins

GUIDELINES

General

■ Aim to make every brochure you produce informative, motivating, attractive.

■ Aim to make them interesting, look interesting, easy to read and understand.

■ Aim to demonstrate how your brand works for your reader's benefit and self-interest.

■ Aim to show your brand in action.

■ Aim to arouse in your reader a desire to try, buy or possess or learn about your brand.

■ Aim to demonstrate by example.

Front cover

- Grab your reader's attention.
- Aim to get the front cover opened – make this your primary objective.
- Make a promise; show a benefit.
- Propel your reader into the inside pages.

Inside pages

- Write a headline which links direct to the promise on the front cover.
- Use AIDA.
- As always, tailor the technique to the target.
- Ensure that your copy and design flow logically to the conclusion you want.
- Ensure your copy is easy to read and understand.
- Use sub-heads and cross-heads.
- Vary sentence and paragraph length.
- Use visual devices.
- For emphasis, use bold type, italics, underlining, small caps, colour.
- Use typography creatively, but not eccentrically.
- Don't use too many typefaces, weights and sizes.
- Make the design look busy, attractive, interesting, but never at the expense of clarity.
- When using a six-page format, make the most effective use of page 5.

Reply element

- Make it visible.
- Write and design it as a promotion in its own right.
- Give it a headline; put a promise into it.
- Give it its own body copy, pay-off and action line.
- Make it interesting, look interesting, easy to read and understand.
- If possible, make it self-addressed; ensure the accuracy of the information.

EXPLOITING THESE TECHNIQUES

Front cover

Grab your reader's attention

As with other forms of promotion, your opening idea must be strong enough to reach off the page and grab your reader by the eyeballs! Look at the key proposition, and find ways of basing your opening idea on that.

Aim to get the front cover opened – make this your primary objective

If you can't do this, your entire effort fails. Tempt, seduce, intrigue, tease. Merely having the name of your company or brand name on the front page is just not good enough when you are promoting a product or service.

Make a promise: show a benefit

Appeal to your reader's self-interest. If you have a solution to your reader's technical, corporate, domestic or personal problems, feature it here.

Propel your reader into the inside pages

This is where you aim to do the main selling job on your customer. It amounts to nothing if you don't get your reader beyond the cover.

Inside pages

Write a headline which links directly to the promise on the front cover

Justify, explain and expand your front cover proposition. Don't just repeat the headline you have used on the front. Start with a headline which you can develop in the body copy.

Use AIDA

Even within the body of a brochure or leaflet, you need to attract your reader's attention, generate interest, get a decision and encourage action. Scattering these elements too widely, however, makes pages look messy. Use your judgement.

For AIDA technique, see Chapter 5.

As always, tailor the technique to the target
Bear in mind your reader's profession, occupation, age, education and location, and the language he uses. I once wrote a campaign for a retail outlet in Scotland. The client ticked me off with the words, 'They don't talk like that in Glasgow!' Rebuked, I revised at once.

Ensure that your copy and design flow logically to the conclusion you want
AIDA is an excellent tool to use for this. Construct the whole production with action in mind. If you want an active response to your mailshot, sit down with your art director and plan it that way. Designers use AIDA for the same reason you do, but sometimes they need to be coaxed.

Ensure your copy is easy to read and understand
Don't expect your reader to assimilate large chunks of copy, unrelieved by adequate punctuation and typography. See Chapter 16 for guidelines.

Use sub-heads and cross-heads
These are signposts, to guide your reader through the copy in the way you have planned. Face it: nobody is going to read your copy from the first word to the last. But you can tempt your reader to look for the things that interest him most. If he likes what he sees, he may read all the interesting bits, and then take action. Therefore, make sure each of your sub-heads and cross-heads is tempting, and reveals the most important benefit contained in the paragraph that follows.

Vary sentence and paragraph length
Although paragraphs may be of intense interest, they may not look interesting enough to read if they line up like bricks in a wall.

Use visual devices
Here are some of the options. Most word-processing and DTP software offer you the capability to generate:

drop caps	illustrations	diagrams
graphs	histograms	pie charts
tables	columns	footnotes
bar-charts	flashes	starbursts
colour	tinted panels	white space

However, avoid the temptation to go over the top; use these devices *sparingly*.

For emphasis, use:

bold type, *italics*, <u>underlining</u>, CAPS, SMALL CAPS, colour

Why not experiment with combinations of these attributes? Exploit your WP software: on some systems you find such features as 'large', 'very large' and 'extra large'. For techniques, see Chapter 16; for contact information, see Chapter 21.

Use typography creatively, but not eccentrically
Where typography interferes with clarity, you may lose the ability to be understood. Try to *gain* intelligibility with appropriate typography, and increase your copy's power to *persuade*. Insist on your right to be read!

Don't use too many typefaces, weights and sizes
It can look messy and amateurish. Keep to two, if you can, as on this page.

Make the design look busy, attractive, interesting
As always, tailor the technique to the target. Consumer print often benefits from a busy look, business print from a more clinical look. However, never, never, sacrifice clarity.

When using a six-page format, make the most effective use of page 5
Most print uses multiples of four pages. If you haven't enough material to fill eight pages, a six-page gatefold is an economical format. You also avoid the expense of complicated finishing.

■ Take a sheet of paper. Fold it twice along its width, in the form of a gate.
■ Number the pages.
■ Now look at page 5. It should be the one facing you on the right after you turn the front page.
■ This is the most important page in the whole leaflet. Exploit it fully, by putting your most persuasive copy on it.

Reply element

Make it visible

If you are serious about getting a response, you dare not hide the coupon, reply card, telephone number or whatever device you have decided on. Don't, for example, dump it on page 48. Your reader may never get there.

Call your reader's attention to the reply element in strategic places throughout the design. Consult your art director before you start writing.

Moscow overnight!
The brilliant new service –
only from Pan-European

Get your freight to your nearest Pan-European depot by 9am, and it's in Moscow next morning. Whatever the weight or size. Guaranteed.

To get things moving now, telephone the new Moscow Overnight Hotline for details:

PAN-EUROPEAN   **01181 090 95056**

Pan-European Transport Group, PanEuro House, London W16 1PE

Figure 9.1 *Business-to-business advertising*

A clear, bold headline and newsy sub-head. Short, benefit-led body copy. Bold contact information. Simple, clear branding.

Write and design it as a promotion in its own right
If you have decided on a coupon, reply card, fax reply sheet or other detachable reply device, make it pay its way. Ensure that it makes a *contribution* to the promotion you are creating.

▨ Give it a headline; put a promise into it.
▨ Give it a short piece of body copy, a payoff and an action line.
▨ Make it look interesting, easy to read and understand.
▨ If possible, include your recipient's full name and address; test this over a split run, to see how it increases the response. Ensure the accuracy of the database information.

Above all, make sure all your reply elements have *positive promotional value*!

10

How to Write Effective News Releases

When a dog bites a dog that is not news, but when a man bites a dog that is news.

— Charles Anderson Dana, in the New York Sun

This is not a specialist book on PR. It is about helping you to communicate successfully with your publics. However, before we start on techniques, it is sensible to establish a few essentials.

DEFINITIONS

The IPR definition
The Institute of Public Relations has devised the following definition. Do you think it covers the field adequately?

The planned and sustained effort to establish and maintain goodwill and mutual understanding between an organisation and its publics.

The Mexican statement
A public relations conference in Mexico came to the following conclusions. Has it done any better?

Public relations practice is the art and social science of analysing trends, predicting their consequences, counselling organisation leaders, and implementing planned programmes of action which will serve both the organisation and the public interest.

Comparison with advertising

Public relations aims to educate and inform, in order to create knowledge and understanding.

Its aim towards its target publics is to achieve a change of attitude:

■ ignorance to knowledge
■ apathy to interest
■ prejudice to acceptance
■ hostility to sympathy.

Advertising, on the other hand, seeks to inform and remind, in order to persuade and sell. It strives to achieve specific action by its target audiences.

THE PUBLICS FOR PUBLIC RELATIONS

■ Primary publics
the media: feature writers
  editors   press photographers
  journalists   TV producers & editors
  reporters   radio producers & editors.

■ Ultimate publics
  academics   general public
  children   health authorities
  competitors   international influencers
  customers & consumers   investment analysts
  distributors   investors
  end users   key opinion-formers
  financial institutions   local community
  foreign governments   local government

medical profession
money market
opinion leaders
parliamentarians
potential employees
resellers
retailers
shareholders

stock market
students
suppliers
teachers
the professions
trade associations
trades unions
wholesalers.

■ Internal publics
    associate companies
    candidate employees
    existing employees
    management

new employees
overseas associates
shareholders
trades unions.

THE TOOLS OF PUBLIC RELATIONS

■ News releases
■ Electronic news releases
■ Feature articles
■ PR functions & events
    news conferences
    press receptions
    media lunches
    facility visits
    open days
■ Documentaries
    radio
    TV
    taped interviews
    studio interviews
    series & serials
■ Competitions and prizes
■ Archival material
    library clips
■ House journals
    external & internal
    sales bulletins

newsletters
digests
newspapers
magazines, monthly and quarterly
poster-newspapers.

MEDIA RELATIONS: HOW NOT TO DO IT

According to some of Britain's leading editors, many PROs commit these top 10 errors:

1. Write long, rambling news releases which don't stand a chance of being published.
2. Send dull, boring photographs that won't be published either.
3. Send these items to inappropriate publications.
4. Send them at the wrong time; sometimes after the deadline.
5. Hold news conferences unnecessarily. Ninety per cent turn out to be a waste of time, effort and money.
6. When holding potentially interesting news conferences, do so in a long-winded, badly organised, ill-timed way.
7. When they have something interesting to say, do not individually tailor their material to individual media. This happens even though they know that the individual PR approach does actually succeed better than the blunderbuss method.
8. Rarely think of creative angles that might interest their target publics.
9. Don't know how to handle bad news. Instead of saying something positive, they freeze up.
10. Commit journalistic and commercial suicide: they don't get editors' names right.

MEDIA RELATIONS: HOW TO DO IT

Fortunately, there are 10 golden positive rules to counteract the 10 top errors:

1. Create short, sharp news releases. Get to the point immediately.

2. Get press photographers to shoot your pictures. Arrange photo opportunities for the nationals; they don't accept contributed photographs.
3. Send news releases to the right journalist, not just to 'The Editor'.
4. Find out journalists' deadlines and 'dead days', and work to them.
5. Hold a news conference only if you really need one.
6. If you must hold a news conference, keep the presentation short.
7. Tailor news releases to appeal to specific media.
8. Be creative: make your stories newsworthy.
9. Interviews: anticipate the negative questions and have your answers ready. Focus on making three key points, whatever the questions.
10. Cultivating and developing personal relationships with journalists beats everything.

CREATING EFFECTIVE NEWS RELEASES

To create successful news release copy, you need to address your mind to:

■ Purpose
■ Format
■ Content
■ Style
■ Final checking.

PURPOSE

Your reason for creating news releases is to supply news and information to those media in which you want it published.

The proper target audience for your PR is not the general public, but editors and journalists. They are the human channels through which you reach your various publics; you must aim to serve their professional needs.

FORMAT

Your copy is bound to compete with material sent in by other companies. It follows that you must present your copy in an acceptable professional format.

■ If you want to be noticed, and taken seriously, provide yourself with PR-viable headed paper.
■ Use white paper of reasonable quality: A4, 297 mm × 210 mm.
■ At the head of the paper, identify the contents with a bold, well-designed heading, such as:

NEWS RELEASE	PRESS INFORMATION
PRESS RELEASE	NEW FROM ...

In selecting a heading, bear in mind that your copy could be going to television and radio stations, as well as to the press.

■ Make sure the heading is no more than 50 mm high, otherwise you waste valuable space.
■ Leave 40 mm between the heading and the title of your story. The gap enables the editor to make notes on where and how to use the story.
■ Don't clutter the heading with irrelevant information – keep it simple. All you need is the name of the company, its logo, address, telephone and fax numbers. Some of this data can appear at the foot of the page if you like.
■ A 'catchline' identifies a story, and is the word or short phrase used when referring to it. Put a catchline in the top left-hand corner. If your story is about a new range of professional books published by Kogan Page, your catchline might be simply: 'Kogan Page books'.
■ An 'embargo' requests an editor not to publish until a certain date and time. Use it only if you have a really good reason. Put 'EMBARGO' before your headline, briefly give the reason, and the date for publication. Editors will usually cooperate, but don't be surprised if they ignore it; it's not binding.
■ Create a margin of at least 30 mm at both edges of the paper. The sub-editor uses this space for typesetting and make-up instructions.

Figure 10.1 *Example of news release*

▓ Use double-spacing. Use only one side of each sheet.
▓ Don't indent the first paragraph; indent all the others. Check for those media on your list that do indent first paragraphs, and prepare a separate release for them. The aim is not to give the editor unnecessary work.
▓ If your copy is long, use sub-heads to break it into logical sections; this will make it easier for the editor to read.

▓ If you have to carry copy over to the next page, do not break up a sentence or a paragraph. Don't use a sub-head within three lines of the foot of a page.

▓ Number all continuation pages in the top right-hand corner. Put the story's catchline in the top left-hand corner.

▓ Date the release and give it a reference number.

▓ Give a name and telephone number for editors to contact if they want more information or a discussion.

▓ Type 'More follows' at the foot of every page on which your copy is carried over. Type 'Ends' at the end, below the final line of copy.

▓ If there is a lot of technical detail to your story, put it on a separate sheet headed 'Technical information', or 'Technical notes for editors'. This avoids cluttering your story proper, which should be as newsy as possible. In writing up your story for his readers, the editor may include some or all of the technical info. In separating technical info from news, you offer the editor the opportunity to add, rather than delete. It's more positive.

▓ Likewise, instead of cluttering your news with background information on your company or product range, attach an extra sheet headed 'Note to editors', or 'Background information for editors'.

Having firmly established the basics, let's now look at techniques for creating effective news releases. See Figure 10.1 for example.

GUIDELINES

Content

▓ Give your story a title.

▓ Start with a short intro paragraph; condense the whole story into it.

▓ Follow this with the complete story.

▓ Use quotations effectively, but sparingly.

▓ End with contact information.

Style

▓ Decide on the type of story you are going to write.

■ Apply the W6H technique: What? Who? When? Where? Why? Which? How?
■ Plan the length according to the weight of the story.
■ Use language the editor can use.
■ Write tersely, in clear, simple English.
■ Write sentences and paragraphs of reasonable length.
■ Keep to the facts you have selected.
■ Apply emphasis sparingly, and only where it really counts.
■ Use correct spelling and punctuation.
■ Avoid self-praise and exaggeration.

Final checking

■ Check spelling, punctuation and grammar.
■ Purge waste words, redundant words and phrases.
■ Check the accuracy of your facts and statements.
■ Read it over for sense and storyline.

EXPLOITING THESE TECHNIQUES

Content

Give your story a title

Your title should tell the editor at one glance what the story is about. If it looks right for his publication, he may read the whole press release. If not, he will stop right there, and bin it.

If you distribute news releases electronically, be aware that some editors use a clever piece of time-saving software. This allows them to view news releases only as far as the end of the first paragraph. If an editor can't detect a promising story by then, he can delete the whole item.

Guidelines for titles:

■ Make your title a simple summary of the key point in the story.
■ Sub-editors usually write their own titles. This is inevitably in their publication's own style, designed to tempt readers. Therefore, don't be witty, waggish or eccentric with your titles; the editorial staff can quite easily do that for themselves. Just stick to the central fact.

■ Your title should be just long enough to cover the key point; 12 words at most. If you really *must* qualify it, or make another point at the head of a story, do it in the form of a sub-title; and keep it short.

■ Whatever your title says, make it *active* by including a verb. 'Kogan Page launches new professional book series' is more active, and interesting, than 'New professional books from Kogan Page'. The word 'launches' does the work.

■ Don't despair if, before you start, you can't think of a title for your story. Do it the other way round. By the time you've completed the body copy, you'll have digested the story and be in a better position to create a viable title.

Start with a short intro paragraph; condense the whole story into it

Your first paragraph should be no more than two sentences. In it, you should put the essence of the whole story. The editor can then assess the story without having to read it all.

Use quotations effectively, but sparingly

Quotes add human interest to a story, and give it extra credibility. Therefore:

■ Make sure what your quoter says is relevant, and actually adds something to your story. Specify the quoter's name.

■ A quote is a personal statement, so use personal words such as 'I' and 'us' and 'we'.

■ As always, keep it simple; use plain English, and simple words and phrases.

■ Self-praise in a quotation can damage a promising story. You don't want your managing director, for example, to sound like King Kong. Avoid smugness, complacency and back-patting.

■ Keep it short.

End with contact information

At the end of the release, give a name and telephone number for editors to contact if they want more information or a discussion. A discussion could lead to a major article based on your story.

Style

Decide on the type of story you are going to write
This can depend on the publications you are sending it to. However, with every story, you need to decide whether it is a consumer story, a product story, an 'event' story, a technical, problem-solving, personality or background information piece. Whatever it is, it needs a core and a lead. You must decide this at the start, to prevent your copy wandering aimlessly to an unsatisfactory conclusion. The best way of thinking about this is in the form of the W6H formula.

Apply the W6H technique: What? Who? When? Where? Why? Which? How?
Whatever the range of information in your story, the editor wants to know certain basic facts. He needs these for two reasons:

1. to decide quickly whether your story is a real story, and whether it is worth running
2. to decide how to run it, and if he needs more information.

You therefore need to plan your story on the W6H formula, so that it includes:

1. WHAT: What the story is about; what is happening; what is new about it; what is unique about it.
2. WHO: To whom it is happening; who is making it happen; who is involved.
3. WHERE: Where the action or event took place, is taking place or will take place. Precise information.
4. WHEN: When it happened, is happening or will happen. Precisely.
5. WHY: Reasons why this has happened, is happening or will happen.
6. WHICH: Which organisations or people are affected by it.
7. HOW: How it is happening; the sequence of events; how people or organisations are affected; how it benefits those affected; how the product works.

While considering this, you need to decide what the main idea of your story is to be, and what should lead it. It should, for example, be:

What-led	Why-led
Who-led	Which-led
Where-led	How-led
When-led	

It is unlikely that a single press release will appeal to every publication on your press list. For example:

■ a personnel magazine appreciates stories about people and companies
■ regional newspapers and magazines go for stories about people and companies in their circulation areas
■ technical journals look for technical success stories.

Ideally, you should apply W6H to suit each publication getting the story, then tailor the story to match each one. However, this is expensive and time-consuming. It is easier to divide the publications on your list into groups, each representing a common interest, and slant the story for each group.

Study the media you are using – see what appeals to each one, and plan your story accordingly.

Plan the length according to the weight of the story

For example, a story about a stolen cat might just make four lines in your local paper. A national competition for Britain's best-looking kitten, sponsored by a major petfood company, could make half a column in a marketing magazine, a column in a national tabloid newspaper, and a page in a petlover's monthly.

Again, it's a good idea to study the media on your list, and judge what weight and style of stories they most easily accept.

Use language the editor can use

Consumer publications use consumer language; even the technical language they use is pitched at the level of consumers' understanding. However, the editor will appreciate a technical appendix. Technical publications need technical data, but remember that editors want stories they can use, whatever the technicalities. Give editors stories in plain English, and the grinding technical detail in appendix form. Editors know their jobs, and know how to combine the two.

Write tersely, in clear, simple English
As with advertising copy technique, 'terse' does not mean 'short' or 'clipped'. It does mean tight, readable, professional writing. Use simple words and phrases wherever possible. Edit your copy efficiently; purge it of redundant words and phrases.

When sending stories to US media, remember that, although they use English, it is not *Queen's* English. Also, their writing style differs from that of the UK and the Commonwealth. Some words differ in meaning from their Queen's English counterparts. Be careful to use US spelling. See Chapter 4 on words in this book.

Write sentences and paragraphs of reasonable length
Aim at one idea per sentence, and no more than two commas. Group related ideas logically in the same paragraph. Make paragraphs of readable length, which do not tax your reader's patience, mind or memory.

Keep to the facts you have selected
If you have selected the right facts for the story, related them to the media you are using, and arranged them in logical order, the story should be easy to write. Don't introduce extra facts unless you first review the story as a whole.

Apply emphasis sparingly, and only where it really counts
An occasional word in italics is fine, if it provides a degree of emphasis in the right place. But avoid dotting them all over your copy. Do not underline words in a news release – this is an instruction to the printer to set in italic type. If you must have italics, go to Chapter 12 to see how it's done.

Avoid self-praise and exaggeration
… like the plague. See your copy from the editor's point of view; if you find yourself using a word which he might regard as self-praise, purge it. Otherwise, your copy may fly to the bin.

Do not mention your brand name more than twice throughout the entire text, or your company's name more than once.

Use correct spelling and punctuation
Your best friends are the *Concise Oxford English Dictionary*, *Fowler's Modern English Usage*, and *Hart's Rules for Compositors and Readers*. See Chapter 22.

Final checking

Check spelling, punctuation and grammar
Do not make the editor do any of the work you should be doing. He may not have the time, and your release will end in the bin.

Purge waste words, redundant words and phrases
Go through it again for a final edit.

Check the accuracy of your facts and statements
The corporate or brand situation may have changed since you received the brief. A quick check will safely update you.

Read it over for sense and storyline
A final read, and see it from the editor's angle.

Make sure your picture and its caption are relevant
A sensible precaution. The picture should be relevant both to your story and the destination media. For technique, see Chapter 11.

11

Improving Your Photographs and Illustrations

If it doesn't sell, it isn't creative.

– Benton & Bowles

GUIDELINES

- Make your publicity pictures active …
- … and motivating.
- Ensure your pictures are effectively captioned.
- Ensure optimum reproduction.
- Take steps to avoid problematic or doubtful pictures.

EXPLOITING THESE TECHNIQUES

Make your publicity pictures active

I would be amazed if you had not at some time wondered about a house-journal photograph showing a line of dark-suited executives staring at the camera. Some of them are clutching their genitals; at least one grimacing in a genuine attempt to smile. You might have asked yourself what they are doing there, what they are illustrating and what prompted the photographer to line them up like that.

Unless you are promoting tailors' dummies, photographs showing people should look alive and active. Preferably, the people in your picture should be *doing* something instead of merely being there. What they are doing should be connected with your brand, or whatever you are promoting.

The essence of this technique – for advertising as well as PR – is making every picture show:

■ something about to happen; or
■ something actually happening; or
■ something that has just happened.

Look at the national press, and learn from their picture editors.

What you show must also be topical. A word of caution: cars, buildings and technology tend to date rapidly.

The secret is in the briefing – every professional photographer appreciates the support of a competent brief.

For advertising and print, base your briefing on the creative brief and on approved layouts. For PR, base it on your assignment brief and the news element of your release.

Take the advice of the photographer. However, don't just hand the photographer a sheaf of papers and hope for the best. To get what you want, and get the best results, *talk* to him. Take his advice.

I can hear you saying: 'What if I'm given a picture taken by a well-meaning amateur, and am obliged to use it?'

■ *Solution 1:* Consult your photographer; he'll probably crop it efficiently and eliminate the worst bits. Or he may recommend retouching.
■ *Solution 2:* Crop it carefully yourself. Cropping is the art of trimming a photograph or illustration to make it fit a space, or to get rid of unwanted visual junk.
■ *Solution 3:* You may have realised that some problems in marketing life have no solution – this may be one of them. I sympathise.

Make your publicity pictures motivating

Photography is expensive. Make sure every picture and illustration you commission and use has a purpose in the promotion you are creating. Make sure every picture you use has Positive Promotional Value. It's amazing how many expensive brochures sent to me use photography just for design – rather than for promotion and motivation.

Concentrate on appealing to the reader's self-interest – again, the magic ingredient. What you show should be relevant to what he is buying, as well as what you are promoting. Bear in mind that these motives may not be the same.

Pictures accompanying news releases must appeal to editors as well as their readers. Editors are not interested in advertising photography; they will bin any shot that looks like advertising. Take care.

Ensure your pictures are effectively captioned

In press advertising and brochures, pictures which show something intriguing, yet don't explain what's going on, are a turn-off. Turning customers off is definitely not what you want.

In editorial PR, any photograph without a caption invites sudden death at the hands of the editor.

Photoprints
A photograph is referred to as a photoprint, but is commonly called 'a print'.

Attaching a caption to a photoprint

■ Type your caption on white paper, and tape it to the back of the print. If you prefer, tape the caption strip to the back of the photoprint so that it hinges forward. The editor can then look at the copy and the photograph together in the same plane.

■ Do not use an adhesive label; the editor may want to remove it, edit the copy and mark it up for typesetting. Rather than take the trouble to steam the label off, damaging the print in the process, he may decide not to use it.

■ Never write on the back of a print. You may damage the photographed side and render it unusable.

■ Never use staples, pins or paper clips. They damage prints.

Transparencies
Attaching a caption to a transparency

■ 35 mm 'trannies' are usually mounted in white plastic frames. Write a short identifying title on the mount in indelible black marker. Enclose the tranny in a translucent paper sleeve or envelope, and include a full caption on a separate sheet or slip.
■ Larger sizes, such as 120 roll-film (57 mm or 2¼ in square), 6 in × 4 in and 10 in × 8 in are usually not mounted. Mark the translucent sleeve with identifying information, and include a caption sheet. Never use staples.

What to put into captions for PR
■ Editors look for stories they can print. Make sure your copy accurately describes what is happening in the picture.
■ Ideally, your picture and caption combination should tell a complete story.
■ Your caption should not only tell the story, but also help to sell the story to target editors. Put PRO contact information at the end.
■ Everyone in a group shot should be identified. Make sure your photographer takes the names after shooting each picture. This is particularly important during a meeting or conference; one group can look very like another.

What to put into captions for ads and print
There are two basic styles of caption:

1. the one-liner
2. the extended caption.

The one-liner is probably the most difficult to write – or, rather, it is often extremely difficult to choose what to put into it. Go for the simple description, a single fact or the main consumer benefit.

The copy style of one-liners depends on the effect you want. If you are showing a disposable oil filter for an industrial hydraulic system, you can make the caption benefit-active even if the picture is just a still-life.

Better, of course, is to show a close-up of the filter actually being changed, and caption it with one main benefit. For example:

Filter Mk 2: a clean change in under 30 seconds.

or:

Easy change-over with clean hands: Filter Mk 2.

An extended caption may be anything up to 10 lines; in this case, you need to write it as a mini-story. For example: the problem; how your brand solved it; the satisfactory result. Because this is in short form, and therefore condensed, it must also be plausible.

Be careful not to make your copy too clipped, which can render it hard to assimilate. This is tempting, especially when showing complicated or high-tech equipment. If an editor wants to butcher a caption, it's up to him.

As always, tailor the technique to the target.

Suggestions for caption content
The content of your captions is as vital as the pictures they illustrate. Therefore, ensure your captions contain:

▪ **Benefits**
Select information your reader wants to see or learn, and which appeal to his self-interest. At the very least, a caption should convey, or strongly imply, the promise of a benefit, solution or pleasure to come.

▪ **Facts**
Make sure you supply useful information. This should start with a description of what is happening in the picture. If you are stuck with a picture in which nothing is happening, refer to something active associated with it.

▪ **Action**
Make sure what is being shown demonstrates an important benefit to be obtained from using your brand, product or service.

▪ **Solutions**
If your customers want to see results, show them, describe them. Present them as results arising from the use of your brand.

▪ **Names**
Wherever possible, name the people in the picture. It makes the

argument in your body copy more effective. I realise that every machine-minder cannot be named in a shot of a factory floor; give them job titles.

Ensure optimum reproduction

The two main considerations are:

1. whether the picture is for advertising, print or PR
2. whether it is to be reproduced in black and white or colour.

Pictures for advertising and print

Make sure they are suited to the media in which they appear. You have total control over this, so it is worth taking care. As always, brief your specialist suppliers and take their advice.

The important factors are:

▓ the printing process used by the various media
▓ the paper being used in each case
▓ the appropriate halftone screen
▓ the contrast and detail you need
▓ Whether you intend to print copy over or out of the illustration. The general rule is: the typeface and size must be readable. A spindly typeface in a small size prints very badly out of four colours. Poor colour registration can render it totally unreadable.

For more information, see Chapter 16.

Pictures for PR

Use the best possible photography for PR. You have less control over pictures sent to publications – indeed, in most cases, you have none at all. So, concentrate on producing the best possible professional news photography to start with! Amateur efforts should be rejected.

Point out, tactfully, that although the chairman's wife may be good with a camera, your local press photographer is better. His career and livelihood depend on being better. What's more, he has experienced, professional picture sense; he understands media, editors and print reproduction, and techniques for getting the best out of poor photo-situations.

That should do it.

Black and white prints

Take care when preparing prints for press. Most newspapers use coarse paper called newsprint. The result is that photographs reproduced on newsprint often turn out poorer in quality than the originals. Therefore, take care when preparing originals for the press, so that your pictures achieve the best impact.

When briefing your suppliers, make sure they know what's on the media schedule, and have the mechanical information provided by the publishers.

▓ Ensure good contrast in the original photoprint. This is because you will lose some of it both during platemaking and printing. Some magazines use better-quality paper, glossy on the surface. This raises the reproduction quality of your photoprint, but you still need good contrast.

▓ Ideally, black and white photoprints should be 50 per cent larger than they will be when printed. This is known in the trade as 'half up'. Enlarging a photoprint to fit a space always loses quality and sharpness; reducing is much safer.

▓ Brochures and leaflets usually use better-quality paper than newspapers and magazines. Next time you are passing a main car dealer's showroom, grab a few brochures and examine their quality. The paper, known as 'stock', is excellent. The best of these has a smooth coating, to provide the best possible surface for printing.

Pay careful attention to the photographic illustrations. Usually, these will be made from first-class photoprints and transparencies, with good contrast, brightness and density.

Try to emulate this high standard of quality in the photography you commission for all your company's advertising, editorial and print output – black and white as well as colour.

Colour photography

The best quality for colour printing is obtained from transparencies, rather than photoprints. Unless you have absolutely no choice, always send colour transparencies for editorial work.

The size of the tranny is not critical, but the larger the better: 35 mm is acceptable, but the image needs to be absolutely pin-sharp; 120 size (57 mm or 2¼ in square) is a reasonable compromise; 6 in × 4 in is better, particularly as this size is easier for picture editors to examine.

What to do about problematic or doubtful pictures

Talk to your suppliers: the photographer, retoucher, platemaker, printer. They are your best allies, so explain carefully and take their advice.

12

How to Read and Correct Proofs

We must never assume that which is incapable of proof.
– George Henry Lewes

GUIDELINES

- Make sure all pages are present.
- Check that all your instructions have been carried out.
- Use red ballpoint for marking corrections.
- Use the system accepted by the printing and publishing industry.
- Mark errors in the text from left to right.
- Correspondingly, give corrections in the margin also from left to right.
- Ideally, two people working together should read and correct proofs.
- Check spelling, punctuation, names and numbers.
- Do not confuse the letter 'O' and the numeral '0'.
- For large insertions of copy, use a separate sheet.
- Check and correct hyphenation and justification.
- Check layout, line spacing, widows and orphans.
- Familiarise yourself with the British Standard for proof-correcting symbols.

EXPLOITING THESE TECHNIQUES

Make sure all pages are present
This saves time in the long run; there is no point in leaving it to the end of the process. You can lose track of where you stopped reading a proof while waiting for missing pages, and may miss something when you get back to it. Make sure the original copy accompanies the proof, together with the marked-up layout if there is one.

Check that all your instructions have been carried out
If this is not so, contact the printer at once.

Use red ballpoint for marking corrections
Different colours identify where different people have made corrections. Copywriters usually use red and blue; printers mostly green. There is no hard rule about this, just convention. Clients usually use blood.

Use the system accepted by the printing and publishing industry
There is a British Standard for proof-correcting: BS 5261: Part 2 1976. Copywriters, authors, printers and publishers are recommended to use the symbols in this system.

This is a more or less international standard, because it does not use words to describe corrections to be made. There is a previous standard, BS 1219, if you prefer to use instructions in words; the effect is much the same.

Mark errors in the text from left to right
Be systematic: mark errors in the text as you go along.

Correspondingly, show corrections in the margin also from left to right
Where there is only a single error to be corrected in a line of copy, use the left-hand margin to show what that correction is.

Where there are several corrections in a line, use a left-to-right sequence. If you run out of left-hand margin, use the right-hand one.

Ideally, two people working together should read and correct proofs
Use a reliable colleague; for proof-reading, two heads are definitely better than one.

Read the proofed copy out loud; your colleague follows it in the original manuscript, calling out every time you read a mistake. You then mark that correction on the proof.

If you are forced to read proofs on your own, do it slowly and carefully. There's a small problem here: you may have written the copy yourself and know it by heart. You could miss errors. In that case, read the proof upside down; hold the proof upside down, I mean, unless you are really keen to stand on your head when proof-reading. It sometimes feels like this after a couple of hours of proof checking.

Check spelling, punctuation, names and numbers
The safest method is to read out absolutely everything, including all caps, commas, full stops and hyphens. You need to take care about reading out words in bold, italics and small caps. For example: where a word is in bold, say 'bold', then read the word. Important spaces need to be read out loud, so that the copy-holder can check them.

Take special care over names, spelling them out carefully – telephone numbers as well. Be ruthlessly pedantic; many an advertising account has been lost over an uncorrected phone number.

Do not confuse the letter 'O' and the numeral '0'
Distinguish between the letter 'O' and the numeral '0', which you should call 'zero', 'nought' or 'null'.

For large insertions of copy, use a separate sheet
Do not cram lengthy corrections, especially new and omitted copy, into the margins. They will probably be unreadable, and may cause further errors – which you will need to correct and return to the printer.

Use a key letter to identify each copy insertion, and mark the same key on the proof where you want it inserted. Leave no doubt where each piece of new copy goes.

Staple the new copy to the sheet to which it belongs. Do not use paper clips, which are insecure and cause more angst than they are worth.

Check and correct hyphenation and justification
If a word-break at the end of a line looks unsightly, or unacceptable for any other reason, correct it at this stage. Hyphenation is usually done by the typesetter's computer, which sometimes cannot discriminate between proper word-breaks and barmy word-breaks. If your typescript does not contain daft word-breaks, you should be entitled to ask your typesetter to correct them without charge if they occur on his proofs.

The *Concise Oxford English Dictionary* is your best friend when proof-reading. Keep a copy on your desk and use it. Insist on your right to be read properly.

See Chapter 22 for dictionary information.

Check layout, line spacing, widows and orphans
A widow is a single word carried over on to a subsequent page or column, sitting there in isolation from the rest of its paragraph. This is always undesirable.

An orphan is a single line at the beginning of a paragraph, stuck at the foot of a page, while the rest is on the next page. This is usually undesirable, but not always. If you allow an orphan to live, make sure it is deliberate and not the victim of a proofing error.

Familiarise yourself with the British Standard for proof-correcting symbols
Figure 12.1 provides a selection of proofreading marks.

PROOF-READING MARKS

CORRECTION REQUIRED	MARK IN THE MARGIN	MARK IN THE COPY	
Insert into copy	New copy, followed by ⅄	⅄	
Insert full-point	⊙⅄	⅄	
Insert comma	⸴⅄	⅄	
Insert semi-colon	⨟⅄	⅄	
Insert colon	⊙⅄	⅄	
Insert single quote-marks	⸜ OR ⸝	⅄	
Insert double quote-marks	⸜⸜ OR ⸝⸝	⅄	
Delete from copy	ꝺ	/	through copy
Delete and close up	ꝺ	⌒	through copy
Close up space	⌒/	⌒	linking characters
Leave unchanged	✓	....	under copy
End of this correction	/		
Set in caps	☰/	☰	under copy
Set in small caps	☰/	☰	under copy
Set in itals	⊔/	―	under copy
Set in bold	∿/	∿	under copy
Change caps to lower-case	≢/		circle copy
Change to full-point	⊙/	/	through copy
Start new para	⌐/	⌐	
Run copy on	⌣/	⌣	linking copy
Transpose characters	⊔⌐/	⊔⌐	between characters
Indent line	⌐/	⌐	
Centre the copy	[ ]/	[ ]	round copy
Take over to next line	⊏/	⊏	
Take back from previous line	⊐/	⊐	

Figure 12.1 *Proof-reading marks*

RAW COPY FOR CORRECTION

Correcting proofs cost monay, These days, changing a single
comma costs you £25 or more; which is downright wicked. So,
it's important to eliminate changes at proof stage - or at
least avoid as many as you can. The proper way to do this is
to get your manuscript read and corrected before submitting it
to the printer. The most efficient technique for reading
proofs is to do it with a reliable colleague. You read the
profed copy out loud; your colleague follows it in the
original manuscript, calling out every time you read a
mistake. You then mark in the corrections on the proof. The
safest method is to read out absolutely everything, including
all caps, commas, full-stops and hyphens You need to take
care about reading out words in bold, italics and small caps.
The most important spaces need to be read out loud, so that
the copy-holder can check them. take special care over NAMES,
spelling them out carefully; and telephone numbers as well.
You can't be too pedantic about this. Or, rather, you need to
be ruthlessly pedantic; many an advertising account has been
lost over an uncorrected 'phone number. Distinguish the letter
'O' and the numeral '0', which you should call 'zero',
'nought' or 'null'. Printers are usually very good at checking
proofs. However, one thing you can't rely on is the printer's
computer spell-checker. Like the spell-checker in your own
computer, it cannot distinguish between properly-spelled
words. If you type 'than', for example, but meant really to
type 'then', the computer won't see this as an error. Beware
of americanisms; some typesetting software is not properly
anglicised. If you have no option but to check proofs without
the aid of a friend, read very slowly and carefully. Time is
money when reading proofs; if you don't spend the time, you
may have to spend money instead. And it can cost you more time
as well! because proofs take time to re-set... and you will
have to check them again, to be really safe. Tip: get a copy
of the British Standard on proof-correcting.

As a useful exercise, correct this copy using standard marks.
Compare your results with the next two pages.

HOW MARKS ARE USED IN CORRECTING COPY AND PROOFS

Correcting proofs cost money, These days, changing a single comma costs you £25 or more; which is downright wicked. So, it's important to eliminate changes at proof stage - or at least avoid as many as you can. The proper way to do this is to get your manuscript read and corrected before submitting it to the printer. The most efficient technique for reading proofs is to do it with a reliable colleague. You read the profed copy out loud; your colleague follows it in the original manuscript, calling out every time you read a mistake. You then mark in the corrections on the proof. The safest method is to read out absolutely everything, including all caps, commas, full-stops and hyphens. You need to take care about reading out words in bold, italics and small caps.

The most important spaces need to be read out loud, so that the copy-holder can check them. take special care over NAMES, spelling them out carefully; and telephone numbers as well. You can't be too pedantic about this. Or, rather, you need to be ruthlessly pedantic; many an advertising account has been lost over an uncorrected 'phone number. Distinguish the letter 'O' and the numeral '0', which you should call 'zero', 'nought' or 'null'. Printers are usually very good at checking proofs. However, one thing you can't rely on is the printer's computer spell-checker. Like the spell-checker in your own computer, it cannot distinguish between properly-spelled words. If you type 'than', for example, but meant really to type 'then', the computer won't see this as an error. Beware of americanisms; some typesetting software is not properly anglicised. If you have no option but to check proofs without the aid of a friend, read very slowly and carefully. Time is money when reading proofs; if you don't spend the time, you may have to spend money instead. And it can cost you more time as well because proofs take time to re-set... and you will have to check them again, to be really safe. Tip: get a copy of the British Standard on proof correcting.

THE CORRECTED PROOF

Correcting proofs cost money, These days, changing a single comma costs you £25 or more; which is downright wicked. So, it's important to eliminate changes at proof stage - or at least avoid as many as you can. The proper way to do this is to get your manuscript read and corrected *before* submitting it to the printer.

The most efficient technique for reading proofs is to do it with a reliable colleague. You read the proofed copy out loud; your colleague follows it in the original manuscript, calling out every time you read a mistake. You then mark the corrections on the proof.

The safest method is to read out absolutely everything, including all caps, commas, full-stops and hyphens. You need to take care about reading out words in bold, italics and small caps. The most important spaces need to be read out loud, so that the copy-holder can check them. Take special care over names, spelling them out carefully; and telephone numbers as well. You need to be ruthlessly pedantic; many an advertising account has been lost over an uncorrected 'phone number. Distinguish the letter 'O' and the numeral '0', which you should call 'zero', 'nought' or 'null'.

Printers are usually very good at checking proofs. However, one thing you can't rely on is the printer's computer spell-checker. Like the spell-checker in your own computer, it cannot distinguish between properly-spelled words. If you type 'than', for example, but really meant to type 'then', the computer won't see this as an error. Beware of Americanisms; some typesetting software is not properly anglicised. If you have no option but to check proofs without the aid of a colleague, read slowly and carefully. Time is money when reading proofs; if you don't spend the time, you may have to spend money instead. And it can cost you more time as well, because proofs take time to re-set... and you will have to check them again, to be really safe.

Tip: get a copy of the **British Standard** on correcting proofs.

13

Printing and Print

Ab uno disce omnes. From one case you may learn all the rest.
— Tacitus

Six printing processes are today used throughout the marketing communications business. Each has its own production characteristics, its own advantages and disadvantages. One thing is common to all these processes: the transfer of images on to paper or other material.

This chapter does not offer you a history lesson on printing through the ages. There are many other books dealing with this aspect of print. What it does is outline the main printing processes, and show how they are best used in marketing communications.

You will find more on printing processes in the Essential Reference chapter.

Process	Printing technique
Lithography	prints from a flat printing surface using thin, flexible metal plates (planographic printing). Also called litho and offset
Gravure	uses engraved copper-plated cylinders (intaglio printing)
Digital	prints electrostatically with toner fusion, without film or printing plates

Flexography	uses thin, flexible neoprene plates with a raised printing surface (relief printing)
Screen	prints through a mesh (stencil printing)
Letterpress	uses heavy, rigid metal plates with a raised printing surface (relief printing)

FACTS ABOUT LITHO

■ This is by far the most widely used printing process, certainly in the UK, the EU and the USA. It accounts for over 70 per cent of all printed matter.

■ It is a printing process based on the use of greasy ink and water, and on the fact that these two do not mix.

■ The printing plate is prepared so that the printing areas attract ink, and the non-printing areas attract water.

■ During printing, the plate is first dampened with water. When the oil-based ink is applied, the image areas attract it and the water-coated areas repel it.

■ Litho uses thin, flexible metal printing plates. These are wrapped round cylinders on the printing press.

■ In offset litho printing, the most common technique, the plates do not print direct on to the paper. The image is first transferred on to a cylinder covered with a rubber or neoprene 'blanket', which then prints the image on the paper. The blanket offsets the image, hence the term offset litho.

■ The use of an offset blanket minimises wear on the metal printing plate. This gives it a much extended working life, and the ability to print longer runs.

■ Offset litho presses have at least three printing cylinders:

1. a plate cylinder, which carries the metal printing plate
2. a blanket cylinder
3. an impression cylinder, which presents the paper to the blanket cylinder for receiving the printed image.

■ The presses use a system of inking and dampening rollers and reservoirs.

■ The printing plate comes into contact first with the dampening rollers, then the inking rollers.

■ There are two types of offset printing press:

1. sheet-fed offset
2. web-fed offset.

Sheet-fed offset press

■ prints on single sheets
■ prints at speeds up to 11,000 impressions an hour
■ presses have single or multicolour units
■ multicolour presses print up to eight colours in a single pass
■ perfecting presses print both sides of the sheet in the same pass
■ sheets can be varnished on the run
■ sheets are delivered at the dry end in a stack, ready for finishing: cutting, folding, binding and guillotining. See Figure 13.1.

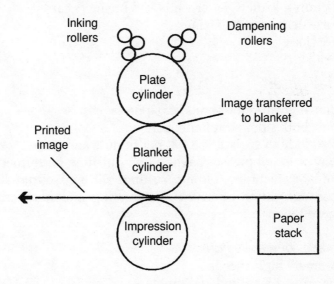

This is sheet-fed offset. The inked image is transferred from the plate cylinder to the blanket, which offsets it to one side of the paper. Each printing unit of an offset press prints a single colour.

Figure 13.1 *The principle of offset litho*

Advantages of sheet-fed offset

- prints all the international sheet sizes
- prints a wide range of materials, from paper to board
- prints well on poor-quality materials
- delivers excellent colour reproduction
- printing plates are economical and easy to make
- make-ready is simple and economical
- economical for short or medium-long runs, from a few thousand to over 50,000.

Disadvantage

- much manual paper-handling, eg manhandling paper to the press, stacking paper at the wet (input) end, removing it at the dry end; manhandling it through the finishing stages.

Optimum and economical uses of sheet-fed offset

- medium-run newspapers, magazines and catalogues; brochures, leaflets, letterheads and business cards
- short-run house magazines
- stationery.

Web-fed offset

- prints on continuous reels of paper – webs
- prints both sides simultaneously
- prints at high speeds, 2,200 ft per minute and more
- many web-fed presses have in-line finishing performed on the run. This includes folding, cutting, slitting, saddle stitching, inserting, gluing of inserts, perforating and numbering. See Figure 13.2.

Advantages of web-fed offset

- extremely high speeds
- long runs, 1.5 million and more
- can compete with sheet-fed litho on medium-short runs, from about 12,000 copies
- prints up to eight colours in a single pass
- excellent colour reproduction
- good depth of colour and gloss, produced by advanced drying processes

There are two sets of cylinders and rollers: the printing unit prints both sides of the paper in a single pass. The inked images are transferred from the plate cylinders to the blankets, which offset them to the paper on each side.

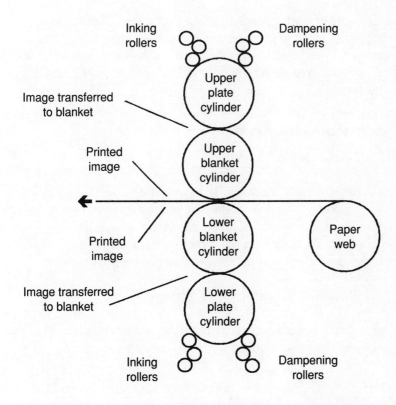

Figure 13.2 *The principle of double-sided offset*

■ economical, easily made printing plates
■ simple make-ready.

Optimum and economical uses of web-fed offset
■ long-run newspapers, magazines and catalogues.

FACTS ABOUT GRAVURE

Gravure, also called photogravure, uses copper-plated cylinders engraved with myriad cells. During the print run, each cell, filled with a thinnish, volatile printing ink, prints a dot on the paper. Surplus ink is removed from the cylinder by a sprung metal blade, called a doctor.

Unlike the other high-speed printing methods, litho, letterpress and flexography (qv), in gravure printing, the entire image area is dot-screened. Type and line-work are screened, as well as halftones. In other words, the whole cylinder is a single, uninterrupted halftone.

Preparation of gravure cylinders

Several methods exist, including:

▦ **Helio-Klischograph.** Artwork is scanned electronically; cylinders are engraved with diamond-tipped engraving heads, in a movement similar to that of a sewing machine needle.
▦ **Lasergravure.** Works direct from computer data. Uses a laser to engrave a special epoxy and plastic coating on the cylinder.

Figure 13.3 illustrates the principle of gravure.

Tip: Before commissioning gravure printing, get specialised advice on origination. Artwork requirements are different from litho.

Advantages of gravure
▦ high speeds: 2,000 ft a minute or more.
▦ uses continuous webs
▦ can print up to 48 pages in one continuous operation
▦ can print 8 colours in a single pass
▦ delivers high-quality colour, in a wide tonal range
▦ prints a wide variety of materials and surfaces
▦ cylinders are hard-wearing and can be made more long-lasting by chromium plating.

Disadvantages of gravure
▦ cylinders are very expensive

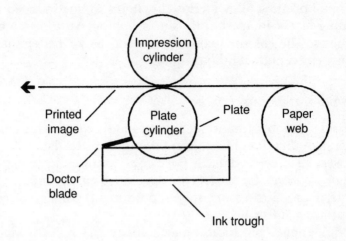

The plate cylinder rotates in a trough of ink. The thousands of etched cells in the plate receive the ink. The surplus is wiped by the flexible steel doctor. The remaining ink forms the image by direct transfer to the paper.

Figure 13.3 *The principle of gravure*

■ machine proofing is exorbitant – dry proofing or computer-aided proofing is cheaper
■ once engraved, pages on a cylinder cannot be changed or modified; a new cylinder is required. Failing that, a specially prepared patch may be possible. Either way, you are in for big money.

Optimum and economical uses of gravure
■ long-run newspapers and magazines; mail-order catalogues
■ security printing, such as postage stamps and share certificates
■ packaging; wallpaper.

FACTS ABOUT DIGITAL PRINTING

Among the most important changes in marketing communications is the rapid development of short-run colour printing technology. Digital printing is at the leading edge, and the main contender for short-run and on-demand printing.

Digital printing allows printed material to be produced without printing plates, imagesetting, film, stripping, halftone screening or scanning. The colour quality is as good as, or better than high-quality conventional litho printing.

Computer-generated data

Probably its most important features is that it accepts computer-generated data. It converts computer-generated data into images. The system accepts data in PostScript form, either direct from a disk or via ISDN. It converts the data into a bitmap image via a RIP (Raster Image Processor), then reproduces the image direct on to the printing substrate.

Origination is produced on a company's own PC or Mac in any PostScript application. After everything has been finalised, the job is saved to disk and sent for printing. It can be sent by modem or ISDN line (Integrated Systems Digital Network, a high-quality data transmission system). The files go straight from the printer's computer system to the press.

One of the first digital colour presses was Agfa's Chromapress, designed for short runs up to 5000 copies. IntelliStream, the version launched in 1997, enables complete jobs to be printed straight from computer output.

The system can produce micro-runs, eg 200 company factsheets in 10 languages in a single pass. With its Electronic Collation feature, IntelliStream enables you to produce, say, five 126-page brochures as a preview for a trade exhibition. With other print technologies, this complex operation can be too costly and time-consuming. See Figure 13.4.

Instant reprints

On-demand printing, and instant reprints of existing print jobs, is an IntelliStream option. It enables past print jobs to be retrieved from the computerised archive, and reprinted immediately.

Other companies manufacturing digital systems include Xerox, MicroPress and Heidelberg. Research programmes by Mitsubishi, Man Roland and Océ, using their own technological techniques, could be under way during the lifetime of this edition of *Creative Marketing Communications*.

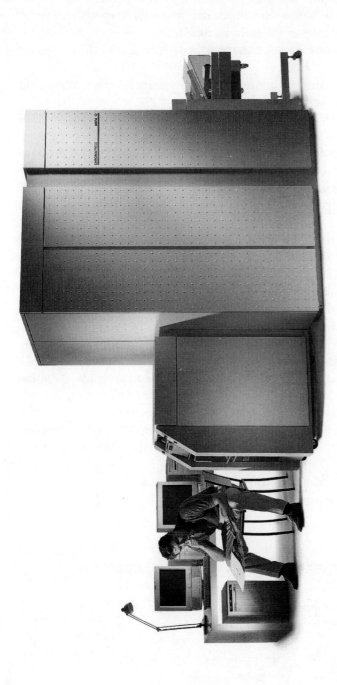

Agfa's IntelliStream digital colour printing system. It enables high-quality brochures, leaflets, books and other material to be printed straight from computer disk. You can print 200 company factsheets in 10 languages, for example, in a single run. The true revolution lies in the total absence of film, photo-processing, colour separations and other time-consuming pre-press procedures. And in the on-demand possibilities if offers.

Figure 13.4 *Digital revolution*

Advantages of digital printing
■ allows you to create promotional material targeted to small groups of recipients, or even individuals
■ a digital colour press can produce over 2,000 double-sided colour pages an hour
■ it needs no film or plates, no imagesetting, film, stripping, halftone screening or scanning
■ make-ready is limited to loading the press with the paper to be used
■ the printer or in-house print manager can complete a job 60 per cent faster than conventional offset litho
■ on 4-colour runs, it can also be more economical
■ every single page can be different. Even parts of a page can be personalised
■ elements can be merged, so that no two sales letters, house journals, leaflets, booklets, posters or news releases need be the same
■ with Xeikon-based printing, the maximum width is 320 mm
■ because the Xeikon press is reel-fed, the printed length can vary up to 840 mm. This makes four-colour process printing economical on any job from a simple compliment slip to a 96-page brochure, even for small quantities.
■ it can be used cost-effectively for quantities as low as 10 copies.

Disadvantages of digital printing
■ So far, I haven't been able to detect any. If you have found some, please send them to me via the publisher of this book.

Optimum and economical uses of digital printing
■ Small- to medium-run print jobs, and those where fast turn-round is vital.

FACTS ABOUT FLEXOGRAPHY

A relief printing process similar to letterpress, but uses flexible rubber, neoprene or photopolymer plates.

■ Most modern flexography is rotary web-fed.
■ It uses fast-drying, water-based inks.

Pre-press
Design or page make-up
Electronic page layout
Laser output of copy and images
Proofs
Repro data conversion
Mono or colour artwork scanning
High-resolution film separations
Film stripping and masking
Colour proofing
Platemaking
Press make-ready

Production
Printing, single or multicolour litho
Finishing
Delivery

Conventional offset

Electronic page layout

Digital proofing

Printing

Finishing

Delivery

Digital printing

Substantial savings in time, effort and cost.

Figure 13.5 *Digital printing vs offset litho*

■ As with letterpress, the printing plates have a raised image. Ink is applied to the raised image surface and transferred by pressure to paper, board or other material to be printed.
■ Modern flexo plates are backed with thin metal sheet to give strength and stability.
■ Plates are exposed photographically and developed chemically.

Advantages of flexography
■ high-speed web printing
■ a simple printing method, and economical for long runs
■ compares favourably with gravure on price and flexibility, especially in terms of shorter runs and special workings, though gravure may have the edge on quality
■ can print difficult materials, eg cellophane, plastic film and metal foil
■ can print curved surfaces
■ prints 4-colour process, or individual colours
■ manual proofing possible; though this is not cheap.

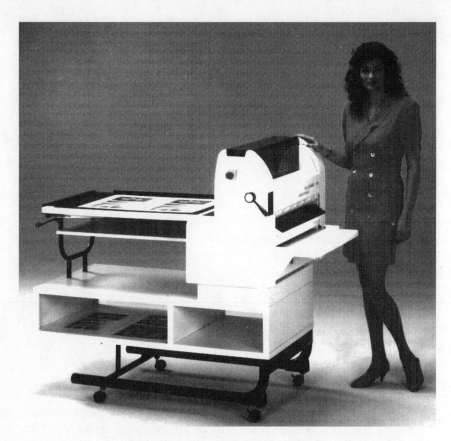

DuPont's Cromalin EasySprint system is used by companies with large DTP facilities, and printers with in-house repro. This is toner-fusion technique, easy to operate and clean. A four-colour proof can be made in about 15 minutes; special colours can be added. There are analogue and digital proofing systems in the range, producing proofs that meet the Cromalin Eurostandard specification. This is a far cry from the old days of 'wet' proofing, where an entire printing press had to be set up for a few proofs.

Figure 13.6 *Proofing without tears*

Disadvantages of flexography
■ print quality depends on the surface of the material being printed
■ good quality can be achieved, but only by using special mechanical techniques
■ being flexible the image carrier, the plate, can distort the printed image

■ small type and fine-screen images are difficult to print
■ make-ready can be expensive; though this is mitigated by the use of a flexible, economical printing plate.

Optimum and economical uses of flexography
■ newspapers; direct mail; packaging; books; wallpaper.

FACTS ABOUT SCREEN PRINTING

■ A stencil printing process method which uses a mesh screen, mounted and stretched in a frame.
■ Screens are of man-made materials such as nylon; often of stainless steel.
■ The stencil is produced photographically on to a light-sensitive emulsion on the screen mesh.
■ Exposing the emulsion to ultra-violet light hardens the non-image areas.
■ The non-printing areas are protected by solid material remaining on the screen after processing.
■ The printing areas are open, the emulsion having been washed away during processing.
■ They therefore let the ink through to the paper beneath.
■ The ink is forced through the screen mesh by a squeegee.

Advantages of screen printing
■ highly versatile – can print virtually any surface, including paper, board, wood, glass, metal, plastics and fabrics
■ uses strong, opaque inks, giving rich depth of colour
■ because inks are opaque, you can print white on black, for example
■ can print curved surfaces, such as bottles
■ prints individual sheets or rolls of material
■ commercial screen presses are highly mechanised
■ these can print up to 5,000 impressions an hour
■ the toughness of screen materials allows long runs and worthwhile economies
■ most useful and practical also for short runs – before commissioning screen printing for short runs, compare with other methods
■ manual proofing is simple and economical.

Disadvantages of screen printing
■ ink takes longer to dry than other processes
■ printed sheets must be separated and racked individually, or put through a drying tunnel
■ ultra-violet curing is also used, but this also takes time
■ accurate registration limits the printing speed
■ because of the relatively coarse nature of the screen mesh, fine detail is difficult to achieve.

Optimum and economical uses for screen printing
■ posters, point-of-sale and other material, packaging.

FACTS ABOUT LETTERPRESS

A relief printing process similar to flexography, but prints from rigid metal printing plates and metal type. As with flexography, ink is applied to a raised surface image and transferred by pressure to the paper or board to be printed.

In the UK, EU and USA, letterpress is little used, most commercial work now being done by offset litho.

■ Print quality depends on the quality of the surface of the material to be printed.
■ Type-matter is composed on Monotype or Ludlow mechanical typesetting machines. This is known as hot metal.
■ Halftones and line illustrations are made into flat plates, called blocks plates. These are produced photographically and etched on copper or zinc.
■ There are three types of press: platen, flatbed and rotary.
■ Platen presses are usually small and fast, mostly used by jobbing printers for small commercial work.
■ Flatbed presses produce larger page sizes, up to broadsheet newspaper dimensions.
■ Rotary letterpress is web-fed, prints at high speed and uses curved metal plates.

Advantages of letterpress
■ rotary letterpress prints at high-speeds
■ economical for long runs

■ good for line and tint work
■ good for monochrome work and spot colour
■ machine proofing is easy, using special small letterpress proofing presses.

Disadvantages of letterpress
■ not the ideal method for high-quality four-colour work
■ small type and fine-screen images are not easily achieved
■ printing plates can be expensive
■ make-ready is complicated, expensive and time-consuming.

Optimum and economical uses of letterpress
■ best suited to small-run newspapers and magazines, books and small jobbing work such as stationery.

14

Writing Successful Television Commercials

There is an inherent drama in every product. Our No 1 job is to dig for it and capitalise on it.

– Leo Burnett

GUIDELINES

The TV environment

- Your message is transient.
- Consider the high cost of TV production.
- Bear in mind the small size of the screen.
- Exploit the programme environment.
- Don't write detailed, heavily reasoned copy for TV.
- Aim for high impact from the start.
- Too many scene changes are confusing and distracting.
- Don't cram copy into a spot too short for it.
- Time your commercial accurately.
- Get your script and production cleared.

Creating the commercial

- First, write a simple word-picture of the action.
- Write the initial script in a simple, two-column format.
- Create strong images.
- Use high emotional pull.
- Start with an attention-grabber.
- Try to look unique, sound unique.
- Leave a unique, sales-promotion image.
- Use movement, colour, sound, demonstration, entertainment, humour.
- Exploit television and film techniques.
- Situation sketches: work fast within the time available.
- Testimonials: use people your target audience can identify with.
- Personalities: ensure they are relevant to your product and your proposition.
- Jingles: use them to sell your brand.
- Titling: synchronise with the action and voice-over.
- Make the response you want absolutely clear.
- Include a pack-shot.
- Allow for a period of silence at each end.
- Put 10 seconds of freeze-frame at the end.
- Liaise with your storyboard artist.

Creating television commercials is a vast subject, and more than adequately covered by specialist books and media.

Outline of the TV environment and creative techniques
This chapter will get you started. It outlines some of the conditions in which your commercials will be competing, and offers you techniques for creating sales messages for this exciting and powerful medium.

EXPLOITING THESE TECHNIQUES

The TV environment

Your message is transient
Blink twice, and your commercial is over and gone. If your audience misses it, you've wasted your money.

You must *set out* to make maximum impact from the start of the commercial, hold the viewer's attention to the end, and finish with a message so strong that the viewer will remember it at the point of sale.

Consider the high cost of TV production

At today's production prices, it could cost you between £20,000 and £75,000 for each second you are on the screen. Airtime, of course, is extra.

Consider carefully if you *really* need television for your brand, and the budget you need to command if you do. You could use a simple colour slide and voice-over, but would this do the job as well as a full-blown action commercial? Think well before spending your money.

Bear in mind the small size of the screen

The TV screen is a lot smaller than life. If you are old enough to have seen *Ben Hur* at the cinema, and recall the chariot race, you will have experienced an entertainment event much larger than life.

You must aim to exploit the TV screen, small though it is, so that it puts larger-than-life images and ideas into your customer's minds. If you cannot do that, you should try another medium.

Exploit the programme environment

Television is a medium that delivers entertainment, news, education material and features of specialised interest. When planning a commercial, take into account the programming conditions it will fit into, and the audience viewing it at the time.

Remember that television viewing is a group activity – most people watch it in family groups, and discuss what is on screen; unlike radio, which is a solitary activity. Can you exploit this useful feature of the TV environment?

Don't write detailed, heavily reasoned copy for TV

Because TV messages are fleeting, and arrive on top of one another during an advertising slot, you cannot safely tax your viewer's powers of concentration. Besides, a commercial costs so much to bring to air, you get a really short time for your money. How much should you put into it? Only as much as you can express *simply and persuasively*.

Aim for high impact from the start
Viewers do not watch television just to see commercials. They do not wait with breathless anticipation for yours to come on the screen. Your commercial will be surrounded by entertainment, news, interesting personalities and aggressive, competitive advertising. When you go on screen, go for the jugular.

Too many scene changes are confusing and distracting
In passive viewing, as with TV, the human brain is comparatively slow to interpret what the eye sees. Changing scenes on screen too rapidly tends to confuse the viewer, who may switch off your message mentally. Keep your scene changes to a minimum.

Don't cram copy into a spot too short for it
Normally, you cannot ask for more airtime without giving your media-buyer high blood-pressure. Media budgets are usually fixed in advance. Therefore, when writing a commercial, you should have respect for your media schedule; changing it in your favour can result in a reduction somewhere else. All media scheduling is compromise, but changing it under pressure is bad campaign planning technique.

On the other hand, what can you do if your marketing director wants *everything* put into a single commercial, and it won't fit the scheduled length? Here are some possibilities:

■ Prepare a list of sales points and other elements; arrange them in order of importance.
■ Get your marketing director to agree this list.
■ Write the commercial in this order. Time it.
■ If what you have written goes over the scheduled length, cut out the least important elements from the bottom up, until it fits.
■ Discuss this with your marketing director. Having agreed the original synopsis, it's now up to him to authorise any increase in running time. Instead, he will probably cut the copy to fit the schedule.
■ Argue for shorter commercials, running at higher frequency, each making a major point.

Time your commercial accurately
Take into account not only each word in your script, but also the pauses between words and phrases. Sound effects also take up time, and so do the pauses between them.

Don't be tempted to stuff a word or sound into every possible pause; every commercial has its natural pace, and you should strive to achieve this. Pacing takes up time too; be prepared.

Get your script and production cleared
All scripts must be approved by BACC. You need to send all completed scripts to the Broadcast Advertising Clearance Centre for vetting. You must submit copies of your finished commercials as well. Why take this trouble? Because no TV station will accept your commercials if you don't get them BACC-approved first.

The BACC is your best safeguard against breaching the law, the Broadcasting Act in particular. The new Act came into force at the beginning of 1992, and could well be updated from time to time. If the BACC advises you to amend your scripts, you can be sure it's necessary.

Why must you have the finished commercial checked, as well as the script? Wouldn't it be sufficient to submit just the script, since you are unlikely to put into the video anything not already in the copy?

Suppose you are advertising garden furniture. The commercial is shot in a garden, with adults and children, householder and several guests. They are enjoying a barbecue. Looks innocent enough at script stage. However, one of the guests is holding a prop, a glass of lager; he takes a sip. If any child is in the frame, if any guest is under 25 years – or even looks under 25 – you may be breaching the Code.

Having your material checked by the BACC helps you avoid problems like these.

Creating the commercial

First, write a simple word-picture of the action
You know what you are putting into a commercial, what is going on in it, but nobody else does. Communicate with your director; put your thoughts into a paragraph. Keep it simple. Just express your intentions. Don't use television technical terminology unless there is no other way of expressing yourself.

For example:

> A woman and her two children get into a taxi. She asks the driver to go to the nearest supermarket. On the way, they chat about baking for her daughter's birthday party, and the benefits in using Sunshine Margarine. The taxi pulls up outside the supermarket; the woman leaps out, leaving the children with the driver. The voice-over repeats the product benefits at the end.

Write the initial script in a simple, two-column format
This should be a simple description of the spoken copy, if any, and the visual that accompanies it. Do not write it as a shooting script; do not put in any stage directions or other technical instructions. Leave this to the director and production company.

See the specimen script at the end of this chapter.

Create strong images
If you want your commercial's sales message to be recalled at the point of sale, use images strong enough to do this difficult job. Every advertiser strives to do this; few succeed in linking these images with major sales points. Link your USP (unique selling proposition) with a powerful visual image. Think what this could do for your sales!

Use high emotional pull
When this book is published, there should still be puppies pulling toilet rolls across your TV screen. Mothers may still be taking their young daughters to the dentist, saying 'I felt so guilty!'

Young families will still be used to sell insurance, grannies to sell low-calorie meals, pre-teenage pirates to sell fish-fingers and teenagers to sell washing powders. See what I mean? If not, watch commercial TV even more closely and critically.

Start with an attention-grabber
Your audience may not be concentrating when your commercial comes on. They may be just about to switch channels. Grab their attention with something so interesting, so startling that they stay with you to the end of your commercial.

A car driving off a roof is one way of doing it; you know the one I mean?

Try to look unique, sound unique
This should be part of your branding policy. Put on the screen an image that can belong only to your brand. It could be something as simple as your house colour. Which computer range is identified with blue? Which dark, fizzy drink is identified with bright red? Which light-coloured fizzy drink is identified by the colour orange? Or use a prop: which sailor has a short, white beard, wears a nautical cap and sells fish-fingers?

Leave a unique, sales-promoting image
At the end of a commercial, a dog licks its chops after a plateful of meaty chunks. The same dog appears on the label of that brand. What does the advertiser expect dog-owners to think and do when they see that label on supermarket shelves?

Use movement, colour, sound, demonstration, entertainment, humour
Exploit the unique creative possibilities of television and cinema. Make your brand move in such a way that the targeted viewer makes a decision in its favour. Use movement, colour and sound to achieve the demonstration you could get if your prospect were right in front of you. In a way, of course, he actually is.

David Ogilvy says that you should not mix entertainment and selling. This is true, I think, if the entertainment *obscures* the selling and the branding. Television is an entertainment environment, and your viewer is expecting to be entertained. Can you exploit this opportunity without damaging your objective or message? What do you think? David Ogilvy is the richest, most successful copywriter in the world, so be careful how you answer.

Exploit television and film techniques
You have a huge library of techniques to call on: live action, conventional animation, computer animation, live action and animation mixed (remember *Jurassic Park* and *Roger Rabbit*?), special effects, black-and-white from end to end, black-and-white mixed with colour, fades, dissolves. The list is growing all the time – see the terminology selection towards the end of this chapter.

Situation sketches: work fast within the time available
You have to perform a minor miracle: set up the situation; sell your brand; convince the viewer; wind up with an action-line ...

all in a few seconds. This demands careful planning and terse writing. Be careful not to make it too clipped, or your audience will wonder what has happened and your branding will fly by unnoticed.

Testimonials: use people your audience can identify with

Stick to ordinary, undistinguished people, characteristic of your target audience. They are easier to understand, to identify with and to believe. Be especially careful with regional accents.

Personalities: ensure they are relevant to your product and your proposition

A celebrity or presenter should be appropriately selected for his or her speciality: a commercial for cars could benefit from an endorsement by a racing driver, for example.

Jingles: use them to sell your brand

Plan to make them sell, as well as entertain. Use sales points; make them memorable; keep them simple. If you hear your jingle on the lips of children in the street, you know you have achieved success. They are selling for you.

Titling: synchronise with the action and voice-over

Words on screen and different words in the viewer's ear can be confusing. How do people act when they are confused?

Make the response you want absolutely clear

Be specific. To get your viewer to take the action you want, you must leave no doubt what the action is. 'Call our credit-card hotline ...', or 'Call Free-phone Kogan Page now ...', 'Send for the full-colour illustrated brochure ...' On the other hand, there is usually no need to tell viewers that they can get soap at super-markets.

Include a pack-shot

Showing your pack on screen increases the chance of its being identified at the point of sale. This is vital during a launch, or after a label change. Consider using the brand logo and campaign slogan, where appropriate.

Allow for a period of silence at each end
The BACC specifies that: 'The running time of the sound should be less than that of the picture by at least one second, starting not earlier than half a second after picture start and finishing not later than half a second before the end of the picture.'

If you can grope your way through the fog of this statement, you will allow for half a second of mute videotape at the beginning of the commercial. There also should be a half a second of silence at the end.

Put 10 seconds of freeze-frame at the end
At the end of the action, you should plan for at least 10 seconds of mute tape. This means you repeat the final frame 250 times, but put no sound on it. Freezing the action is better than having the actors look as though they have been suddenly struck dumb at the end of your commercial.

The mute overrun allows a particular broadcasting station to extend a commercial break by a few seconds while the others catch up.

You may be grieving that the half-second of silence at the beginning of your commercial is costing you thousands of pounds. However, if your commercial is the final one in a break, you could get an extra 10 seconds of free airtime.

See Chapter 21 for details of the BACC and other organisations.

Liaise with your storyboard artist
A storyboard is a series of drawings, each showing an important stage in the commercial. Usually it is presented with the script, copy being pasted below the drawings it relates to. Figure 14.1 shows an example of a storyboard.

Many creative teams prefer to present their ideas on separate boards. The text is spoken by one of the team as the boards are flipped by another.

Sometimes, when there is little speech and much action, the storyboard alone is the presentation.

This stage of creation is nearly always the product of liaison between writer and art director. More than ordinary cooperation is required for this work; it needs to be inspirational.

The whole idea is to show the sequence of key shots in the commercial, and highlight some of its production values. This can be cheaper than making an 'animatic' – a very basic representation of the commercial, using artwork and a camera in the studio. It is an economical way of showing the approvers what the commercial will look like.

Eventually, the production team will get the script and storyboard for realisation. That's when the big money starts to roll.

TELEVISION TERMINOLOGY: A SELECTION

Audio   Sound or sound-related instructions.

Caption   Artwork board.

Close-up   Camera instruction: head and shoulders shot.

Cut   Stop shooting; change camera shots.

Dissolve   One shot faded out as another is faded in.

Establishing shot   Long, scene-setting shot.

Exposition   How the viewer is told who or what the characters are.

Exterior sounds   Noises off: traffic, aircraft, etc.

Extreme close-up   Camera instruction: an ear, eyebrow, nostril.

Fade   Picture gradually disappears from screen. Sound gradually fades out.

Fade in   *Video:* picture gradually appears. Audio: sound gradually builds up.

Fade up   Same as Fade in.

Fade out   *Video:* picture gradually disappears. Audio: sound gradually fades.

Film-clip   Piece of film used as a spliced insert.

Fix   Firmly establish in the viewer's mind

Flashback   Shot of a previous action.

Format   Style of script or programme.

Frame   What the camera 'sees'.

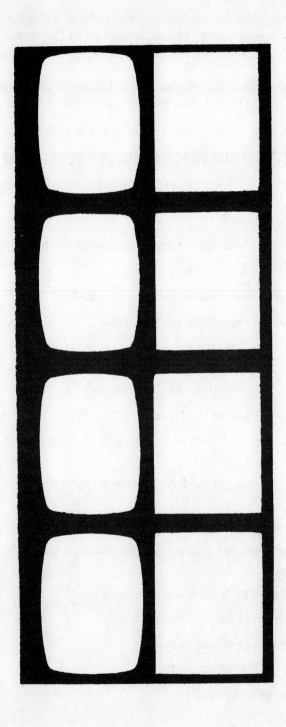

Figure 14.1 *TV storyboard: four blank frames from a TV storyboard layout sheet. Each frame represents a highlight or sales point in the commercial. Drawings of the action are inserted into the TV-shaped frames. The copy is typed and goes in the rectangles beneath. This text can either be dialogue copy or a description of the action, or both. Sound effects are also shown in the text boxes.*

Freeze-frame   The effect of a still image; a frame repeated.

Go to black   Blank screen in black.

Image   The picture shown on the screen.

Interior sounds   For example, aircraft sound from within the plane.

Key sounds   Sounds indicating a complete environment.

Lap dissolve   A slow dissolve, superimposing two frames.

Lip sync   Voice and lip movements synchronised.

Live   Action shot involving real people.

Location   Any non-studio venue.

Long-shot   A long view as seen from the camera.

Medium close-up   Human figure shot from head to belly-button.

Mid-shot   Human figure, shot head to foot.

Miniature   Scale model used during shooting.

Mix   Slowly fade one picture while fading another in. At one point both are visible.

Narrator   Storyteller.

Opticals   Optical effects: dissolves, fades, wipes, mixes, split screens, etc.

Pan   Move camera from side to side.

SFX   Sound effects.

Slate   Clapperboard, used to mark the film with production details, eg advertiser, brand name, title, scene, take, date.

Tilt   Move camera up or down.

Voice-over   Words spoken by invisible actor over screen action.

Zoom in   Camera closes in on subject without interrupting the action.

Zoom out   Camera draws away from subject.

TELEVISION COMMERCIAL SCRIPT

Title: 'Taxi'
Product: Sunshine Margarine   **Length:** 60 secs

Vision	**Sound**
Open on a suburban street. It is raining. A woman and two children emerge from a house just as taxi pulls up. They approach the taxi.	*½ sec silence* *SFX* *Cabbie:* Where to? *Lady:* Supermarket, the High Street.
They get in. Drive off.	*SFX*
Cut to taxi interior.	*Cabbie:* Doing the weekend shopping then? *Lady:* No, I did that this morning. *Cabbie:* What's the hurry? *Lady:* Forgot the Sunshine.
Driver raises eyebrows in an aside to camera	*Cabbie:* It's pouring. Haven't you noticed? *Lady:* It's Jackie's birthday tomorrow. I've got more baking to do. *Cabbie:* Ah. (Puzzled)
Cut variously to taxi struggling through traffic; interiors and exteriors. Intersperse with tense close-ups of all faces.	*Lady:* Can't you hurry up? They close at five. We'll miss the Sunshine.
Cut to taxi clock. It shows 4.45 pm.	*Cabbie:* I'm doing my best. What's all this about sunshine then? *Lady:* It's in the shop.

Driver raises eyebrows to camera.	*Cabbie:* She's barmy!
	Jackie: Can I have a cassette player for my birthday?
	Lady: Shut up.
Taxi pulls up outside supermarket.	*Cabbie:* What's so special about the sunshine, then?
Woman gets out. She leans into driver's window.	*Lady:* Sunshine Margarine. It's perfect for baking. The kids love the taste as well.
	Cabbie: Eat it on their bread, do they?
	Lady: Of course. You ought to know that. Spreads like a dream, straight out of the fridge. Don't go away. I'll be back in a minute.
	Cabbie: (Aside to camera) They all say that. *(To woman)* Don't be too long, sunshine.
	Jackie: I want a cassette player.
The children quarrel silently together.	*Cabbie:* Shut up or I'll give you one.
	Jackie: Thanks, dad.
Pack shot.	*Female voice over:* Sunshine Margarine. Great taste. Great for baking. Great for kids. Use it straight from the fridge. At your supermarket now.
	SFX: Cab horn hoots twice.
Hold for 10-sec freeze, mute.	**End**

15

Writing Successful Radio Commercials

Short words are best, and the old words when short are best of all.
— *Winston Churchill*

GUIDELINES

- Write a word-picture of your commercial.
- Write a short description of each character.
- Keep copy simple.
- If possible, use only one voice; two at most.
- Write true dialogue.
- Use realistic dialogue.
- Establish a clear relationship between the characters.
- Avoid too many scene changes.
- Write a buffer zone at each end of the commercial.
- Don't cram your copy into a running time obviously too short for it.
- Get the copy cleared by the BACC.

EXPLOITING THESE TECHNIQUES

Write a word picture of your commercial
Aim to give the director a good idea of what the commercial should look like in your listener's mind. Summarise the scenario, action, emphasis and content. It helps him and his team to create what you really want, and get it right first time.

Write a short description of each character
This helps the actors to realise the parts they are playing. Don't forget the voice-over character. If it will help, give each character a name.

Keep copy simple
When you've something really interesting or striking to communicate, the simpler the better. Avoid long, complicated technical arguments and figures. Complications are distracting to the listener's ear and mind, and a strong turn-off.

If possible, use only one voice; two at most
There are few propositions which cannot be sold using just one voice. Sometimes, however, as in domestic situations, your appeal may be aimed at husband and wife together. You may wish one partner to influence the other, or to stimulate discussion, leading to a decision in favour of your brand. The same applies in business advertising – partners and colleagues may be encouraged to talk to and influence each other.

Write true dialogue
Make sure there is a real reason for having a conversation. Then write your copy as true dialogue, rather than a monologue for two voices. It is unconvincing when two actors pretend to be old friends, yet talk as though they had just met for the first time. Dialogue is not realistic when it sounds as though it has been lifted from the pages of your company's product catalogue.

Use realistic dialogue
The way your listeners speak may not be the way you do. Study your targets and write for them, not for yourself.

Establish a clear relationship between the characters
When writing to influence business or domestic partners, find out how your targets actually talk to each other. To do a good job, you must express a clear relationship in the minds of your listeners.

Avoid too many scene changes
As with TV commercials, jumping from one sound-effect location to another can confuse and distract your target audience. You may turn people off before you have convinced them about your brand.

Write a buffer zone at each end
This could be a striking sound effect, a few bars of music, a bit of atmosphere. It helps to separate and protect your copy from the junk around it. Entertainment may be a good environment for your commercial, but you need your listener to switch into your message.

Don't cram your copy into a running time obviously too short for it
When you've finalised your copy, read it aloud using a stopwatch. That's the proper length. You may have to fight for more airtime. Otherwise, edit it down to the running time shown in the media schedule. Nobody can have it both ways, I'm afraid.

Get the copy cleared by the BACC
Make sure your copy is acceptable for transmission. Get it checked and cleared by the Broadcast Advertising Clearance Centre. You then can be sure it is 'legal', and conforms to the Radio Authority's Code of Advertising Standards and Practice. The procedure takes a little time, but it's better than having to start again because your finished tape has been rejected by a radio station.
See Chapters 21 and 22 for information.

RADIO COMMERCIAL SCRIPT

'Taxi'.   Video Dynamics 1 min 15 secs.

SFX: *A busy street. Traffic.*

1st male voice

    Taxi ... TAXI! What do I have to do to get some attention round here?

2nd male voice

    That's easy. Make a video. You'll get noticed where it counts.

1 MV   Anything's better than waiting here.

2 MV   You should talk to Video Dynamics.

1 MV   Video Dynamics? What can they do for me?

2 MV   They'll make a video that'll hit your target audiences right between the eyes – and the ears.

1 MV   Target audiences? Such as?

2 MV   Your customers. Your sales force. Your shareholders. Your suppliers.

1 MV   What about my employees?

2 MV   Sure. A dynamic video helps you train them. And it's cost-effective.

1 MV   Can it help my sales force?

2 MV   Of course. How else can you demonstrate a fork-lift truck without actually sending it to a potential customer?

1 MV   I see what you mean. What did you say they're called?

2 MV   Video Dynamics.

SFX: *Taxi pulling up.*

Driver   Where to, guv?

2 MV   There you are. You've only got to *mention* Video Dynamics to get dynamic results!

(Cut SFX)

3 MV   Call Video Dynamics, the creative video professionals. They'll make sure you hit your targets
where it really counts. They're fast, reliable and
competitive.

Call Freefone Video Dynamics – for advice, for
help, for a discussion or an information pack.
Freefone Video Dynamics. Send for our showreel;
you'll soon see how dynamically a video can work
for you.

End

16

Design Techniques for Press and Print

The creative man with an insight into human nature, with the artistry to touch and move people, will succeed. Without them he will fail.

– Bill Bernbach

This is yet another vast subject covered by a huge volume of literature. I have suggested books on design, typography and production in Chapter 22.

Bear in mind that communications technology is changing at high speed. You can find yourself out of date in the space of a few months, so do take care to keep yourself informed.

There is also an impressive range of technical journals on the market dealing with these subjects. Some of them, you will be pleased to learn, are controlled-circulation and free of charge. Consult BRAD, *British Rate and Data* – see Chapter 22. The equivalent in the USA is *Standard Rate & Data Service* (SRDS). In Germany, *Media Daten*; in France, *Tarif Media*. Counterpart directories exist in most industrialised countries.

This chapter does not therefore attempt to cover the whole field of design and typography for marketing communications. It is an outline of techniques you need to get started. It also helps you liaise with art directors, visualisers, designers, publishers and printers.

PREPARE AN EFFECTIVE DESIGN BRIEF

Objectives
Before you brief a designer, be absolutely clear about what you want; all participants must be of one mind. The alternative leads to a waste of time and money.

Scope of job
Establish the basic scope, limitations and facts about the job. This applies equally to press and print assignments.

Checklist
Prepare a checklist covering all eventualities, so that nothing is overlooked. It is prudent to get the whole design assignment briefed-in at the same time.

Flowchart
Work out a flowchart for the job. This should show every stage of the assignment, from the first meeting to the delivery of the finished job. It should show who is involved at each stage of the operation. Remember to allocate time for approval of work. Circulate the chart to everybody involved; there should be no doubt about who does what, and when. See Figures 16.1 and 16.2.

DESIGN CHECKLIST

Commit everything to writing
This reduces the risk of errors and misunderstandings. Don't rely on your memory, or anyone else's. And don't rely solely on the telephone for giving instructions and making changes. Sooner or later you'll pay a heavy price for breaking these rules.

Job number
This should follow the job from stage to stage, so that budgeting, invoicing and payment are achieved efficiently. If planning, liaison and copywriting have been done by this time, you should already have a job sheet and a job number.

Job description
A description of the nature of the job is essential; it should appear at the head of the job sheet.

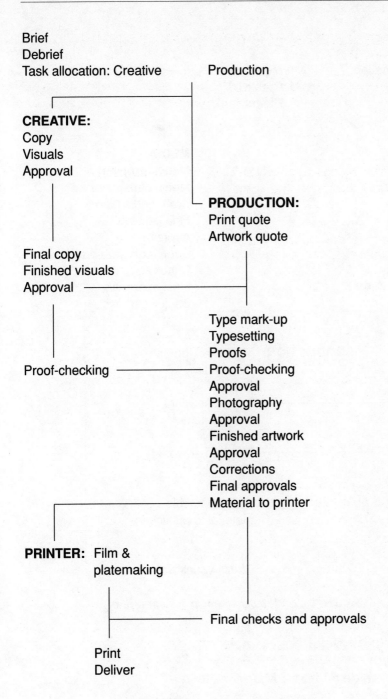

Figure 16.1 *Flowchart for printing*

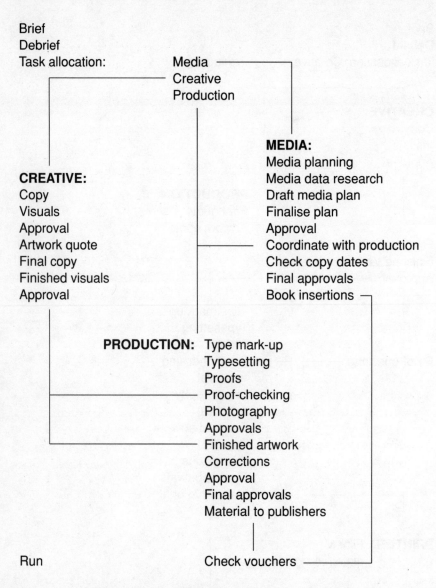

Brief
Debrief
Task allocation: Media
                   Creative
                   Production

MEDIA:
Media planning
Media data research
Draft media plan
Finalise plan
Approval
Coordinate with production
Check copy dates
Final approvals
Book insertions

CREATIVE:
Copy
Visuals
Approval
Artwork quote
Final copy
Finished visuals
Approval

PRODUCTION: Type mark-up
                  Typesetting
                  Proofs
                  Proof-checking
                  Photography
                  Approvals
                  Finished artwork
                  Corrections
                  Approval
                  Final approvals
                  Material to publishers

Run   Check vouchers

Figure 16.2   *Flowchart for press advertising*

A tag-line is useful. For example:

'4-page trade folder for Miaou cat-food'

'6-ad consumer campaign for Sunshine Margarine'

'45-sec commercial for Video Dynamics'

Budget and fees
If a production budget has already been agreed, you can abstract the design element and show it here. If not, you should establish it now. If the designer is a freelance, agree a fee and show it here. Make allowance for any change in job specification.

Design stages
Decide at the start, if you can, the design stages you need to go through. This saves time and money, and keeps the approvers to pre-set limits of both.

There are four basic stages of design preparation:

1. *Scamps*. Basic sketches on layout paper.
2. *Roughs*. Better quality visuals, but still quite rough in treatment. One-stroke display lettering and greeked-in body copy are good enough for this stage. Mainly for developing ideas and internal decision-making.
3. *Finished roughs*. Good enough to present to the approvers. This means using properly lettered headlines and Letraset 'body type', with illustrations, logos and other elements accurately mounted in place.
4. *Presentation visuals*. For approvers at board level, or those without the imagination to read the copy, look at the finished roughs, and see them as a finished production. Headlines and body copy are typeset; colours are accurate; all elements are accurately mounted. Everything is mounted on board and covered with transparent acetate.

   This is also often done electronically, and presented to management on computer screen. You may still need hard copy, if only so that managers can scrawl their amendments on it.

Photography and illustrations
These two items can carve a huge chunk out of your budget. Put either an agreed list of pics and illustrations in here, or agree guidelines for development later.

Printing process
Establish which processes are involved. This is usually determined by the quality of the finished job and length of the print run. Consult art director, production manager and printer at this stage, rather than leave it until the printer is asked to quote.

Ask the printer for a print specification form; this should enable you to give all the information needed for him to advise and estimate.

THE PRINTED PAGE

Paragraphs

Paragraphing is an essential tool. It helps to show the reader that you have come to the end of one stage in your argument, and are about to start another.

Paragraphs help to prevent your copy becoming a wall of words. You cannot force your reader to climb such a wall; he is more likely to avoid reading the copy altogether. Don't give your reader any work to do.

Paragraphs work most effectively when confined to groups of related ideas. When one group comes to an end, start a new paragraph. Where a paragraph you are writing looks like getting too long, try breaking it into two. Word-processing systems make this kind of manipulation quick and simple. Use related ideas as your guide.

When used with sub-heads and cross-heads, paragraphs help to hold your reader's interest. They encourage your reader to go through your copy with the least effort.

Aim to write paragraphs that are short and easy to read. Don't make them too short, however; it looks scrappy. Short paragraphs, however, are useful for emphasis and dramatic impact. If you are going to use this technique, make sure you do it deliberately. And use it in moderation.

A paragraph can even be a single sentence.

Avoid writing paragraphs of uniform length; the copy will look boring and tedious to read. At worst, uniform paragraphs look like bricks in a wall of words. Why put your readers off before you've put your case?

Sentences

Write copy in sentences of a length that is easy to read. Research shows that, to be readable, a sentence should contain 12–17 words. This is too arbitrary to be a really practical rule, but it is a useful target.

Vary the length of your sentences; it avoids monotony, both in the writing and the reading. If all your sentences are short, it looks messy on the page.

Aim for sentences that do not stretch your reader's patience or memory. Do not string out the length so far that, when your reader arrives at the end, he cannot remember how it began.

Short sentences are usually easier to follow and assimilate than long ones. This applies especially when you need to get complete ideas and arguments across.

A couple of important rules to follow:

1. Keep to one idea per sentence. If you cram multiple ideas into a single sentence, you create a log-jam in the reader's mind. Your writing then becomes difficult to read. Do not give your reader any unnecessary work to do.
2. If you've written a sentence containing more than two commas, it's too long. You won't find many in this book.

Sub-heads and cross-heads

Whether you call them sub-heads or cross-heads depends where you received your professional training. The difference is marginal.

Whatever you call it, a sub-head marks the division between two paragraphs. In writing sub-heads for press advertisements and print, you should have four objectives:

1. to signal to your reader that another group of ideas is coming up
2. to entice the reader to continue reading your copy
3. to signal that what he is about to read is of benefit
4. to make it easy for the reader to get into the copy at any point he chooses – breaking up walls of words makes this easier.

Aim for good visual contrast between the sub-head and the copy. For example, increase the size and weight of the sub-head. Use CAPS, **BOLD CAPS**, *italics*, ***bold italics***. You will find many examples in the pages of this book.

Measures

In printing, a measure is the width of a typeset line, the width of a column of type.

The design of an ad or printed page is usually a compromise. If the measure is too wide, the reader can find himself fruitlessly re-reading lines. If too narrow, he may have to scan back and forth rapidly. Either way makes for difficult reading; both are a turn-off.

In designing an ad or a printed page, aim for *readability* above all other considerations. If you want to know what that means to your reader, try it on yourself: what do *you* find reasonable and readable?

Leading

This term comes from former times, when type was set by hand in lead alloy. Compositors would space lines of type with strips of lead.

Points to remember:

■ Type set without any spacing between the lines is known as 'set solid'.

■ The thickness of leading between lines is measured in 'points' – another relic of printing history. This is also the case with many desktop publishing programs. Scalable fonts are given in point sizes and fractions of a point.

■ The distance from the top of a lower-case 'x' and its foot is called the 'x-height'. See Figure 16.3.

■ As a rough rule: the wider the measure, the larger the type, the greater the x-height, the more leading your copy needs.

Copy set to wider measures benefits from larger type.

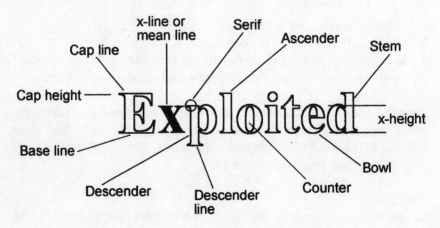

Figure 16.3 *The anatomy of type*

12pt TIMES ROMAN, SET SOLID, FULLY JUSTIFIED

Setting copy fully justified can produce a number of unwanted effects. Uneven word-breaks can disturb the reader's concentration. Rivulets of white space can meander down pages and columns, diverting your reader's attention from your message. At the ends of lines, hyphens can appear from nowhere, breaking up words in unnatural configurations. A copywriter's nightmare. The end-result can be brick-like. Brick by brick, justified typesetting can build into a wall of words, which the unfortunate reader must climb before he gets to the meaning. Every copywriter knows that no reader is actually compelled to climb the wall; he may easily turn away and read something less daunting. Prevention is better than cure: liaise with your art director and typographer.

12pt TIMES ROMAN, SET SOLID, JUSTIFIED LEFT, INDENTED

When you are planning a brochure, the total number of pages must be divisible by four. You cannot, therefore, have a 10-page brochure. If you have too much copy for, say, a 16-pager, you just have to go up to 24 pages if you want to preserve the design concept. On the other hand, there are some surprising tricks you can build into dull-looking brochure designs to make them more exciting and motivating. You need an appropriate budget, of course, and a willing marketing manager. Notice how much easier this passage is to read than the brick wall above.

Figure 16.4 *Examples of justification and indentation*

12PT UNIVERS, SET SOLID, CENTRED

Consider introducing a couple of pull-outs into your next brochure. They can be made to concertina away from fixed pages, revealing a range of ideas and product applications. You can incorporate slide-out cards, coupled to elastic bands so that they snap back into their sleeves. You can have holograms glued to pages, and holes to see them through. Blind embossing is popular, even though you can hardly read the copy.

12pt TIMES ROMAN, WITH 28PT BOLD RAISED INITIAL

Nothing improves the look of a page or column of type like a raised or drop cap. This is a capital letter several sizes larger than the rest of the copy. Sometimes it is in the same typeface, sometimes in another, or in bold. It shows – with some impact – where a main section begins. It is an important device to use when you want to retain control of your reader's attention. As with all special effects in typography, use sparingly.

Figure 16.4   *Examples of justification and indentation (cont.)*

Justification, indentation

To make your writing easy to read, and avoid the brick-wall effect, consider how your copy looks at the edges. Compare the examples in Figure 16.4.

A copy brick is set absolutely square, with both vertical edges lined up dead straight. This is often the most difficult to read, especially where margins are narrow. The copy often suffers from uneven word-spacing, and much hyphenation down the right-hand edge, where the typesetting system tries to cope with word-breaks.

A viable, more readable alternative is known as 'justified left'. Copy is set with the left edge vertically straight, the right edge somewhat ragged. Word-spacing is normal, and hyphenation kept to a minimum.

Justified-left copy is not favoured by some art directors and typographers. They regard un-square copy as imperfect, untidy. They may also demand perfect bricks, with no short lines at the feet of paragraphs, columns and pages.

Paragraphs which start with a line butted right up to the left edge are considered modern. Indentations, on the other hand, are thought old-fashioned.

Art schools, I fear, seem to know little about marketing, or how copy is actually read off the printed page.

Consider the following suggestions, seen from the reader's point of view rather than the designer's:

■ An unjustified right edge helps the reader's eye to jump more easily from line to line.
■ A short line at the end of a paragraph helps the eye to jump the gap to the next.
■ Indentation helps the eye to get into a paragraph.

My advice: **Insist on your right to be read!**

Typography
Today's typographer has tens of thousands of typefaces to choose from. The main classifications are those with serifs, those without, fancy faces and specially designed faces. Figure 16.5 shows the typeface Times Roman.

■ Among the serifed faces are old-style, transitional, modern, egyptian and decorative.
■ The sans serif faces include grotesques and gothics.
■ The fancy faces include scripts, graphics and decoratives.
■ Companies such as Letraset, Adobe and Monotype produce vast quantities of specially designed typefaces.

Times 8pt
Times 9pt
Times 10pt
Times 11pt
Times 12pt

Times 14pt

Times 16pt

Times 18pt

Times 20pt

Times 22pt

Times 24pt

Times 26pt

Times 28pt

Times 36pt

Times 48pt

Times 72pt

Times Roman, surely one of the world's most *legible* typefaces. You can get an incredible number of classified ads on a broadsheet page with this delightful face.

Figure 16.5 *An example of a serifed typeface: Times Roman*

Serif faces:

Bodoni, a modern face
Cooper Black
Garamond, an old face
Grail
Palatino
Times New Roman

San serif faces:

Arial
BLYPA
Eros
Futura
MOTORIST
SHADOW
Univers

Slab serif faces:

Ardwolf
Courier
GHOST TOWN
Looby
Memo

Exotic faces:

ANGIE
Arnie
DIGITAL
Frankenstein
LOGO
Medieval
Mondine
MONTEREZ
NEON
SHADOW
Uncial

Script faces:

BALLOONIST
Calligraphic
Casual
Church Script
Florentine
Freedom
Mistrelle
Park
Technical

Figure 16.6   *Typefaces: a sampler*

SCREEN DENSITIES

SCREEN ANGLES

Lines per inch	Lines per cm
50	20
55	22
60	24
65	26
70	28
80	32
85	34
90	36
100	40
110	44
120	48
133	54
150	60
175	70
200	80

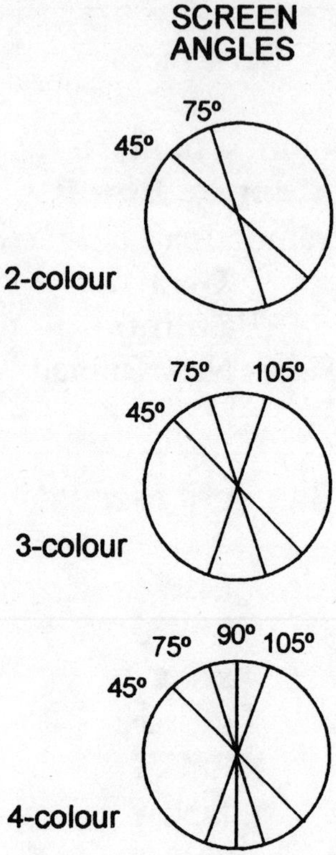

Figure 16.7 *Halftone screen densities and angles*

Serifs are tiny 'handles' at the ends of main strokes on type characters. Their effect is to help the reader's eye to group characters, words and phrases together more easily. They are an aid to comprehension.

People do not read printed material one character at a time; or even one word at a time. The brain seems to prefer small groups of words. If this were not so, it would take a month to read a newspaper.

Aim to help your reader assimilate and comprehend your marketing communications easily and quickly. Here are a few guidelines.

- In sizes up to about 12pt, serifed typefaces are easier to read than sans serif faces.
- Sans serif faces are difficult to read in small sizes. They are excellent in display sizes, 18pt and larger.
- To enhance readability, match the typeface to the paper and printing method you are using.
- When reversing type – white on a black or coloured background– make sure the type is large enough and heavy enough to be readable.
- Small type sizes on a 4-colour halftone background can spell disaster. Slight variations in registration can destroy the legibility of your message. Figure 16.7 shows halftone screen densities and angles.

This, of course, is only the beginning of the process. To increase your skills in design, typography and production, you need organised and structured study. Many colleges hold courses in these subjects; I have given one in Chapter 21.

17

Assessing Creative Work

If I only had a little humility, I would be perfect.
— *Ted Turner, President, CNN*

This is a highly practical guide to creative analysis. You apply it to test the viability of creative output.

Although it was compiled mainly with printed media in mind, you can use it on all marketing communications: broadcast and narrowcast, press and print, business-to-business and consumer.

It has three important uses:

1. As a self-test of the viability, accuracy and power of your own creative work.
2. To help you evaluate the work of your colleagues, agency and suppliers.
3. As a weapon to use when your work is under critical scrutiny by superiors and colleagues.

Do not underestimate the power of self-analysis. At this honest, intellectual level, it should be carried out right through the creative process, not just at the end.

This is time well spent, because it can save you much time, labour and heartburn. It can also help you to avoid perfecting the wrong message.

It gives you three important advantages:

1. it helps you create the right message, and avoid creating the wrong one
2. it avoids the frustration of perfecting the wrong message, and therefore...
3. it avoids your having to start again.

GUIDELINES

■ Does it answer the creative brief?
■ Does it progress through AIDA?
■ Is there a promise in the headline? What is it?
■ Is there a consumer benefit in it? What is it?
■ Does it grab attention?
■ What exactly achieves this?
■ Does it compel the reader into the copy?
■ There should be no doubt about what is on offer.
■ What is the USP?
■ Is it clear and unambiguous?
■ Does it leave a memorable image?
■ Does the copy say too much? Not enough?
■ Is it convincing?
■ Does it appeal to the reader's self-interest?
■ Where exactly in the copy is that appeal?
■ Does it propel the reader towards making a decision in favour of your brand?
■ Does it clearly direct the reader to action?
■ Are the illustrations captioned?
■ Are the branding, and the consumer benefits, easy to recall at the point of sale?
■ Where a sales call will follow the message, does the message create a strong bridge between the two?

Style

■ Is the writing terse and to the point?
■ Does the creative technique overshadow the branding?
■ Does it enhance it?
■ Is the creative idea glued firmly to the branding?

■ Does it have a 'big idea'?
■ Does the typography add to the readability of the copy?
■ Or does it make it more difficult?
■ Is it in character with the branding?
■ Is the layout clear or cluttered?
■ Do all illustrations play their full part in the sales process?
■ Are they captioned effectively?
■ Is there a good balance between copy and illustrations, taking full advantage of the medium?

EXPLOITING THESE TECHNIQUES

Message

Does it answer the creative brief?
Go through each point and check the copy against it, especially the research findings. Check also whether any changes in marketing policy or situation have taken place since the brief was raised.

Does it progress through AIDA?
Above all, you need the disciplining of AIDA to progress you through to the action you want the target audience to take. It has to be sound to be safe. For the technique, see Chapter 5.

Is there a promise in the headline? What is it?
In an advertisement, where there is no promise or benefit in the headline, what drives the reader to start reading the ad?

On the front of a brochure or leaflet, what *real* reason does the recipient have for picking it up and reading it? What drives him into the inside pages?

Take a red pen and underline it.

Is there a consumer benefit in it? What is it?
It has to be a *specific* benefit, with real substance. There has to be a real fact or product feature behind it.

Does it grab attention?
The attention-grabber you have used must reach off the page and grab the reader by the eyeballs. Nothing less will have the impact you need.

What exactly achieves this?
Words, pictures or both working together?

Does it compel the reader into the copy?
Is the promise strong enough to do this? Is there a stronger promise you could use?

There should be no doubt about what is on offer
Be honest. If you can't see it, neither can your potential customer. This may ruin your chances of getting the enquiries and making the sales you have banked on.

What is the USP?
Is it the one you decided on in the creative brief? Does it work? It's the brand's unique selling proposition. Underline it in red.

Is it clear and unambiguous?
As with the main offer, your USP must be clear in the mind of your reader. They should be closely linked.

Does it leave a memorable image?
The benefits you offer, and how they are worded, must leave a lasting impression on the reader's mind. This must reach as far as the action you are asking him to take – and beyond: when your salesman makes contact, your copy should already have opened the door in your reader's mind.

Does the copy say too much? Not enough?
Have you crammed into your copy absolutely every fact and benefit in the brief? This may be cluttering the persuasion in your argument. It may be stretching your reader's patience and powers of concentration. Can you delete some of the less persuasive material and cut the copy to a readable length? You must be able to do this without damaging the argument, the proposition and the persuasion.

Is it convincing?
Your judgement should tell you. If this is too difficult an exercise, try the copy out on a colleague or associate not involved with the promotion.

Does it appeal to the reader's self-interest?
The magic ingredient again: is it clear and unambiguous?

Where exactly in the copy is that appeal?
Satisfy yourself. Take a red pen and underline the words and phrases where the reader's self-interest resides.

Does it propel the reader towards making a decision in favour of your brand?
Before action comes decision. Does your copy arouse an irresistible desire to try, examine or discuss your brand or proposition? If not, rewrite it so that it does. Then use the red pen as before.

Does it clearly direct the reader to action?
Many ads ask for action in more than one place in the copy. Nearly all the brochures I have written in the past 10 years do that. Have you injected a call to action on *each spread* of your current brochure, on *each page* of your current leaflet? If not, do it now.

Are the illustrations captioned?
Captions can sell as effectively as headlines. Do yours?
   See Chapter 11 for techniques.

Are the branding, and the consumer benefits, easy to recall at the point of sale?
There is usually a time-lapse between viewing a commercial, seeing a press ad, reading a brochure, and reaching out for your brand at the point of sale. Your branding and benefits must be strong enough to bridge the gap.

Where a sales call will follow the communication, does the message create a strong bridge between the two?
You must make it easy for the salesman to open his sales pitch without having to explain everything from the beginning. When your copy is a strong foot in the door, your sales force will thank you for it.

Style

Is the writing terse and to the point?
Can you purge redundant words and phrases – those that don't

pay their way? If you have begun any leading paragraph with a generalisation, you may have done this to ease yourself into the argument. We all do it from time to time. Edit all such passages so that you start with a specific *benefit* or *fact*, one which appeals to your reader's self-interest.

Does the creative technique overshadow the branding?

Clever-clever ideas, illustrations, typography and other creative monstrosities can cause the persuasion in your argument to be rendered invisible. The all-important branding can disappear, swallowed up in the dominating technique.

Take a dispassionate look at the work you have done. Put yourself in the customer's shoes. Does the creative technique you have used work *with* the branding? Then ask yourself ...

Does it enhance it?

Does the creative technique add *significant value* to the proposition you have put before the reader?

For example: the range of vacuum cleaners you are promoting is coloured orange. This is its most distinguishing visual feature, and is important at the point of sale. Have you built this into your product branding? Or have you wasted the uniqueness of the idea, ignored it, diluted it, rendered it invisible?

Is the creative idea glued firmly to the branding?

Canon copiers are positioned as problem-solving. The campaign slogan they are currently using claims that if anyone can solve your copying problems, you and Canon can. The copy, the visuals, and the strapline with its clever alliteration, work in harmony. They create the *total* effect the advertiser needs to get enquiries, demonstrations, trials and sales.

Does it have a 'big idea'?

Volvo recently drove one of its cars off a roof into its backyard. Just before it landed, a huge white bag on the floor inflated and prevented a catastrophe. What product feature was the ad demonstrating? Was the idea *big* enough? Was it memorable?

Does the typography add to the readability of the copy?

Whatever else it does, typography must ensure that your creative work is *readable*. This applies to ads, mail shots, brochures, leaflets, posters, packaging, TV and cinema commercials. Everything, in fact, from sky-writing to book-matches.

By all means accept typography which enhances your message but only if it is part of the message, and makes a real contribution to it.

Or does it make it more difficult?

If you have the slightest doubt about the typography you are presented with, reject it. Do not tolerate eccentric typography.

Insist on your right to be read!

Is it in character with the branding?

Usually, you do not want typography which clashes with your branding. However, you may want contrast, which may enhance its attention value. Whatever you decide, be deliberate about it, and make typography work in harmony with your creative ideas.

Is the layout clear or cluttered?

Every layout you commission must drive the reader to the conclusion you want. The coupon, the Freepost address, the e-mail address and the telephone number must do the work if you want a worthwhile response. It doesn't matter much whether your layout is clinically 'clean' or messy-looking – as long as you get a logical flow towards the response element. Be pragmatic.

If there is no response element ... you may have a different problem. Take another took at Chapter 9.

Do all illustrations play their full part in the sales process?

In your press ads, have they been selected to work in harmony with words to get your ideas across, to attract attention; generate interest? Are they benefit-led?

In print, do they punctuate the copy, work in harmony with it? Do they reinforce claims and statements made in it, demonstrate your product, and show important user-benefits achieved by using it?

For more on techniques, see Chapter 11.

Are they captioned effectively?
Captions generate high interest, and get high reader attention. Are you using them constructively – to explain what is going on in the illustrations? Are they written to sell your ideas to the customer, to reinforce your claims?

Is there a good balance between copy and illustrations, taking full advantage of the medium?
Do any of the elements dominate at the expense of others? Is the main selling idea or proposition obscured by eccentric typography or bizarre illustrations, or do they work in harmony?

THERE IS NO POINT IN PERFECTING AN INCORRECT MESSAGE

What exactly is an incorrect message? Every marketing professional knows how important it is to get all the elements in the marketing mix exactly right. But that's the challenge, and the threat, to every marketing planner and communicator.

An incorrect message is one which:
- is not aimed at the right target audience or segment
- does not reach the right target audience
- does not appear in the media the target audience sees and hears
- does not appear at the right time
- does not make an *appropriate* offer to the target audience
- contains no deal, offer or proposition
- contains no promise, benefit or solution
- does not contain the *right* promises, benefits or solutions
- does not stem from the appropriate key proposition
- is *not actively persuasive* from the start
- does not contain the right branding elements
- highlights product features and facts, but omits the associated benefits
- contains the incorrect appeal for the selected target audience
- is not relevant to the *self-interest* of the target readers, viewers and listeners
- does not appeal actively, *dynamically* to their self-interest
- does not demand or encourage a decision in favour of your brand

■ does not show why the target audience should buy from *you*
■ does not ask for *action* by your target audience [NB: there are exceptions. Some kinds of corporate promotion need no immediate action. They may lay the groundwork for action at a subsequent stage, however.]
■ asks for *inappropriate* action
■ does not take into account the ability of your target audience to respond.

18

Creative Marketing on the Web

As a marketer, you should regard your Web site as a sales tool. See it as a tailor sees his sewing machine: it is there to help you earn a living.

An initial word of caution: creativity must always be at the service of marketing, not the other way round. Although a Web site can be stylish, good-looking, attractive and even creative, it is not an art form. You should therefore treat your Web site as you treat all your marketing tools: professionally; with promotion and persuasion in mind; with customers in mind; and with sharp focus on the bottom line.

In constructing a Web site, six factors are paramount:

- clarity
- accuracy
- simplicity
- communication
- persuasion
- navigability.

While I have no doubt that most designers are well trained in their discipline, many are untrained or inexperienced in marketing. A creative team's track record of commercial success in Web site design can make or break a business or campaign in which a Web site is a key element. Make sure your design team is marketing-trained and marketing-minded. If you don't, it's your funeral.

According to Philip Walker, managing director of Ebeon, e-business specialists, recent research (2000) reveals that 30 per cent of consumers in the UK have a PC. This implies that 70 per cent do not. It may also be true that every business of any size in Europe and the United States has at least one computer. This is not to say that every consumer and business can access the Internet. What can be said with certainty is that the current state of PC ownership and use, and Internet access, is increasing, worldwide; and that the technology continues to improve. It is therefore worth taking care over your Web site, if only because trading opportunities for your company are now truly global.

PLANNING YOUR WEB SITE

Guidelines

1. **Assess your company's needs**. This fundamental measure applies whether you are selling to consumers or businesses, selling gardening equipment or fork-lift trucks; whether you are seeking enquiries, sales leads or orders.
2. **Can you handle it?** Having decided that you actually need a Web site, look again at your organisation, and see how well it can handle business derived from the Web. You may need to invest in new people, new equipment, extra office space and new software.
3. **Allocate a realistic budget**. Once you have decided to create and run a Web site, you should aim to do it properly. Having and operating a new Web site can be exciting, especially if you have an exciting new product. But you need to update it frequently; giving adequate attention to a Web site costs money. Consider it a good investment, and put the cost into your marketing plan.
4. **Study the competition**. Learn from their mistakes and omissions. It's much cheaper than learning from your own. Creatively explore ways in which you can appeal to and cater for their customers, and do it better. Make sure your site actively demonstrates how much better your offerings actually are.

5. **Create and develop** attractive offers which particularly appeal to Web site customers in a Web site environment. Promote them attractively and appealingly on your site. And, like every successful salesman, always ask for the order.

6. **Involve your specialist teams**. Put your key marketing, sales and operations personnel in the picture; consult and discuss everything with them. Test the new situation on paper, or with a computer model, including the finance and running costs. Demonstrate that you can operate it professionally and cost-effectively.

7. **Allocate resources appropriately**. Match the new Web site to the resources you have or hope to have. For example, do you really know how to evaluate a Web site design? Do you have an executive who does, or should you hire one?

8. **Simple or sophisticated?** Before you begin designing and constructing a Web site, you must decide whether you need simple copy and design, or a sophisticated multimedia site requiring visitors to download plug-ins.

9. **Consider your customers**. Match the design and copy on your Web site to meet your customers' level of language and technical sophistication. It must contain offers and appeals that customers can respond to, and which make a profit for you. A brilliant-looking but over-complicated site that turns visitors off is a waste of time, effort and money.

10. **Communication style and tone**. If your visitors are consumers, develop a simple, natural style for communicating with them. Avoid corporate language and marketing jargon. If your site is for businesses, use some of the terminology they use – you must do this to remain credible. Don't overdo it – still keep it simple and natural.

11. **Plan for updates**. You will need to update your site frequently. Customers are easily bored by old material, and you need to keep them interested. You need to allocate resources for updating at least the basics, such as prices, discounts, incentives, new products and services, and special offers. Take an active interest in the site and its results, and evolve it as your experience with it grows.

12. **Concentrate on useful information**. Potential customers visiting your site are primarily looking for useful information. It is the most important component of your on-site offerings.

What customers see on screen is literally what they expect to get. You cannot ask them to select, decide and order from you without adequate information. Moreover, if the information you give them is unclear, complicated or long-winded, they won't look around for explanations; they'll go to another site. After all, it's just a click away!

13. **Aim for a dynamic response**. Your Web site should be interactive, so build in a lively response mechanism. Make it attractive, friendly, simple and easy to use – and easy to reply to immediately. In the questionnaire, keep the personal details you require to a minimum, so that the customer stays with it to the end. If you are greedy in your demand for data, the customer may get frustrated and abandon you without completing the enquiry or order. Aim to make the most of each visit – both for you and the customer.

14. **Make it easy to do business with you**. Guide the customer through your site, and make it *look easy*. Then make it easy to decide, select and order. Consider, for example, creating an animated cartoon character to do the guiding in a friendly way. Giving the character a name makes it even friendlier. You may consider animated cartoons rather naff; if so, do something more effective.

15. **Make your site easy to find**. Register it with as many search engines as possible. Consider carefully the classifications used by other sites; you may want to avoid those in which you are submerged and rendered ineffective. Take advice on the keywords you specify, and use those which make your site easy to identify.

16. **Feature your site everywhere**. Give its address prominence on every page of your company's product and corporate literature; on letterheads, business cards, handouts, gifts and giveaways. Highlight it in your e-mails, advertising, PR, house journal, direct mail, posters, sales promotions, PowerPoint presentations, seminars, conferences, press and trade briefings, exhibition stands, fleet vehicles; and anywhere else you think has good promotional value.

17. **Actively promote your site**. When launching your site, run press advertisements and PR activities. Take banners on friendly sites on an ongoing basis, to generate site traffic for your own. Reciprocal arrangements for banners on comple-

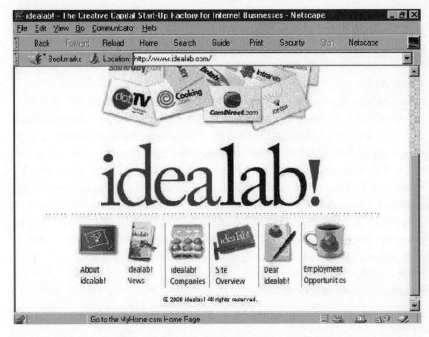

Figure 18.1 *Idealab! home page. Clear and unambiguous, with excellent use of typography, graphics and white space. No doubt about what's on offer here, or how to access it.*

mentary and non-competing sites can be helpful, and cost little or nothing.

MARKETING AND PROMOTION ON THE WEB

The promotional mix

Press

On the printed page, it is easy to distinguish editorial from advertising. Editors and advertisers are careful to design their presentations to emphasise the difference. Advertisers sometimes use advertorial: advertisements closely resembling the editorial environment in which they appear. With online marketing, editorial is also advertising. What's more, the marketers can also be the publishers. Anything on screen can be treated as advertising; you can use logos, headlines, body copy, brand names, symbols and pack designs. In Britain the Advertising Standards Authority's remit extends to online promotion, and it investigates complaints.

Television

Television offers you movement, animation, colour, sound and contact information. It cannot target individual consumers, but it can address the interests, needs and wants of well-defined groups of consumers. On the other hand, consumers using the Internet cannot at the same time be watching TV. In the UK, prime-time TV is about 7–10.30 pm. Internet usage usually peaks in the early evening, around 7.30–9 pm. One of the things people do when arriving home from work is check their e-mails. This online activity, including surfing the Internet, may continue until late in the evening. With 300 million or more European households expected to be online by 2003, this represents worthwhile opportunities for Web marketers.

Radio

Some of the conditions mentioned above apply to radio. In industrialised countries, there is at least one radio set to every household. Radio is often described as audible wallpaper; listening to it demands no concentration. A listener can be carrying out other activities at the same time: reading, designing, ironing, using the loo or washing a car. On the other hand, while surfing the Net, reading e-mails or studying online offers, the consumer concentrates on the screen. As an online marketer, you must therefore make your promotions as interesting and motivating as possible. Don't forget, the consumer may also have the radio on in the background.

Direct response

Direct mail marketers know how to track response. Key numbers in coupons are popular and proven. With radio and TV, it is more difficult to achieve a traceable response, but key words and telephone hotlines help to make tracking viable. Evaluation of response to online promotions are not only possible but essential. It helps you to compare online advertising with the best results obtained from other direct-response methods.

Some online marketers take the conventional direct response

route to evaluation, basing it on cost of response or enquiry. The real test for effective advertising, of course, is cost per sale. Independent measurement of Web site use, with directly comparable audit reports, allows marketers, media buyers and planners with decision-making. A company in the Audit Bureau of Circulation group, ABC//electronic, audits Web sites; see details below.

Outdoor
Nobody has yet come up with a technique for tracing actual response to posters at individual sites. This is because there is no foolproof way of determining how many passers-by look at a poster. Even on underground transport systems, where passing human traffic at poster sites can be estimated fairly accurately at various times of the day, there can be swings in either direction. A UK specialist research company, POSTAR, has gone some way to remedying this situation. However, the nature of posters as an advertising medium does not lend itself to relating, with accuracy, exposure at the site to sales at the check-out. Web surfers, on the other hand, can interact with online advertisements, and accurate calculations are possible.

Banner advertising is sometimes compared to posters. Like a poster, a banner can direct users to another Web site where they can get product or other information. But while posters are static, and cannot be changed frequently, banners encourage users to interact immediately. They can be changed as frequently as you like. A mouse-click or key-stroke links the visitor to an interactive information source or product offer. Each click on a banner or Web site is recorded, and it needs no great effort to calculate the cost-effectiveness for the banner or Web site (Figure 18.2).

WEB SITE MARKETING

Web site marketing activity is not unlike opportunities offered by TV: colour, movement, sound, graphics and animation are all possible. In addition, customers can download your information and print it. The unique advantage to you is the ability to offer products and services to consumers worldwide, and take orders

Figure 18.2 *Banners: the size, shape and content is limited only by your imagination – and the site owner's permission*

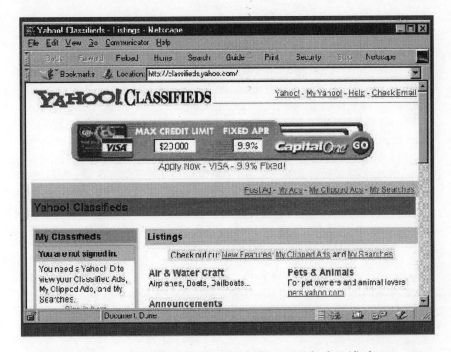

Figure 18.3 *Classifieds on the Web. Treat Web classifieds as you would treat the conventional kind. Be clear about what is on offer. Keep copy terse; which means tight, not condensed or unreadably short. Give your contact details, and indicate what you want the visitor to do. Note the hypertext link at the foot of the banner. It indicates that the banner is clickable.*

and receive payment, direct from your Web site. The creativity you put into constructing your Web site should aim to achieve this, above all else.

Web site classifieds

As with newspaper classifieds, you can buy lineage from the owner of the site. Popular directory and search sites such as Yahoo! offer this service (Figure 18.3). Lesser-known organisations offer similar services, often at cheaper rates, or even free of charge. You therefore need to establish the reach and track record of such sites before investing in them. With conventional TV, radio and print-based advertising, this is standard practice; Web site advertising is no different.

Always test any site you select for advertising before entering into contracts. The tests should include evaluation of quality as well as quantity. An advertisement rate card and media information should be obtained from each site you are considering.

There are some advantages to be gained from using classified advertising on the Web. Sites that charge fees are often of higher quality than free sites. They may also receive more visits from potential customers looking for particular products and services – if that is what you want. On the downside, some sites offering free classified advertising may be using the sites to collect e-mail addresses. If you take classifieds on such sites, you may sooner or later be involved with multiple junk e-mail lists, which are bought and sold at random to all-comers. The practical quality of these addresses for your needs may be questionable. This is especially important when you are planning to reach a specified target audience for a product or service.

Banners

A banner is a strip of advertising on a Web page, usually appearing close to the top. The page can be a home page of another company's Web site, or some other page which receives a great deal of visitor traffic.

A banner can be any size, depending on the limitations of the owner's page. A large banner might even be a half page, provided that the site owner permits it. As with other media, appearing within editorial is to your advantage. Banners are usually 17 cm wide by 2.5 cm deep, with variations in height and depth for the requirements of graphics and typography.

The main function of a banner on someone else's site is to direct visitors to yours, where they can get more information and place orders. Once at your site, a visitor can be dynamically motivated to purchase your products or services. Press advertisements can offer information, which the visitor can send for by filling in a coupon or making a telephone call. Your Web site, because its size is theoretically limitless, is capable of holding all the information your potential customer needs for making decisions there and then. Bear in mind that too much information on a site can be counter-

BANNER GUIDELINES

Select the right host. Some sites out-perform others in terms of response. A banner may perform better when incorporated into a site which appeals to a predetermined target audience. This is simple common sense. It is also sensible to post a banner to a host Web site for a limited period as a test, before entering into contracts or financial commitments.

Position. Test each host Web site for the best pages; and the best positions on those pages. You may discover that the best position on a poor site out-performs a poor position on a good site. Continuous testing will give you the answer.

Monitoring visitors. Monitor carefully and continuously. Experience shows that visitors are most likely to take action on the first or second visit to a banner. After a second visit, response is likely to decrease.

productive. As always, it's a matter of exercising your best business judgement.

Banner designs vary widely, limited only by the demands of the brief, the budget and the imagination of the designer. However, nearly all banner advertisements have one feature in common: a request for the visitor to 'click'. It can say 'click here', 'click now', 'order now', 'order here', or something similar. Banners can be made interactive, encouraging visitors to carry out an action on the banner itself. An interactive banner can, for example, prompt the visitor to ask questions, using a pull-down menu. Or, a pull-down menu can refer the visitor to specific pages on your main Web site. The visitor clicks on the menu strip he has chosen, or on 'click here'. The software jumps straight to that page, where the full information or sales pitch is displayed.

Some banners are designed as self-contained units, interacting with visitors without jumping to another page or Web site. They briefly show what's on offer, and also take the order. 'Click here' is replaced by 'order here' or 'buy here'. For you this is an ideal situation. Instead of spending substantial amounts of time and money constructing a complex Web site and building brand recognition to entice customers, the whole transaction is concentrated in a single banner. This also saves visitors time and effort. You could describe it as the electronic equivalent of the impulse purchase. You will, of course, have made sure that the product or service being offered is suitable for this kind of promotion.

E-MAIL PROMOTIONS

There are two main types of e-mail promotion. First, straight, 'push' techniques, of which the easiest to operate is ordinary e-mail. Electronic mailshots delivered in this way are sent direct to users' mailboxes, without waiting for them to go online. Users receive a mailshot whether they have requested it or not, just like a mailshot delivered by post. Constraints and controls on this type of advertising are now in force, so take legal advice before you take action.

Some companies are currently offering free e-mail access to users. As always, there is a reciprocal element. The e-mail software displays paid-for advertising on the consumer's screen. Hotmail and Juno were among the pioneers of this useful arrangement. Hotmail operates in the way just described. Juno provides free software and dial-up connection, in exchange for a demographic questionnaire completed by the consumer. The result enables Juno to compile and operate a highly detailed mailing list, based on the questionnaire. Its client marketers can target users with great accuracy, using the demographic information provided by Juno. This can reach virtually any e-mail user with a Windows-compatible PC and a modem.

Discussion groups and e-newsletters

Another route to target audiences is the sponsored discussion group. A marketer sponsors discussion groups by providing the software and the access free to users. In exchange, the marketer benefits from a precisely targeted audience. Participants are those who have taken a decision to subscribe to that particular discussion group, rather than casual Internet surfers. This makes the sponsorship all the more valuable to the marketer, and participation valuable to the user.

A discussion group is a number of individuals with a common interest. This can be anything from marketing, finance or computing, to gardening, coin-collecting, bookbinding or babies. Subscribers get together on the Internet for an exchange of ideas and advice, or merely to chat about their common interest. Although they are said to 'subscribe' to the group, the subscription is usually free. Any subscriber wishing to contribute to the discussion sends a message to the e-mail address of the group, and this is read by all subscribers.

An e-newsletter is a similar technique. Its content is material created by an organisation or individual, and distributed by e-mail to subscribers. The subscription is free to participants. You can insert your copy to be read on screen by all subscribers.

As a marketer sponsoring e-mail discussion groups and newsletters, you benefit in a number of ways. First, the content is text-only, free from distractions and diversions offered by conventional commercial Web sites. Second, because announcements in group newsletters promote products and services related to the interests of the group, subscribers are more likely to take up your offerings. For example, if you are promoting cameras, film and processing materials at worthwhile discounts, you are likely to receive an unusually high degree of attention and interest from subscribers with an interest in photography. Provided that the offer is appropriate and viable, and the copy persuasive, you can convert this interest into orders.

There are thousands of e-discussion groups and e-newsletters currently online. You can sponsor such a group or e-newsletter for as long as your budget allows and the sponsorship remains commercially viable. Usually, sponsorship is conducted on a weekly or monthly basis. One major disadvantage is that discussion groups can come and go. They often arise spontaneously and decline or disappear without warning when the subject matter becomes trite, stale or exhausted.

CREATING A WEB SITE

Every company's marketing culture and trading needs are different, and this is often reflected in its Web site. However, most companies are competing for the same customers in their marketplace, and this should influence how a Web site is written and designed. As always, tailor the technique to the target audience.

Follow the tried and tested professional marketing philosophy: see it from the customer's perspective, do it with the customer in mind.

Guidelines

Although visitors have taken the trouble to get to your Web site, you still need to attract their active attention and hold their interest while they are looking at your screens. Do not take this for granted. Although a Web site is not a press advertisement, brochure or leaflet, the same people who see your press ads will be visiting your Web site. You must fulfil their expectations, or they will move to another site very quickly. Remember, it's just a click away!

As with your other advertising, use proven copy and design techniques.

Grab visitors' attention

Instead of repeating the tired old 'Welcome to our Web site...', use the space for a major promise or customer benefit, or a unique selling proposition (USP). The welcome message is useful, but you can exercise much more imaginative and motivating approaches. Where your product or service helps to resolve a problem or issue, say clearly and immediately what it is, and how you can help through your Web site.

Keep it simple

Many Web sites are incredibly cluttered. Home pages are often so crammed with material, especially with small blocks of conflicting text, that it is difficult to know where to look first. Every item on the page seems to shout out loud; there is simply no focus. Press advertisements which do this are usually regarded as bargain basements. Some of the boxes on the Web page scintillate or blink; some are animated. Others change text and colour frequently, sometimes at high speed. The designers' intentions are worthy, but the effect is confusing to the visitor. What you want is for the visitor to concentrate on your screen, understand the offer, make a decision and click.

An excellent example of a clear, focused and professionally designed site is that of the Central London Branch of The

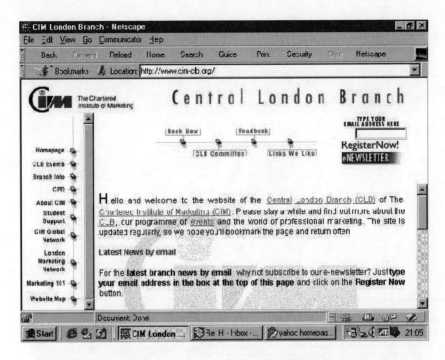

Figure 18.4 *Home page of the Chartered Institute of Marketing's Central London Branch. Clear, uncluttered, easy to read and to navigate. On a site like this, the needs of the organisation's members come first.*

Chartered Institute of Marketing (CIM), shown in Figure 18.4. The home page is simple, uncluttered and easy on the eye. There is a lot of interesting and useful material on the site, aimed at professional marketers and students. It is very easy to navigate and to find any item quickly, including forthcoming events, and there are links to other useful sites. Try visiting the site yourself: www.cim-central-london.org.

Headlines

They do most of the promotional work on a page. If you have several offers on your home page, organise them so that they do not compete for attention. This is easier briefed than implemented. Two sites to watch for this technique are Tesco and Boots, whose sites are shown in Figure 18.5.

Figure 18.5 *Shopping online. It is vital to be absolutely clear as to what is on offer and how to get it; otherwise even the most loyal of customers may be tempted to look elsewhere. It's just a click away!*

Body copy

Tailor the technique to the target audience. For consumers, use plain English, not marketing jargon. If your product or service is technical, you may need to use some technical language; keep it to a minimum. If you are selling insurance, for example, explain the jargon you are using in the kind of English the ordinary consumer visitor can actually understand. It must be clear enough to encourage decision and action on the spot! Business and technical products and services may need business and technical terminology, but the promotional and persuasive styles of your copy are better considered in plain English.

Typography

Use bold, chunky type for headlines. For body copy use sans serif fonts rather than ones with serifs. Spindly type is often broken up or distorted by the lines or pixels on screen. Fancy typefaces can make a page look interesting, but use them in moderation. Don't use any typeface which clashes with or denigrates your company's logo (Figure 18.6).

Banner copy

Keep it short, clear, simple and to the point. Encourage the visitor to go for the click button. Do not crowd a banner with text; it can confuse or mislead the visitor, so that no action is taken.

Colour

Use few colours, and use them in moderation. If you use bold colours on your site, make sure they are for focus rather than emphasis. Too much emphasis is no emphasis. Boxes and panels in pastel colours are easier on the eye, and also make accompanying copy easy to read. Slavish concentration on your company's house colour is foolish, especially where it adds nothing to the promotional value of the site or page. For banners, use colours which make the banner stand out from the material round it. This may differ for each host site.

Animation

Movement, blinking, sparking, wipes or other simple visual effects will grab attention, but can be distracting if you overdo it. If you must animate, just animate the main item or USP. Where the rest of

Typefaces for Web sites

Absolute clarity is the quality to aim for.

Basic rules for Web site fonts

1. Keep it simple
Simple shapes translate best to low-resolution viewing. Spindly ones, or those with sharp contrasts between thick and thin strokes, fare worst; thin strokes can be lost in low resolution. Caveat: don't use too many faces on the same page. It looks messy, confusing and amateurish.

2. Bigger the better
The bigger the typeface, the more pixels you have to define the characters on screen. Big faces are easier to read on screen than smaller ones; bold is easier than light. However, don't overdo it.

3. Sans serif is safer
Sans typeface design tends to work best on Web site pages, particularly in body copy. In a screen environment, fancy typefaces can be a distraction, diluting message content and impact; unless, of course, they are used deliberately and are relevant to the promotion.

Some typefaces are better than others for overcoming the drawbacks of low screen resolution. Here are a few.

Sans serif faces to select:

Arial. **Arial narrow bold**
Eros. **Eros black**
Franklin gothic demi-bold
Franklin gothic book
Franklin gothic medium condensed
Futurist. Futurist narrow
LOGO
Lucinda sans
Ultra-sans
Verdana

Serif faces to select:

Cooper black
Bernard MT condensed
Bookman old style
Century schoolbook
Courier new
Lucida bright
Palermo
Rockwell & condensed
Also called Slab, Egyptian, Memphis
Times new roman

NB: Times Bold in its press version is usually narrower than roman; in the screen version, it is wider

Fancy faces to try:

Aristocrat
BALLOONIST
Casual
COPPERPLATE
Comic sans
Francis

Hobbit
Mondine
Monotype corsiva
Scripty
STYLISTIC
STENCIL

Figure 18.6 *Typefaces for Web sites*

the page is static, a banner featuring animation can divert attention away from other material on the page. Caution: the host owner may not care for too much distraction from your banner.

Getting action

Where you want action from the visitor, feature a click button or line of text saying 'Buy here', 'Buy now', 'Order here', 'Click to order', 'Click here', Click now' or similar instruction. Banners should be organised to link with your own Web site, or straight though to your ordering system.

Banner incentives

Encourage the visitor to click on a banner by giving an incentive or compelling reason for doing so. This can be anything from a worthwhile discount or a closing date, to a prize or free gift. If this is not included, the visitor may leave the banner, and even the site, without taking the action you want.

HOW WELL ARE YOU DOING?

Monitoring your Web site

To be cost-effective, promotion on the Internet must satisfy the demands of the brief. You can use software to monitor the effectiveness of your Web site. However, the monitoring of your banners and promotional material on other Web sites needs more than the owners' statements of visitor traffic.

For estimating cost-effectiveness of your marketing promotions in the conventional media your company uses, you rely on independent third party audits. This is also possible with the Internet. Most visitor traffic claims rely on 'hits'. This is doubtful for proving the effectiveness of the Internet as an marketing medium. Hit reports can be inflated at the site operator's whim without any real increase in traffic.

Page impressions, where specific information on pages is requested, give a clearer picture. This has given rise to the establishment of independent auditing services. ABC//electronic, an associate company of the Audit Bureau of Circulations, was formed in 1996 in response to demand by advertisers, publishers and media buyers. It provides marketers, advertisers and Internet publishers with information, independently audited and reported, to agreed standards. This is a reliable aid to the buying and selling of promotional space on UK-based Internet sites.

Web site auditing

The ABC//electronic auditing process comprises:

- A questionnaire, to gain as much information as possible on a Web site before auditing begins.
- An individual auditor assigned to each site.
- The use of census-based measurements reflecting actual total activity, rather than ratings or sampling-based research.
- For registration-based sites, two-way communication with Web users, allowing for validation of site visits by individuals.
- Audited Web information is augmented by analysis and diagnosis, which helps with demographic profiling.
- Audit reports are designed to indicate not only the number of visits, but also the types of visitor. This takes place where the site captures the information, allowing for validation of the demographics of individual visitors.

Audit certificates

Ten steps are taken for the issuing of an ABC//electronic Web site audit certificate:

- The site is registered for ABC audit, and the site commits to ABC membership and first audit.
- An auditor visits the site to observe access logs and databases, taking sample segments of data.
- Interim fixes of record numbers and file sizes are also monitored.
- The auditor also observes the registration building for registration sites.
- Using e-mail, samples of registered visitors are checked.
- The site compiles the statistics it is claiming for the audit period; this is usually once a month.
- The site sends the information to ABC//electronic for verification.
- The auditor verifies the data claimed on site.
- Site statistics are checked, to ensure that they have been compiled using ABC//electronic definitions.

■ The ABC//electronic certificate is issued. Each ABC//electronic certificate carries the following information:
   - Top level URL
   - Definitions
   - Audit opinion
   - The period covered by the certificate
   - Page impressions
   - Description of site content
   - A breakdown of registered and non-registered traffic for sites declaring registration. To be claimed, a registrant must be contactable by the auditor.

MAINTAINING STANDARDS

It is often claimed that the Internet is a free-for-all and unregulated. Even if this were the case at present, it is due for substantial change in the near future, certainly within the life of this edition of *Creative Marketing Communications*.

As use of the Internet as a commercial tool increases, governments across the world will inevitably strive to regulate it. That process is now under way, and you would be advised – and professionally obliged – to keep up to date with it.

In the UK, controls are already in place, influencing the conduct of Internet marketers and advertisers. All general British law applying to general commerce also applies to the Internet. The Advertising Standards Authority's British Codes of Advertising and Sales Promotion apply to Internet activity. They govern 'advertisements in non-broadcast electronic media such as computer games' (1.1c). According to the ASA's information department, this includes Internet activity.

A number of other regulation measures either are already in force or being considered. The main generator is the European Union. Regrettably, many of their directives are issued without public consultation, or democratic or parliamentary debate.

You should make a note of some of the more important and far-reaching regulations:

■ The Data Protection and Telecommunications Directive; currently in force. Article 12 applies to unsolicited faxes and telephone calls, but not to unsolicited e-mails. This may change.

■ The Data Protection Act, 2000. Applies to all electronic commerce in the UK.
■ The Distance Selling Directive.
■ The EU's Data Protection Directive. No specific application in place for e-mails.
■ The E-Commerce Directive. Now being debated in the EU.
■ The Electronic Commerce Bill. A UK parliamentary White Paper, tabled March 1999 by the Department of Trade and Industry (DTI).

Two organisations have the task of accrediting e-commerce codes of practice: the Direct Marketing Association (DMA) and the Consumers' Association. The DMA is a founder member of the Alliance for Electronic Business, and in this case is acting within the Alliance's initiative, TrustUK. As part of this initiative, the DMA has established access to a global e-mail preference service (EPS). This is an opt-out scheme for unsolicited e-mail. Consumers wishing to register their e-mail addresses for the EPS need to access the DMA Web site and link to the EPS.

If you intend to send unsolicited e-mail messages, you are required to purge your lists against the master EPS file. TrustUK provides companies using e-commerce with an e-hallmark. This enables consumers to identify at a glance companies signed up to codes or practice, which helps to ensure high standards of customer service.

The White Paper states: 'For business, e-commerce will be the trade route of the new millennium'. It sets out proposals for enhancing consumer protection and service to consumers, giving particular emphasis to electronic commerce. It looks to TrustUK to help raise consumer confidence in e-commerce by ensuring that UK Web sites subscribe to stringent codes of practice. These set out clear trading principles, respect the privacy of the individual's data, and ensure robust procedures are in place for cross-border resolution and redress of consumer complaints.

You should be aware that, in Internet affairs, what is possible is not always legal. For example, in the UK the distribution of pornography via the Internet is a criminal offence. The mere possession of pornographic images on your computer can land you in prison.

19

Creative Marketing and the Law

Despite the fact that marketing is the engine of prosperity in market economies, it is every interfering busybody's Aunt Sally. Marketing is a profession that by its very nature attracts legislation. In Britain, the United States and other industrialised countries, the volume of new government Acts, regulations and orders which affect marketing is expanding hugely. This also applies to existing national and local legislation, which is constantly being updated, amended and augmented. On top of that, the European Union imposes its own laws, directives, regulations and decrees on member states. Some of these compulsorily overlay or supersede individual state legislation.

Bear in mind that e-commerce and Internet traffic are actively regulated by local national legislation. This will certainly increase and become much tighter as time goes by.

It is important therefore to take legal advice for every stage of marketing operations, especially during the planning of creative work. More important still, ensure that your creative ideas, concepts and campaigns are legally watertight before investing money in them, and before signing artwork, print and media contracts (Figure 19.1).

> # £100 REWARD
> WILL BE PAID BY THE
>
> ## CARBOLIC SMOKE BALL CO.
> TO ANY PERSON WHO CONTRACTS THE INCREASING
> EPIDEMIC
> ### INFLUENZA,
> Colds, or any diseases caused by taking cold, AFTER
> HAVING USED the BALL 3 times daily for two weeks
> according to the printed directions supplied with each Ball.
>
> ## £1,000
> Is deposited with the ALLIANCE BANK, REGENT-STREET,
> showing our sincerity in the matter. During the last epidemic
> of Influenza many thousand CARBOLIC SMOKE BALLS
> were sold as Preventives against this Disease, and in no
> ascertained case was the disease contracted by those using
> the CARBOLIC SMOKE BALL.
>
> One CARBOLIC SMOKE BALL will last a family
> several months, making it the cheapest remedy in the world
> at the price -- 10s. post free. The BALL can be RE-FILLED at
> a cost of 5s.
>
> Address:-
> ## CARBOLIC SMOKE BALL CO.,
> 27, Princes-street, Hanover-sq, London, W.

Figure 19.1 *Carlill vs the Carbolic Smoke Ball Company – a leading sale of goods and consumer protection case of the 19th century. Mrs Carlill saw an advertisement for the product, bought it and used it as directed. She contracted influenza shortly afterwards, sued the advertiser and won.*

As an example of how legislation controls marketing activity in Britain, here are 175 items to be going on with.

Accommodation Agencies Act 1963
Administration of Justice Act 1985
Agriculture (Safety, Health and Welfare Provisions) Act 1956
Alcoholic Liquor Duties Act 1979
Architects Act 1997
Banking Act 1987
Banking Act 1987 (Advertisements) Regulations (1988) as
    amended
Betting and Gaming Duties Act 1981
Betting Gaming and Lotteries Acts 1963–85

Bingo Act 1992
Bread and Flour Regulations 1995
British Telecommunications Act 1981
Broadcasting Acts 1990 and 1996
Building Societies Act 1986
Business Advertisements (Disclosure) Order 1997
Business Names Act 1985
Cancer Act 1939
Charities Act 1992 and Regulations
Children Act 1989
Children and Young Persons (Harmful Publications) Act 1995
Children and Young Persons Acts 1933 and 1963
Civil Aviation Act 1982
Civil Aviation (Air Travel Organisers' Licensing) Regulations 1995
    as amended
Civil Aviation (Aerial Advertising) Regulations 1995
Cocoa and Chocolate Products Regulations 1976
Coffee and Coffee Products Regulations 1978
Companies Act 1985
Competition Acts 1980 and 1998
Condensed Milk and Dried Milk Regulations 1997
Conduct of Employment Agencies and Employment Businesses
    Regulations 1976
Consumer Credit Act 1974
Consumer Credit (Advertisements) Regulations 1989
Consumer Credit (Exempt Advertisements) Order 1985
Consumer Protection Act 1987 and the Code of Practice for
    Traders on Price Indications
Consumer Transactions (Restrictions on Statements) Order 1976
    as amended
Control of Misleading Advertisements Regulations 1988
Control of Pesticides Regulations 1986 as amended
Copyright Designs and Patents Act 1988
Cosmetics Products (Safety) Regulations 1996 as amended
Crossbows Act 1987
Customs and Excise Management Act 1979
Data Protection Act 1984
Data Protection Act 1998
Defamation Act 1952
Defamation Act 1996

Dentists Act 1984
Deregulation and Contracting Out Act 1994
Deregulation (Betting and Bingo Advertising etc) Order 1997
Deregulation (Casinos) Order 1999
Disability Discrimination Act 1995
Education Act 1996
Employment Agencies Act 1973
Endangered Species (Import and Export) Act 1976 as amended
Energy Act 1976
Estate Agents Act 1979
European Communities Act 1972
Fair Trading Act 1973
Finance Act 1981
Financial Services Act 1986
Financial Services Act 1986 (Investment Advertisements)
    (Exemptions) Orders 1995–97
Firearms Act 1968 as amended
Fireworks (Safety) Regulations 1997
Flavourings in Food Regulations 1992
Food Labelling Regulations 1984 and 1996 as amended
Food Safety Act 1990 and Regulations
Food Intended for Use in Energy Restricted Diets for Weight
    Reduction Regulations 1997
Forgery and Counterfeiting Act 1981
Friendly Societies Act 1974 and 1992
Gaming Act 1968 as amended
General Optical Council (Rules on Publicity) Order of Council
    1985
Geneva Convention Act 1957 as amended
Hallmarking Act 1973
Hearing Aid Council Act 1968
Hearing Aid Council (Amendment) Act 1989
HIV Testing Kits and Services Regulations 1992
Human Organ Transplant Act 1989
Human Rights Act 1998
Income and Corporation Taxes Act 1988
Indecent Displays (Control) Act 1981
Industrial and Provident Societies Act 1965
Infant Formula and Follow-on Formula Regulations 1995
Insurance Brokers (Registration) Act 1997

Insurance Brokers Registration Council (Code of Conduct)
Approval Order 1994
Insurance Companies Act 1982
Insurance Companies Regulations 1994
Jam and Similar Products Regulations 1981
Knives Act 1997
Licensing Act 1964
Local Government Act 1992
Local Government (Miscellaneous Provisions) Act 1982
London Cab Acts 1968 and 1973
London County Council (General Powers) Act 1938
Lotteries and Amusements Act 1976 and amendments
Mail Order Transactions (Information) Order 1976
Malicious Communications Act 1988
Marine etc Broadcasting (Offences) Act 1967
Meat Products and Spreadable Fish Products Regulations 1984
Medicines Act 1968
Medicines (Advertising of Medicinal Products) Regulations 1975
and 1975 (No. 2)
Medicines (Advertising) Regulations 1994 as amended
Medicines (Advertising and Monitoring of Advertising)
Amendment Regulations 1999
Medicines for Human Use (Marketing Authorisations)
Regulations 1994
Medicines (Monitoring of Advertising) Regulations 1994
Metropolitan Streets Act 1867
Milk and Milk Products (Protection of Designations) Regulations
1990
Misrepresentation Act 1967
Mock Auctions Act 1961
Motor Cars (Driving Instruction) Regulations 1989 as amended
National Lottery etc Act 1993 as amended
National Lottery Regulations 1994
Natural Mineral Water Regulations 1984
Nurses Agencies Act 1957
Nurses, Midwives and Health Visitors Act 1997
Obscene Publications Act 1959
Olympic Symbol etc (Protection) Act 1995
Opticians Act 1989 and Regulations
Organic Products Regulations 1992 as amended

Package Travel, Package Holidays and Package Tours Regulations
1992 as amended
Passenger Car Fuel Consumption Order 1983 as amended
Personal Pension Schemes (Advertisements) Regulations 1990
Post Office Act 1953
Prevention of Corruption Acts 1889–1916
Price Indications (Method of Payment) Regulations 1991
Price Marking Order 1991 as amended
Private Hire Vehicles (London) Act 1998
Professions Supplementary to Medicine Act 1991
Property Misdescriptions Act 1991
Protection of Children Act 1978
Protection of Children (Tobacco) Act 1986
Race Relations Act 1976
Registered Designs Act 1949
Registered Homes Act 1984
Representation of the People Act 1983
Restriction of Offensive Weapons Act 1959 as amended
Restriction on Agreements (Estate Agents) Order 1970
Restrictive Trade Practices Act 1976
Road Traffic Act 1988
Sale of Goods Act 1979
Sex Discrimination Acts 1975 and 1986
Social Security Act 1986
Solicitors Act 1974
Specified Sugar Products Regulations 1976
Spreadable Fats (Marketing Standards) Regulations 1995
Sunday Entertainments Act 1932
Sunday Observance Act 1780
Sunday Theatre Act 1972
Sunday Trading Act 1994
Supply of Goods and Services Act 1982
Surrogacy Arrangements Act 1985
Tattooing of Minors Act 1969
Telecommunications Act 1984
Telecommunications Apparatus (Advertisements) Order 1985 as
amended
Telecommunications Apparatus (Marking and Labelling) Order
1985 as amended
Telecommunications (Data Protection and Privacy) (Direct

Marketing) Regulations 1998 as amended
Textile Products (Indications of Fibre Content) Regulations 1986
Thefts Acts 1968 and 1978
Timeshare Act 1992
Timeshare Regulations 1997
Torts (Interference with Goods) Act 1977
Trade Descriptions Act 1968
Trade Descriptions (Sealskin Goods) (Information) Order 1980
Trade Marks Act 1994
Trade Union and Labour Relations (Consolidation) Act 1992
Trading Schemes Act 1996
Trading Schemes Regulations 1997
Trading Stamps Act 1964
Unfair Contract Terms Act 1977
Unfair Terms in Consumer Contracts Regulations 1994
Unsolicited Goods and Services Act 1971 as amended in 1975
Vagrancy Act 1824
Venereal Disease Act 1917
Veterinary Surgeons Act 1966
Weights and Measures Act 1985
Wildlife and Countryside Act 1981
Wireless Telegraphy Act 1949

Part 3
Essential Information

20

Essential Reference

There are a number of essentials that professional marketing communicators need to know. These are fundamental to successful marketing communications practice. Indeed, you simply cannot do without this prior knowledge, since it is a vital management tool. What's more, virtually everything connected with the technology of our business is in constant change. You must keep abreast, or fall behind.

An important aspect of this reference section will be of intense interest to CIM's working students, including those striving towards the DipM. Also those studying for CAM examinations. Concepts in this Essential Reference are not only accurately defined, but also properly explained. This means that you will not only be able to identify the most important tools of marketing communications, and understand how they work, you will also be able define and express them competently in your exam answers.

Abbreviations and other categories used in this reference:

Art	Finished art and studio work
CAD	Computer-aided design
Creative	Copywriting, visualising, concept and design, of press advertising, brochures, leaflets, direct mail, and all forms of promotional material, printed or otherwise
DTP	Desktop publishing

EP	Electronic publishing
Media	Media planning, scheduling and buying
Planning	All forms of planning for campaigns
Platemaking	Preparing printing plates
Print	Printing and presswork
Production	Pre-press work
Research	Marketing, media, copy and other research
qv	Quod vide; see the named cross-reference
TYP	Typography and typesetting
WP	Word processing

A, B, C1, C2, D, E.   Planning and research:
Socio-economic classification of target audiences, used by marketing planners.

This is a simple and practical system for differentiating target groups. It is pragmatic, in the marketing sense, not political.

Social grades used in UK marketing communications

Grade:		Members:	% of UK population:
A	Upper middle class	Top businessmen; other leaders; key opinion-formers	About 2.7%
B	Middle class	Senior executives; managers	About 15.2%
C1	Lower middle class	White-collar, white-blouse office workers	About 24.1%
C2	Skilled working class	Blue-collar factory workers	About 27.1%
D	Working class	Semi- and unskilled manual workers	About 17.8%
E	Lowest level of subsistence	Poor pensioners; disabled; casual workers	About 13.1%

**Identification of consumer needs and wants,
UK socio-economic groups**

Class   Needs and wants

A   Status-conferring products and services of high quality, eg investments, school fees, luxury travel and travel services; 5-star hotels and cruises; expensive leisure activities; special interests, eg fine arts, music, wine and antiques.

B   Products and services with cachet, conferring aspirant status; banking, investment, insurance and life assurance; weekend breaks; three- and four-star hotels; good restaurants, nightclubs.

C1   Products and services of above-average quality, conferring aspirant status; above-average-quality foreign holidays, fashion products, personal and domestic possessions; restaurants of slightly above-average quality; takeaway meals; convenience foods; efficient kitchens; improving quality of home decor. Popular sports activities.

C2   Average-quality products and services; mass-produced fashion and personal products; packaged holidays; convenience and fast foods; DIY products and personal effort in home improvements. Popular sports activities.

D   Economy-emphasised products and services; fast foods; above-average, routine consumption of fish and chips; packaged holidays and holiday camps. DIY activities. Much time and money spent on popular sports and leisure activities.

E   Product purchases of the most basic kind, heavily angled towards the best economic value. Occasional use of services, especially those most economically priced.

ABC   Media research and planning: Audit Bureau of Circulations:
A private organisation dedicated to auditing the circulation figures of newspapers and magazines. The figures issued by the Bureau accurately represent the number of copies actually sold. They also monitor exhibition attendance.

The certificates of circulation issued by the Bureau are trusted by media owners, advertisers and agencies, and used as a true basis for comparison among media competing for advertising money. Circulation should not be confused with readership.

The ABC was founded in 1931 as a non-profit organisation, by the forerunner of the Incorporated Society of British Advertisers (ISBA) (qv). This was done in response to concern shown by advertisers and publishers about false representations and claims made by some unscrupulous publishers.

Since then, the publicity industry has recognised the ABC as the UK's only independent system for confirming the circulation credibility of the press. The ABC claims to be the country's only independent system for the validation of circulation and exhibition attendance data. It ensures that its members' figures are accurate, objective and comparable. In this way, it helps media owners and buyers in the effective selling and buying of advertising space.

Today, the ABC is run by a full-time staff, governed by a general council of permanent and elected members, representing advertisers, agencies and publishers.

The ABC Council has 28 seats. The five permanent representatives comprise the chief executives of the Institute of Practitioners in Advertising, the ISBA, the Periodical Proprietors' Association, the Newspaper Society and the Newspaper Publishers' Association. The remaining seats are split between representatives of media-owner and media-buyer member companies, elected every two years.

ABC's staff include inspectors and auditors, responsible for certifying audit returns. They visit publishers' offices to check that the audit rules and procedures are adhered to, and to provide circulation advice to existing and potential members.

The ABC has three main divisions: the Consumer Press, the Business Press, and Verified Free Distribution (VFD).

The ABC's Consumer Press Division administers national newspapers, paid-for regional newspapers, consumer magazines and specialist journals, international and world regional newspapers.

The Business Division administers business magazines, annual publications and directories; and exhibitions, for which the validation of audited attendance is carried out.

See Circulation, Controlled circulation, Penetration, Profile, Rate card, Reader, Readership, Television rating points, VFD.

Above the line   Advertising campaign planning:
The metaphorical horizontal line drawn by advertising planners, to differentiate between those media which allow agency commission, and those which do not.

Above the line:	press
	television
	radio
	cinema
	outdoor
The line	

Below the line:	print
	point-of-sale material
	sales promotion
	sponsorship
	retail display and merchandising
	public relations
	packaging
	direct mail
	exhibitions
	advertising gifts
	mini media
	body media

Account executive   Advertising agency personnel:
An executive responsible for the day-to-day management of a client's business within an advertising agency. At its most basic, akin to a ball-boy on a tennis court. At its most sophisticated, a person responsible for the planning, organisation supervision, implementation and analysis of clients' advertising campaigns.

An agency's contact with its clients is done mostly through account executives. It follows that the executive represents the agency to the client, and the client to the agency. This executive, however, is expected to sell the agency's services, as well as provide advice and expertise.

Acknowledgement
The written or spoken expression of thanks to an individual or organisation for the use of their material.

Absolute placement   DTP:
The exact position on a page where a line of copy is to start; the position of the corner of a graphic element is to be anchored.

Access   Computing:
To find or go to an area of computer memory or auxiliary storage for storing or retrieving information.

ACORN   Research: A Classification of Residential
                 Neighbourhoods:
A research system which classifies people according to where they live.
   Some years ago, it dawned on a certain bright research team that the places people choose to live are directly related to their spending power. Of course, the fact had been staring us in the face for centuries, but these particularly fertile and disciplined minds saw its commercial potential.

Adaptation   Art direction:
A press advertisement or piece of print in one size or shape modified to another size or shape. This is usually referred to as an 'adapt'. Adaptation of the creative concept for a press advertisement is routinely made for other media, such as posters and point-of-sale material.

Address   Computing:
Location in computer memory or auxiliary storage.

Ad hoc survey   Research:
A one-off research survey on a specific topic.

Adshel   Outdoor advertising:
A poster illuminated from within a transparent or translucent shell. Usually sited in high streets, shopping precincts and other busy locations. Popularly used at main-road passenger bus-shelters, rail and bus stations. Adshel is also the poster contractor's trade name.

Advance   Authorship, publishing etc:
Money paid to a writer or artist in advance of publication of his

work. This sum is offset against any royalties which the work may produce.

Advertising
Many people have attempted to define and describe this difficult subject. The answer depends on who you are, and also what your investment is. Here are a few ideas to be going on with:

■ For advertisers, it is presenting the most persuasive message to the right prospective customers for the product or service, at the lowest possible cost. This is the official IPA definition.
■ For marketeers, it is an economical communication system, aimed at achieving fast pay-off of marketing investment.
■ For agency account management, it is a means of reaching and influencing a chosen group of people quickly and cost-effectively.
■ For academics, it is a specialised form of communication used in marketing, to influence choice and buying decisions.
■ For creatives, it is a highly skilled creative trade, demanding imagination and creative flair of an extremely high order.

If you have a single definition which describes advertising to perfection, dear reader, please send it to me, care of the publisher of this book. You'll get proper credit for it in the next edition; possibly achieve a degree of immortality as well.
    See Public relations.

Advertising research   Marketing research:
Includes: pre-campaign research
           concept research
           copy testing
           mid-campaign research
           post-campaign research
           media research
           motivational research
           tracking studies.

Pre-campaign research:
To determine the likely effect of advertising effort before any serious money is spent on it. Includes research into:

consumer behaviour
product use
brand share.

Concept research:
Determining the most motivating copy themes and platforms before the creative specialists get to work on building the campaign.

Copy testing:
The use of panels of consumers to assess press advertisement copy and visuals, TV and radio scripts and other creative effort. This takes place, of course, before any money is spent on production proper. The results either confirm the creative team's judgement, or indicate how it can be modified to achieve the best chance of success. Or scrapped.

Mid-campaign research:
Quizzing and discussing with panels of readers, listeners or viewers, while a campaign is in progress. Often, depending on the research brief, this is done by interviewing consumers in the street or in panels. For business-to-business campaigns, it is sometimes done by telephoning respondents during office hours.

Post-campaign research:
As above, but after a campaign has ended. Useful for comparing the results with pre-campaign and mid-campaign findings. Later, for matching the money spent on the campaign with the product sales anticipated and actually achieved.

Media research:
◼ evaluating the circulations or audiences of media during the media planning stage of a campaign.
◼ a form of research in which readers, listeners and viewers are studied. The objective is to find out who has seen or heard the advertising, and how many of them there are; then to evaluate their response to it.

Motivational research:
Seeks out the motives of people in relation to their behaviour. For

example, why mothers buy toothpaste; why executives buy certain types of car.

Tracking studies:
Usually carried out before a campaign breaks, then again after the campaign has finished. It seeks to compare the awareness of the brand at both ends of the research; the take-up of the product; consumers' declared intention to try the brand compared with the actual take-up; their knowledge of what the product is, and what it does; awareness of the advertising, or selected features of it.

There is a problem here. Although advertising does make marketing run, it is not the only measure which does. Sales-force effort, public relations, sales promotion, distribution and other marketing tools also influence the progress of marketing campaigns and their results. Tracking studies are usually injected with control features, so that they are able to indicate with more accuracy the value of the advertising effort.

Advertising Standards Authority   Advertising controls:
This is the independent organisation which polices and regulates the advertising industry. According to its own statement, the Advertising Standards Authority promotes and enforces the highest standards in all non-broadcast advertisements in the UK.

The Authority acts independently of both the government and the advertising industry. It operates in the public interest, and in cooperation with the whole of the industry, by ensuring that everyone who commissions, prepares, places and publishes advertisements observes the British Codes of Advertising and Sales Promotion.

Together, the Codes require that advertisements and sales promotions should be:

▓ legal, decent, honest and truthful
▓ prepared with a sense of responsibility to consumers and society
▓ in line with the principles of fair competition generally accepted in business.

The Codes are devised by the Committee of Advertising Practice. CAP members include advertising, sales promotion and media businesses. The CAP provides a free and confidential copy advice service for the industry.

If an advertisement or promotion breaks the Codes, advertisers are asked to amend or withdraw it. If they choose not to comply, a number of sanctions are available:

■ Adverse publicity. The ASA's monthly reports contain details of complaint adjudications. These include the names of the advertisers, agencies and media involved. The reports are circulated to the media, government agencies, the advertising industry, consumer bodies and the public. Published cases receive media coverage.

■ Refusal of further advertising space. Media can be asked to enforce their standard terms of business which require compliance with the Codes. They may decide to refuse further space to advertisers.

■ Removal of trade incentives. Advertisers and their agencies may jeopardise their membership of trade and professional organisations. This could result in the loss of financial and other trading benefits.

■ Legal proceedings. Ultimately, the ASA can refer a misleading advertisement to the Office of Fair Trading. The OFT can obtain an injunction to prevent advertisers using the same or similar claims in future advertisements.

See ASA, British Codes of Advertising, CAP, ITC and Sales Promotion.

AIDA Creative:
An acronym for Attention, Interest, Desire, Action. An important communication discipline employed in creating advertisements and print.

Advertising is not an art form: it is part of the tough business of competitive marketing communications. A discipline for creating those communications effectively is therefore vital. This may sound academic, possibly a little naïve, but it's simple common sense.

Those of us in the marketing communications business know that the arena we work in is not the supermarket, the chain store or the showroom. It is not even the press advertisement, the TV or radio commercial. Nor yet the leaflet, brochure or poster. It is the human mind. It is here that we get the reactions to marketing communications, advertising, public relations and sales promotion messages we create and deliver. It is where the action that produces a sale begins to take place.

AIDA is a discipline of progressive steps in the process of promoting a product, a service or an idea. It is an intellectual tool which helps you to achieve:

■ the levels of understanding you need to write sales-winning copy, produce motivating visuals and dynamic illustrations
■ the levels of understanding you want your target reader to achieve, so that you achieve the response you want.

As every successful salesman knows:

A   First, you must seize your reader's, viewer's or listener's ATTENTION.
I   You must then tell him something important which appeals to his self-INTEREST.
D   You must arouse a strong DESIRE to try or buy your product; or send for your literature; or make an enquiry; or ask for a sales representative to call. Or all these things at different times. Your primary objective at this stage is get a decision in favour of your proposition, product or brand.
A   Finally, you must urge your potential customer to take the ACTION you want.

This action must be in line with your marketing plans. For this reason alone, is it essential to plan your AIDA before you begin writing and designing any marketing communication.

Why do we need this carefully structured thinking? Because *they don't want to read it, look at it or hear it.* Your job, of course, is to entice and seduce them into reading, viewing and listening to your promotional material – and with enthusiasm!
See Conviction.

Aided recall   Advertising research:
A multiple-choice interviewing technique during which interviewees choose responses to questions from a list.

Airbrush Art, Production:
A studio tool for retouching and illustration work. Basically a
spray gun, powered by compressed air. The operator directs a fine
spray of coloured ink or paint on to the artwork or photoprint
being retouched.

Air date Radio, TV:
The date on which a radio or TV commercial is broadcast.

Airtime
The amount of time during which radio or TV entertainment or
advertising is allocated or actually transmitted.

Algorithm Computing:
A set of rules which a computer uses to solve problems, translated
into a sequence of instructions.

Alignment Art, DTP, Production, TYP:
The positioning of type or graphics on a page, so that the horizon-
tals and verticals are accurate.

Alphanumeric
A mix of letters and numbers.

Alterations Art, DTP, TYP, WP:
Amendments made to text after proofing. Sometimes called
'corrections'. Where the typesetter makes a mistake, he pays for
the alteration. Where the originator or author makes the mistakes,
these are called 'author's corrections', and the author pays.
Bearing in mind that it often costs £50 to amend a proof by even a
comma, copywriter beware.
   See Corrections.

Analogue
Varying continuously along a scale, rather than in fixed steps or
increments. A clock with hands and figures, in which time is represented as a continuous circle, can be considered analogue. Spelled
'analog' in American English.
   See Digital.

Anamorphic scan   Computer graphics:
Scanning a piece of artwork so that the width and height are not enlarged or reduced in proportion. The image is modified to produce an image taller and narrower, or shorter and fatter, than the original.

Animatic   Film, TV Commercials, Video:
A pre-production technique, in which a commercial is presented to the client without incurring the mega-pound expense of an actual production. A sequence of illustrations is prepared, showing the progress of the commercial, and shot on a video camera.

The illustrations usually follow the script and storyboard (qv). The client can then see what the commercial will look like, more or less. Sometimes, audio tape is employed for any accompanying music and sound effects. Many producers dislike animatics, since they do not present the full production values of the real thing. However, advertisers with a spark of imagination like them because they save money.

See Storyboard.

Animation   Art, Film, TV:
A technique for film-making, using individual frames. These are usually drawn by hand, or generated by computer. When projected at 24 or 25 frames per second, the effect on screen is an optical illusion of movement. *Snow White and the Seven Dwarfs* was the first major commercial animation production.

See Cel.

Answer print   TV Commercials, Post-Production:
A check print of a commercial after colour grading (qv). Release prints (qv) are produced when the director approves the answer print.

'A' paper sizes   Print, Production:
The international standard for paper sizes. The basic unit of this standard is the square metre, dubbed A0. The sizes then run in descending order, corresponding to the way the paper is folded or cut. All the folded sizes have the same proportions, 1:1.414. Curiously, the higher the A number, the smaller the paper size. Thus:

A0	841 × 1189mm
A1	594 × 841mm
A2	420 × 594mm
A3	297 × 420mm
A4	210 × 297mm
A5	148 × 210mm
A6	105 × 148mm
A7	74 × 105mm
A8	52 × 74mm

Application Computing:
A task to be carried out.

Art
Any visual element, whether photograph, illustration, drawing, lettering, graph, chart or pictogram.

Art paper Print, Production:
Paper stock coated with china clay or similar substance. This gives it a smooth surface for printing of the highest quality. Remember, the better the surface presented to the printing plate, the higher quality of the finished product.

Artwork Art, Print, Production:
Material prepared for reproduction in print. The basis of artwork is graphics, illustrations and photographs; but it commonly includes text. 'Complete artwork', 'artwork ready for camera', and 'camera-ready artwork' always mean the complete material ready for making film and printing plates. At this stage, the implication is that no more material needs to be added.

ASA
1 Photography:
American Standards Association. A universally accepted measure of light-sensitivity of photographic film; the 'speed' rating of film stock. The higher the ASA figure, the 'faster' the film speed, and the greater its sensitivity to light.

The speed of film stock determines the aperture of the lens and exposure time. For example, in bright light, a fast film needs less exposure; a slow film needs more.

If you are filming in low light conditions, a cave perhaps, you will need film stock with a high ASA rating, and probably a wider aperture. Maybe a slower shutter speed as well. If you are filming at Le Mans, and need to capture fast-moving vehicles as they go by on the track, you will definitely need fast film and high shutter speeds.

On the other hand, if you are covering a garden party on a brilliantly sunny day, and are aiming for sharp portraits, consider a slower film, wider apertures and slower shutter speeds.

Confused? There's a vast literature on photography and photographic materials.

See Film speed, ISO.

2   Advertising controls:
Advertising Standards Authority. This is the independent organisation which regulates and polices the advertising industry. It was set up by the industry itself to protect the public from misleading and offensive advertising, and to protect the industry from unwanted legislation. It also administers and enforces the British Codes of Advertising and Sales Promotion (qv).

The ASA is responsible for ensuring that the system works in the public interest. Its activities include investigating complaints and conducting research.

The Authority's responsibility, and its codes, cover:

advertisements in newspapers, magazines, brochures, leaflets, circulars, mailings, catalogues and other printed publications, facsimile transmissions, posters and aerial announcements

cinema and video commercials

advertisements in non-broadcast electronic media such as computer games

viewdata services

mailing lists, except for business-to-business

sales promotions

advertisement promotions

advertisements and promotions covered by the Cigarette Code.

The Codes do not apply to broadcast commercials, which are the responsibility of the ITC (Independent Television Commission) or the Radio Authority (qqv).

Ascender   DTP, TYP:
In type, the part of a lower case character rising above the 'x' height. The characters affected are b, d, f, h, k, l and t.
   See Descender.

Aspect ratio   DTP, TV, Print, Production:
The vertical to horizontal ratio of a TV screen or sheet of paper. The domestic TV screen ratio is 3 to 4; that is, 3 high to 4 wide. Some of the new wide screens are ratio 3:7; others have an even greater aspect ratio.

Auxiliary storage   Computing:
External magnetic or optical storage outside a computer's own internal memory.

Availability   Media planning:
Where advertising space in a newspaper or magazine is free for booking into, it is said to be available. The same applies to advertising slots in broadcasting air time. The dates and times of publication and transmission need to be specified.

BACC   TV: The Broadcast Advertising Clearance Centre.

Back matter   Print:
Pages following the main text of a printed document, containing appendix, glossary, index and other reference material.

Back-up   Computing:
Work done on a computer copied to external or auxiliary storage. This can be retrieved if the original is lost, damaged or corrupted.

Balance   Advertising design, Art, Creative, DTP, EP, TYP:
The relationship between elements in a layout. Balance aims at achieving a comfortable relationship between copy, graphics, illustrations and photographs. Balance is also applied to the overall look of a printed page. You can usually see when a layout is unbalanced. Sometimes, a reader may not easily see why it

is unbalanced, and the effect may be disturbing. If you are aiming for this reaction, all well and good, but it is not what advertisers usually want.

Balloon   Art, DTP, TYP:
The area containing speech in a cartoon.

Banner   Art, DTP, EP, TYP:
A main headline. In newspaper and magazine publishing, the term banner headline means one running across the full page width. The term also is used in brochure design.

BARB   Audience research: Broadcasters' Audience Research Board.

The Board commissions research into audience ratings for independent television and the BBC.

BARB's purpose is to provide ratings, forming an acceptable basis for comparison for buyers and sellers of television advertising. Advertising agencies and TV contractors negotiate on the basis of these ratings. BARB also provides much other data, but for advertising agencies and TV contractors, this particular basis cannot be obtained by any other means.

The current basis is *consolidated ratings* – the live audience viewing a programme, plus those who record a programme and view it within seven days.

For the television contractors, it is important to see how well their transmission schedules are doing, in comparison with the BBC. The BBC uses the information for the same purpose. It also gives the programme-makers an indication of how well a production is doing. It may also suggest a good time to screen a particular programme.

BARB was set up in 1980 by the BBC and ITCA (now called ITVA), and began operations in August 1981. Its function was to provide a single system for TV audience research in the UK.

The ITV audience research system was operated by JICTAR, the Joint Industry Committee for Television Advertising Research. The system consisted of electronic meters attached to the televisions of a representative sample of viewing audience. The meters recorded when the televisions were switched on and off, and which channels were being viewed. Every week, each householder had to remove from the meter the tape which carried the information, and post it to the researchers.

In addition, a questionnaire had to be completed by the house-holder. This indicated the number of people viewing each programme. This was posted to the researchers week by week.

The system was not always reliable, since it depended on complete and consistent questionnaires.

The BBC used a daily survey to obtain recall of programmes viewed the previous day. From this survey, the size and make-up of the audience to each programme was calculated.

JICTAR was concerned with minute-by-minute viewing, because of the need to know how many people were watching commercials. The IBA (now called ITC, Independent Television Commission), carried out a small audience appreciation survey.

The move towards a joint system was stimulated by the 1977 Annan Report on the future of broadcasting. This recommended a *combined* audience measurement system. This would eliminate the argument about which audience size information was correct. Resources could then be released to enable more attention to be directed to research on the reactions of audiences to the content of programmes.

The BBC and ITCA designed a system to provide a common database, to meet the needs of all interested parties, offering acceptable reliability and cost.

By 1980, they had announced the formation of BARB to manage the joint research programme.

Currently, the BBC and ITVA are sole and equal shareholders in BARB Ltd. The company's board comprises representatives of both, under an independent chairman.

The organisation operates through a committee system. The work of BARB devolves into two areas:

1. audience measurement
2. audience appreciation.

A management committee and technical sub-committee control these activities. The ITV companies, the BBC and various interested parties serve on the committees.

On the audience measurement committee, the IPA (Institute of Practitioners in Advertising) represents the advertising agencies.

The IPA is also represented on the main board. The ISBA (Incorporated Society of British Advertisers) represents the advertisers. As users of television advertising, they have a direct interest in the way audiences are measured. For this reason, they have an equal voice with the shareholders on the committees.

The ITC is represented on the audience appreciation side; it too has an equal voice with the shareholders.

Channel 4, Welsh Channel 4 and the satellite broadcasters are subscribers, and represented on appropriate committees.

In August 1991, a new seven-year BARB service was begun.

BARB has allocated the work to two research contractors, RSMB Television Research, a joint subsidiary of Millward Brown, and RSL (Research Services Ltd). These are responsible for all survey and field work, including the recruitment and operation of the audience panels.

The data supply and processing contracts are operated by AGB (UK) – Audits of Great Britain – which has awesome computing and number-crunching power. They service the panel homes, maintain the meters, retrieve the data, edit the data supply and the data-processing output.

The edited data is provided to subscribers electronically, with minimal paperwork. The amount of data supplied each time could equal a fair-sized encyclopedia if committed to paper.

See IPA, ISBA, ITC, ITVA, JICTAR.

Bar code   Retailing:
A pattern of vertical lines printed on a product, pack or printed material. Its function is to identify the product precisely. The information in the bars includes the price, date of purchase, point of sale, country of origin and the manufacturer. To retrieve the information, the bar code needs to be scanned by a computer.

Until recently, there seemed to be little compatibility among the various systems used in Europe. However, like many electronic techniques we now use in marketing, industry standards are being applied. We may have total compatibility by the middle of the 21st century.

Base-line   DTP, TYP:
An invisible horizontal line on which the bases of alphabetical and some numerical characters sit. Characters g, j, p, q and y fall below the base-line. In some fonts, the figures 3, 5, 7 and 9 fall below.

Battered   Art, DTP, EP, TYP:
A typeset character with a blemish. This term is relic of the days when type was set in metal. Occasionally a character emerged imperfect from the typesetting machine. Usually, this was detected only at proof stage, and the proof-reader would make appropriate marks to have the battered character replaced. Today, imperfect characters are rarer, but proof-readers still need to be vigilant.

BDMA   British Direct Marketing Association.
An organisation representing advertisers, agencies and suppliers in the direct marketing industry.

Below the line   Marketing jargon:
A metaphorical, invisible, horizontal line dividing various marketing communications media. By convention, those media granting commission to advertising agencies are above the line; the rest are below it.

Above the line:	press
	television
	radio
	cinema
	outdoor
The line	_____
Below the line:	print
	point-of-sale material
	sales promotion
	sponsorship
	retail display and merchandising
	public relations
	packaging
	direct mail
	exhibitions
	advertising gifts
	mini media
	body media (T-shirts, hats etc).

BCU   Filming, TV:
Big close-up.

Bit Computing:
In computer-speak, the smallest unit of electronic information, a BInary digiT.

Bit-mapped Computing:
In computer typesetting, the characters and their shapes are stored digitally as 'dots' in the computer's memory. When retrieved from the computer's bit-map for printing, they are reproduced as dots.

Black
1 Print:
The colour used with the subtractive primaries yellow, magenta and cyan in four-colour printing.
    See all these, and Process colours.

2 TV, Video:
When the screen is showing neither pictures nor 'snow' it is said to be showing 'black'. In post-production jargon, 'Going to black' means inserting a section of black in the tape. Most commercially produced videos, training videos for example, start with about 20 seconds of black.

Blanket Print:
A rubber-coated roller used on offset litho machines. This to prevent undue wear on the printing plate, since printing paper is abrasive. The blanket takes up the image from the printing plate and deposits it on to the paper or other surface to be printed. There is no contact between the printing plate and the paper.
    See Dry offset, Litho, Offset.

Bleed Art, Creative, Print, Production:
An illustration which prints beyond the trimmed edge of the paper. This brings the image right to the edge after trimming; no margin is visible.

Blind embossing Print, Production:
An image raised up on paper or board above the common surface, but not printed. The paper is usually pushed up from the back by a die or other mechanical device.

See Copperplate, Die-stamping, Embossing, Relief printing, Thermography.

Block
1 Computing, DTP, WP:
A group of characters or words treated as a single unit.

2 Letterpress printing:
An illustration etched on a metal plate.

Blocking out Art, Platemaking, Production:
See Masking.

Blow-up Art, Photography:
An enlargement of a photo negative or photoprint.

Board Paper, Papermaking, Print:
Material used in printing and packaging, heavier and stiffer than paper. In print, board is extensively used for brochure covers.
See Paper.

Bodyline capacity Typesetting:
The number of lines on a page to be printed.

Body copy Copywriting, DTP, EP, TYP, WP:
The small print of advertisement and brochure copy. Most body copy is set in sizes under 12pt. Copy over 12pt, usually headlines, is referred to as display copy.

Body type DTP, EP, TYP, WP:
Printing type smaller than 12pt. Also known as text type.

Boiler-plate DTP:
Copy stored as a standard unit. Different parts of this can be rearranged and combined with new copy to produce new documents.

Bold, Boldface DTP, EP, TYP, WP:
Heavier versions of roman or standard type, with thicker strokes and curves. Also known as heavy.

Booting up   Computing:
Starting up a computer, during which operating software is auto-
matically loaded. Most computers do this internally when
switched on. Nowadays, fewer if any are booted from floppy
disks.

Border   Design, Art, DTP, Print, Production, TYP:
A simple or complex rule, or a decorated one, positioned round
type and illustrated matter on a printed page.

Box   Art, DTP, EP, TYP, WP:
A rule border round a piece of copy, isolating it from other matter
on a printed page.

BRAD   British Rates and Data.
A monthly publication giving advertising rates, circulation figures
and mechanical data for British media. European equivalents
include *Tarif Media* in France and *Media Daten* in Germany. In the
USA, the counterpart is the Standard Rate and Data Service.

Brand image   Creative, Media, Marketing, Research:
Generally speaking, this is the *total personality* of a company or
product. It is this, rather than any trivial technical differences,
which determines a product's position in the market. Brand identity is concerned with how a company *presents* the brand to its
market. Brand image is how that market *perceives* the brand identity.
   See Branding, Positioning.

Branding   Creative, Media, Marketing, Research:
See Brand image, Brand loyalty, Positioning. See the Branding and
Positioning chapter of this book.

Brand loyalty   Creative, Media, Marketing, Research:
Allegiance by customers to a particular brand. This varies a great
deal, and can be complicated by swings of buying patterns by
brand-loyal groups. Research, particularly rolling research, can
determine the fads, fancies and swings, so that marketers can
decide on their marketing and advertising investment programmes with minimum risk.
   See the Branding and Positioning chapter of this book.

Break   Cinema, Radio, TV:
A break during news and entertainment programming, in which advertising is inserted. Also called a commercial break. Usually planned at a natural break point in the programming.

British Codes of Advertising and Sales Promotion
Advertising controls:
A compendium of rules by which the British advertising industry has agreed that the majority of advertisements it produces should be regulated. It is under the general supervision of the Advertising Standards Authority.

Radio and television advertisements are not covered by this code. They are covered by similar codes operated by the Radio Authority (qv) and the Independent Television Commission (qv).

The BCASP establishes a standard against which advertisements and sales promotion may be assessed. It is a guide to those concerned with commissioning, creating and publishing advertisements and sales promotion activities. It is also available to those who believe they may have reason to question what an advertisement says or shows. In this capacity, it helps to protect the public against misleading and offensive advertising.

The Committee for Advertising Practice is the self-regulatory body that devises and enforces the Codes. CAP's members include organisations that represent the advertising, sales promotion and media businesses:

Advertising Association
Association of Household Distributors
Association of Media and Communications Specialists
Broadcast Advertising Clearance Centre
Cinema Advertising Association
Council of Outdoor Specialists
Direct Mail Services Standards Board
Direct Marketing Association (UK)
Direct Selling Association
Incorporated Society of British Advertisers
Institute of Practitioners in Advertising
Institute of Sales Promotion
Mail Order Traders' Association

Mailing Preference Service
Newspaper Publishers' Association
Newspaper Society
Outdoor Advertising Association
Periodical Publishers' Association
Proprietary Association of Great Britain
Royal Mail
Scottish Daily Newspaper Society
Scottish Newspaper Publishers' Association.

In the opening pages of a previous version of the Code, the Committee outlined the essence of good advertising practice as follows:

All advertisements should be legal, decent, honest and truthful.
All advertisements should be prepared with a sense of responsibility both to the consumer and to society.
All advertisements should conform to the principles of fair competition generally accepted in business.

I don't think anyone could fail to subscribe to those sentiments.

Broadcasting Act 1990
See Radio Authority, ITVA, AIRC.

Broadsheet   Production, Print:
A paper size used in newspaper and magazine printing. The trimmed page size is about 600 mm high × 380 mm wide, depending on the printing house. *The Times, Daily Telegraph* and *Independent* are broadsheets.
See Tabloid.

Bromide   Photography:
A photoprint on silver bromide paper. Alas, this is a technique disappearing into photographic history, since more modern materials and techniques are now used. However, the terminology lingers on. To achieve different degrees of photographic contrast, papers of different 'hardness' are still used.
See Photograph.

Bug   Computing:
An error in a computer program. Correcting errors in computer software is called debugging.

B/W   Creative, Art, DTP, Print, Production:
Black and white.

Byte   Computing:
A group of eight bits of electronic data.
  See Bit.

CAD/CAM   Computer graphics, Design:
A combination of computer-aided design and computer-aided manufacture. This term is usually used to express graphic output, both on-screen and printed.

Calender   Paper, Papermaking, Print, Production:
A metal roller used in papermaking.

Calendering   Paper, Papermaking, Print, Production:
During papermaking, passing paper through a series of calenders to condition it for printing. The surface of the paper can be made smoother by calendering, which is much cheaper than coating it.

Callout   Art, DTP, WP:
Depends on which software manual you are using. Usually describes a caption to an illustration, in which the copy is connected to the illustration by a thin rule. In some DTP and WP software, callout describes a box in which copy is inserted. Often, the callout is not a box proper, but single or double rules above and below the copy. Or at the sides.

Camcorder   Video, TV:
A video camera which has a tape cassette built in.
See U-matic, VHS.

Camera-ready   Art:
Finished artwork, ready to be filmed. All the elements are in position with a high degree of accuracy. Printing plates are then made from the film.
  See Copy date.

Cancellation   Media planning and buying:
Cancellation of media bookings. All media have deadlines by which bookings may be cancelled without penalty. The lead time varies with the individual publication. For example, with some national newspapers, the cancellation deadline can be as short as three days. With national magazines, especially those carrying full-colour advertising, cancellation dates can be as long as four months preceding publication.

Capitals   Creative, DTP, TYP, WP:
The capital letters in an alphabet.
   See Caps, Lower case, Upper case.

CAP   Controls: The Committee of Advertising Practice.
The Committee responsible for the preparation, amendment and enforcement of the British Codes of Advertising and Sales Promotion (qv).
   See AIRC, ASA, British Code of Advertising and Sales Promotion, Independent Television Association, Independent Television Commission, Radio Authority.

Caps   DTP, TYP, WP:
Capital letters.
   See Capitals, Lower case, Upper case.

Caption
1   Art, Creative, Print:
Copy attached to a halftone or other illustration, describing or explaining what is going on. Captions are usually positioned underneath a picture; they can be anywhere, as long as you make sure they do relate to the picture and are closely attached to it.

2   Film, TV:
Usually written CAPT in the left-hand column of a script. More accurately, a caption board. A board containing an illustration to be shot, usually in the studio. Often used to make animatics (qv).

Cartridge
1   Paper, Print:
A tough, uncoated, matt paper with a slightly rough surface. Sometimes used for litho printing.

2 Radio:
A tape cassette containing a jingle, station announcement or commercial. Usually called a cart.

Cast off TYP:
To calculate the amount of type space – type area – which will be taken by typescript copy when set in a given typeface and size. Older typographers may still do this with slide rule or calculator. Computer typesetting, however, has rendered this technique and, sadly, those who practise it, obsolete.

Catchline Journalism, PR:
A word placed at the head of an article, and at the top left-hand corner of continuation pages. This is done to identify the piece as concisely as possible; essential when several hundred pieces are passing through a newsroom at the same time. It is also a handy, colloquial way of referring to a piece when discussing it at meetings and on the telephone.

Cel Film production:
In film animation, a single frame in a sequence of frames, drawn on clear acetate. Each cel is different and progressive, so that when the finished sequence is shot and run through a projector, the illusion of movement is created. In film animation, there are normally 24 frames for every second of movement. Think of the people who animated Tom and Jerry, and genuflect. The word is a corrupt abbreviation of celluloid, on which early animators used to work.
  See Animation.

Cell
1 Printing:
On a gravure printing cylinder, one of the tiny impressions or pits which hold the ink.

2 Computer spreadsheeting:
A rectangle containing a single unit of information.

Centre spread Printing:
The true centre of a newspaper or magazine. Both pages face each other, carry consecutive page numbers, and are printed on the same plate. In the USA, these are known as centrefolds.

Centred   DTP, EP, TYP, WP:
Type positioned in the centre of a page, a column or a box.

Certificate of insertion   Publishing:
Confirmation that a loose insert in a newspaper or magazine has actually been inserted and distributed in the publication. The publisher or printer issues this to the advertiser.

CGI   Video: Computer-generated images.

Certificate of transmission   Radio, TV:
Confirmation issued by a broadcasting station, that a commercial has actually gone out on air. It contains air-date, time, channel, air-time and other relevant information.

Character   DTP, EP, TYP, WP:
A single typeset letter. Often also used to refer to punctuation marks, letter-spaces and, sometimes, numerals. Numerals, however, are a separate case.
   See Monotype, Nought, Null, Proof, Proof-reader, Proof-reader's marks, Quote.

Character count   DTP, EP, TYP, WP:
The number of characters and spaces in a piece of copy.

Chroma   Art, Print:
A colour print made without an intermediate negative.

Circulation   Media publishing:
The number of copies actually sold of each issue of a publication. Do not confuse with readership (qv).
   See ABC, Controlled circulation, Rate card, Readership, VFD.

Classified   Press advertising:
Newspaper and magazine advertising sold by the line, rather than by the page unit. Copy is set in straight caps and lower case; no illustrations or logos are allowed.
   A variation of this format is semi-display classified, sold by the single-column centimetre. In this case, simple illustrations, headlines and logos are often allowed. In the USA, this is called classified display.
   See Display.

CMYK Print:
The four colours used in four-colour process printing: cyan, magenta, yellow and black. The initial K is used to denote black, presumably to avoid confusion with blue and brown.
See Primary colours.

Collar Sales promotion:
A paper or plastic collar designed to fit over the neck of a bottle. Offers, competitions, giveaways and other promotional material are printed on the collar.

Colour bars
1 Print:
Small rectangles in four-colour process-printing colours, yellow, magenta, cyan and black. These enable the printer and production team to check the density of the colours on the printed page; and also to a limited extent the registration of the colours being printed, though this is done more accurately by register marks (qv). The same check scheme appears on wet proofs (qv), and on Cromalins (qv).

2 Television:
The test signal for TV cameras; a series of vertical colour bars on screen.

Colour display Computing:
A colour VDU (qv); a multicoloured screen.

Colour filter Photography:
A tinted glass disk attached to the front of a camera lens. Its function is to change the colour values of the light reaching the film. The tints vary widely, according to the modification the photographer wants. A red filter, for example, will produce spectacular sky and cloud effects. A yellow filter is often used to correct flesh tones.

Colour grading Film, TV, Video:
A laboratory procedure in which the colour values of the master footage are adjusted, and for consistency.

Colour negative   Photography:
A type of photographic film producing the colour image in negative form. Used for making photoprints.

Colour reversal   Photography:
A type of photographic film which produces the colour image in positive form. Used for making transparencies.

Colour separation   Print:
Separating full-colour artwork into its component colours for 4-colour process printing: yellow, magenta, cyan and black. In the photographic technique, colour filters are used. Each filter produces the colour values for a single printing plate, captured on film from which the plate is made.
   See Screen angle.

Column   Art, DTP, EP, TYP, WP:
A block of text and other copy set vertically on the screen or printed page. The unit of horizontal measurement of the column is its width. So, you describe the type area of a column on a page like this: an area of copy 20 centimetres high and 1 column wide = '20 centimetres by 1 column', or '20 column centimetres'. The height is always given first. The same type area over several columns may be given like this: '10 centimetres by 2 columns'.
   For advertising media planning in Britain and the EU, type area is measured in column centimetres. In the USA, column height is measured in inches, and type area in column inches.

Column rules   DTP, EP, TYP:
Thin rules separating columns of copy in newspapers and magazines.

Command   Computing:
An instruction in computer language, in the form of a character string or a mix of letters and numbers.

Commercial   Film, TV, Video:
Shorthand for a televised, videoed or filmed commercial advertisement.
   See Still, Voice over.

Commercial break   Radio, TV:
A break during news and entertainment programming, in which advertising is inserted. Mostly, simply called a break.

Commission
1   Advertising:
Reward money in the form of a discount, paid to advertising agencies for placing advertising space and airtime bookings on behalf of clients.

2   To subcontract a job to an outside specialist, such as a photographer or artist.

Compatibility   Computing etc:
When one machine can use the same software, data and components as another without modification, it is said to be compatible.

Competition   Sales promotion:
A consumer activity designed to revive flagging sales, or respond to competitive attack. The punters are asked to compete for prizes by testing their skills and provide solutions or answers to questions. There is usually a tie-breaker, a device for ensuring outright winners. Proof of purchase is often required. Do not confuse with prize draws.

Many newspapers and magazines run competitions sponsored by advertisers or companies mentioned in editorial. The proof of purchase in this case is usually the entry coupon itself.

Competitions and prize draws are tightly controlled by legislation and voluntary controls.

See ASA, British Codes of Advertising and Sales Promotion.

Composition   DTP, EP, Print, TYP:
Originally meant setting metal type, either by hand or machine. It still means this, even though computers have now taken over most composition. One of the most useful advances computers have brought to composition is automatic hyphenation, justification and page formatting. The person composing the type is a compositor.

See Make-up, Mark-up.

Computer graphics Computing:
Any graphic created and generated on a computer, and which can be processed, modified and stored electronically. Drawings, graphs and charts, for example.

Condensed TYP:
A tall or narrow version of a roman or standard typeface.
See Extended.

Consumer Research:
A buyer or user of a product or service. This is not a straightforward, watertight definition, however. Children, for example, are indeed consumers of household products, but do not buy them. However, they can heavily influence purchases made by the parent or householder.

Another example: in medical and pharmaceutical marketing, the manufacturer promotes his product to the general practitioner. However, the GP does not buy the product, and may not even handle it; he prescribes it for the patient. The patient is the end-user, and pays for the product, but has no influence over the choice of its selection. The patient takes the prescription to a pharmacist, who dispenses it from his stock. Under the National Health Service, the government pays the pharmacist.

Although the manufacturer may promote the product to the pharmaceutical profession, the pharmacist has no choice but to supply the product specified by the GP. Confused? You ought be.

In consumer and business-to-business marketing communications, the table of decision-makers looks something like this:

identifiers
influencers
specifiers
deciders
buyers
end-users
gatekeepers.

Industrial consumers are not normally referred to as such, but that is what they are in the final analysis. The chain of influence and decision-making is fairly straightforward, however, bearing in mind the table in the previous paragraph.

Contact print   Photography:
A photographic print made when the negative or positive is in
intimate contact with the photographic paper. The contact is direct
between emulsion and emulsion; that is, both light-sensitive
surfaces. Colloquially known as 'contacts'.

Contact screen   Art, Photography, Platemaking:
A halftone screen on film or glass, consisting of ruled lines laid out
in a pattern to produce halftone dots. The screen is positioned in
intimate contact with the receiving film or plate; emulsion to emulsion for the sharpest definition.
See Halftone.

Continuous tone   Art, Photography, Platemaking:
In original photographs, the colours and shades are reproduced
from black to white, in a seamless range of tones. Because the tones
are continuous right across the range, this manifestation is referred
to as 'continuous tone'. Technically, it is an image in which tonal
gradation is produced by changes in density.
See Contrast, Halftone.

Contrast   Art, Photography, Platemaking, TV:
Although photographically produced material is continuous in
tone, there is a degree of separation between tones. If there were
not, you would see just a blotch of coloured mud on the print,
rather than the proper image. Contrast, therefore, is the ability of
the photographic material to separate the degrees of light and
shade in an image, so that it is intelligible. The same applies to
electronically produced images on screen.

Controlled circulation   Media planning:
A publication which circulates to a pre-selected target audience
is described as having controlled circulation. Many professional,
trade and specialist publications are distributed using this system.
The main difference is that they are free to the reader.
Circulation is determined by the precise description of the category of reader. The qualification system is common to all controlled circulation magazines.
Marketing Week, for example, circulates to the marketing and
advertising industry. To receive your free copy, you must first fill

in, date and sign a reader application card. The personal details you are asked for are:

■ personal title
■ initials
■ surname
■ company name
■ company address
■ town
■ county
■ postcode
■ telephone number.

You are then asked for two main items of information. First, your company's main area of business:

■ manufacturing
■ media owner
■ consultancies
■ agencies
■ services.

This is followed by:

■ the number of full-time employees in your company
■ your responsibility for part/all of your company's marketing/advertising expenditure
■ your involvement in any marketing/sales/promotion activities in Europe
■ your involvement in decisions on recruitment advertising
■ your involvement in your company's selection or purchase of various products and services
■ if you are with a client company/consultancy, your company's total marketing/advertising spend
■ if you are with an advertising agency, your company's approximate billings.

You must then sign and date your application.

If you fail to complete *any* of these sections, including signature and date, the publisher will send the card back to you for completion.

The publisher will then consider your application, and decide if you really do qualify for a free 'subscription'. If you do qualify, you get the publication free for a year, after which you will be asked to fill in a further application. If you don't qualify, you can still get the publication, but you'll have to pay for it, and the publisher will tell you so.

The whole point of this procedure is that the circulation is audited by an independent third party, such as the ABC (qv). That is how advertisers know they are getting the utmost value for that part of their budgets spent with controlled circulation publications.

See ABC, Circulation, Rate card, Readership, VFD.

Conviction   Creative:
Part of the communication discipline, AIDA, designed to attract the attention and hold the interest of potential customers; get a decision in favour of your brand; and get the action you want.

Essentially, you need to convince your reader, viewer or listener that:

■ you have attracted his attention for a good reason
■ what you are telling him is *truly* in his self-interest
■ your promise and benefits help him to fulfil an unsatisfied need
■ the desire you arouse will lead to that fulfilment
■ the action you are asking for will lead to it
■ that when he has taken it, his life will be improved – in terms of that unsatisfied need:
    in his business life
    in his domestic life
    in his social life
    in his personal life
■ that you are offering this certainty on a reliable and permanent basis.
    See AIDA.

Copperplate   Print:
An intaglio printing process (qv), which uses copper or steel plates. The printing image is cut into the metal, either by hand or machine, or chemically etched. The sunken image is filled with ink. The paper to be used is first slightly moistened, then applied

to the plate with considerable pressure. This draws the ink into the paper, producing a dense, crisp image of very high quality. The surface of the paper ends up slightly embossed on the printed surface, with a slightly dented impression on the back.

Copperplate printing used to be very popular for letterheads, business cards, invitations and share certificates. The advantage was the high quality of the paper and the printed image, and the status it conferred on the sender. Nowadays, it is much less used, but still admired when it turns up on a letterhead or card – by those who recognise it.

Today, copper plates are used for short, high-quality print runs. They are comparatively expensive to produce, and therefore best used where the budget, and the desired promotional effect, are appropriate. For longer runs, steel or chromium-plated copper plates are used. Also known as steel-die engraving.

See Blind embossing, Die-stamping, Embossing, Thermography.

Copy
1   Copywriting:
The text of a manuscript; the text of a typescript.

2   Print:
All the material to be printed, including text, illustrations, graphics, halftones, ornaments and borders.
Confused? *See* Hard copy, Manuscript, Print, Typescript.

Copy date   Advertising production, Public Relations:
The deadline by which the publisher must receive advertising or editorial copy. This usually also means copy ready for camera.
See Camera-ready.

Copywriter   Creative:
A writer specialising in conceiving and writing advertising copy. Often also applied to a writer involved in public relations work, principally writing news releases and house journals.

Corrections   Art, DTP, TYP, WP:
Amendments made to text after proofing. Sometimes called 'amendments'. Where the typesetter makes a mistake, he pays for the alteration. Where the originator or author makes the mistakes,

these are called 'author's corrections', and the author pays. Caution: it often costs up to £50 to amend a proof, by even a comma.

See Amendments.

Coupon   Creative, Sales promotion:
A response element in a press advertisement or catalogue page. Its main function is to give the customer or reader an opportunity to send for information, sales call, a demonstration or a product. The coupon should be designed so that readers can fill in their requirements and personal details, then cut the coupon from the page and post it to the advertiser.

At first sight, this is quite a simple response device for building-in to an advertisement. In practice, it is usually the reason why the advertisement was created in the first place. Yet it is often so badly and inefficiently done, I'm not surprised that some advertisers are convinced that their advertising doesn't work.

David Ogilvy says that to get the best results from coupons, you should write and design them like mini-advertisements. I heartily agree.

Give every coupon a motivating headline, with a promise or a benefit in it. Include a couple of lines of motivating body copy.

Show the reader what the product looks like; it needn't take up much space – a thumbnail illustration will do. Even a tiny illustration can increase the response by a worthwhile amount. Then ask for action. How many coupons you have seen in the last three months actually follow this important creative discipline?

Another problem with coupons is the information advertisers expect to get from them. When you decide to include a coupon in an advertisement, you also should also estimate its value to your database. Any database is only as effective as the information it contains. Therefore, when using coupons to build a database, you need to consider the importance of the information you are asking your respondents for.

Coupon offer   Creative, Sales promotion:
A coupon offering a discount on a product. When a product is being introduced or otherwise promoted, a coupon or voucher offering consumers a discount can encourage them to try the product. It can lead to long-term brand loyalty.

Cover date Publishing:
The date shown on the cover of a publication. Often, particularly in the case of full-colour monthlies, the publication is on the street well in advance of the cover date. It sometimes means, for example, that the April issue of a magazine is available on the first of March. Don't forget that copy dates are always correspondingly early.
See Issue date.

CPS Computer printers: Characters per second.
A measure of speed, indicated by the number of characters a computer printer can produce in one second.

CPT Media planning: Cost per thousand.
The cost to the advertiser of reaching a thousand members of the target audience he is aiming at. This is one of the generally accepted bases for comparing one publication with others in the same field.

CRCA Commercial Radio Companies Association.
The trade association for independent commercial radio companies in Britain. It is voluntary, non-profit-making, incorporated as a company limited by guarantee; formed by the first radio companies when independent radio began in 1973. Formerly called AIRC, Association of Independent Radio Companies.

CRCA enjoys the support of the radio industry; all but a handful of stations are members. It is funded by the subscriptions of its member radio companies, who share the cost of CRCA in proportion to their shares in the industry's broadcasting revenue.

CRCA's affairs are managed by a board of eight directors: the Association's chairman and six other non-executive directors elected annually. In addition, one executive director, the Director and Chief Executive, manages the eight-person directorate.

Industry forum:
The CRCA board meets five times a year. There are also two general meetings of all member companies: the AGM in January and the Annual Congress in June or July.

Reporting to the board are six standing committees: copyright, finance and general purposes, marketing, programming, research, and technical matters. There are also a number of specialist sub-committees.

Representations:
Since 1984, CRCA has been active in representations to government, the Radio Authority (qv) and other bodies. CRCA had a significant input to the 1987 Green Paper, 'Radio: Choices and Opportunities', to the 1990 Broadcasting Act, which substantially deregulated independent radio, and to the BBC Charter Review.

Copyright:
CRCA's Copyright Committee negotiates on behalf of members with the principal music copyright bodies, the Performing Rights Society, the Mechanical Copyright Protection Society, and Phonographic Performance Ltd. With the aid of consultants, the Committee monitors copyright developments outside the UK, and lobbies European institutions and bodies such as the World Intellectual Property Organisation.

Marketing:
CRCA's Marketing Committee is the focal point for liaison between radio companies, national sales houses and the Radio Advertising Bureau.

Audience research:
Radio audience research is conducted by RAJAR – Radio Joint Audience Research Ltd (qv). RAJAR is jointly owned by CRCA and the BBC, but all broadcasters contract with it direct. CRCA's Research Committe monitors the performance of RAJAR on behalf of CRCA members, and formulates independent sector research policy which, after approval by the CRCA board, is taken forward to the various RAJAR committees by CRCA representatives, who are all members of the Research Committee.

Copy clearance:
The Radio Authority's Code, and almost 60 acts of parliament, determine what can and cannot be said in radio advertisements. To protect advertisers and broadcasting stations, a central script clearance system is operated by the Broadcast Advertising Clearance Centre, on a basis agreed by CRCA. All stations contribute to the cost, and the Radio Authority collects the fees.

Information and involvement:
CRCA is the prime source of up-to-date information about aspects of independent radio. Members' requirements have priority and, in addition to swift response to enquiries, regular guidance. Enquiries are handled from the media, advertisers and agencies, financial analysts, other researchers, and people seeking careers in radio.

Programming:
CRCA's Programming Committee liaises with the Radio Authority over programming issues, and develops network projects that provide attractive programming and additional revenues for member stations.

New members:
New radio companies are eligible to join CRCA as soon as they are granted a licence by the Radio Authority. There is a small joining fee, and no further subscription is due until the company begins broadcasting. After that, members' subscriptions relate direct to broadcasting revenue. The smallest companies – often those which find CRCA most valuable – therefore pay least.
 See Essential Contacts.

Credit   Art, DTP, EP:
A reference, usually a line of copy, showing the name of the individual or organisation supplying the material. The material can be text, a graphic, an illustration, photograph or artwork.

Cromalin   Print:
A proofing system, using coloured toners rather than inks. This is DuPont's brand name for their process; 3M do another.
 See Agfa, DuPont, Kodak and 3M in the Directory section. *See* Press proof, Proof, Wet on wet.

Crop   Art:
To trim an illustration or photograph. This is done physically on the drawing board, or electronically on computer screen. The objective is to cut off unwanted parts of the photograph, such as dustbins standing outside the front entrance of your new office or factory; or to improve the shape of the print; or make it fit a column width.

Cross-head   Copywriting, Creative, DTP, Editing, EP, TYP, WP:
See Sub-head.

Crown   Outdoor advertising:
See Double crown

CRT   Computing, TV: Cathode ray tube.
A fancy name for a computer screen or TV monitor. This is a proper technical term used by manufacturers of oscilloscopes and early TV equipment. Nowadays, in the mouths of end-users, it sounds a bit 19th century-ish, and pretentious.

Cursor   Computing, DTP, WP:
A flashing vertical or horizontal bar, rectangle or graphic device on your computer screen. This marks the current working position, and the place where text will be inserted when you type. You can move it by using the keyboard or mouse.

Cut-out   Art:
A photograph or illustration with the background cut away.

Cutting copy   Film, video:
The first version of a film or TV commercial.

Cyan   Print:
One of the subtractive primary colours used in 4-colour process printing.
   See Black, Cromalin, Magenta, Pantone, Primary colours, Process colours, Yellow.

Cylinder press   Print, Printing processes:
A letterpress printing press in which the type and illustrations are locked up in a flat frame called a forme (qv). The paper is laid on top of the forme; the cylinder rolls across it, pressing it on to the inked type. In most modern presses of this type, the forme moves along under the cylinder. This delivers sharp, crisp, dense copies (provided, of course, that the inking, make-ready and paper are ideal for the job).
   See Flatbed, Forme, Letterpress, Make-ready, Plate, Pull.

Daisywheel Computer printers:
A detachable printwheel containing a complete type font of characters, numbers and symbols. This type of printer uses impact for getting characters on to the paper. The reproduction quality is high, usually described as 'letter quality'.

Database Computing:
A computer file containing information and facts on a specific subject, eg names, job titles, addresses and other useful data. Usually organised for fast access and retrieval.

Deadline Advertising, PR, Publishing:
The date or time planned and set for the completion of a job.

Deck Copywriting:
Copy, such as a sub-head, between a headline and a section of body copy.

Deep-etched Art, Print:
The treatment of a printing plate, in which some of the printing area is removed. This ultimately leaves areas of unprinted white space, usually for the brightest of highlights, for example.

Definition Computing, Print, TV:
The sharpness or resolution of a printed image, and its TV screen equivalent.
See Dot, Pixel, Resolution.

Demographics Planning, Research:
The division and classification of populations and target audiences, by age, sex, occupation, social status and other characteristics.

Density
1 Photography, Platemaking, Print:
The tonal value of an image, or part of an image.

2 TYP:
The amount and tonal quality of a typeset area. Type set solid, and with minimal word- and letter-spacing can look very dense. Where

it becomes unreadable, the term dense can also be a quality ascribed to the typographer who made it so.

Densitometer Print:
An instrument for checking and measuring the colour and tone density of printing inks. This is used in proofing, and on print runs, to control inking levels.

Depth of field Photography:
To produce a sharp image, a lens needs to be focused at a certain point in front of it. In front of and behind this point, the image continues sharp, depending on how far the subject is from the lens. Outside these areas, the image becomes blurred as it goes further and further out of focus. The areas of acceptable sharpness on either side of the focal point is the depth of field.

Descender TYP:
That part of a character which descends below the base-line (qv); especially lower case characters g, j, p, q and y. In some fonts, the figures 3, 5, 7 and 9 fall below the base-line. Some exotic and fancy typefaces have other descending characters, depending on the whim of the designer.
See Ascender.

Die-stamping Print:
Printing by pressure from lettering engraved into copper or steel plates. The die is the engraved plate.
See Copperplate, Blind embossing, Embossing, Thermography.

Digital Communications, Computing, Radio, TV:
Any data, image or calculation which can be accessed, processed and stored electronically, and later retrieved and re-formed. Until recently, this term was usually applied to the processing of images by computer. It is now current in radio and TV transmission and reception equipment.
A digital clock is one which shows the time by digits, rather than by the use of hands.
See Analogue.

Digital image   Computer graphics:
Any computer image which has been encoded electronically. This applies both to graphics and type.

Direct mail   Advertising, Sales promotion:
A form of advertising in which selling is done by sending promotional material through the post. Selling by post. Do not confuse with mail order, which is *buying* by post.

Direct response   Direct marketing
Advertising, and other promotional activities, in which a measurable response is obtained direct from the target audience. The media used include press, television, radio, mail, telephone, fax, and the Internet. Direct marketing by Internet is now firmly established, especially in the USA.

Display   Press advertising:
Newspaper and magazine advertising sold by the unit of a page. Units are fractions of a page, eg whole page, half, quarter, eighth, sixteenth and so on.
   See Classified.

Display highlight   Computer graphics, DTP, WP:
Any image on a computer screen highlighted to call attention to it. This is done by the use of bright bars or other areas, some of which flash or blink. In DTP and WP, highlighting is done by a procedure called selecting, and used for dragging items to different positions on screen (qv).

Display type   TYP:
Type sizes 14pt and larger. Used mainly for headlines in press advertisements and print.

Dissolve   Film, TV, Video:
Otherwise known as a cross-fade. When changing from one scene or shot to the next, the first is faded out as the second is faded in.
   See Fade, Wipe.

Doctor   Print:
In gravure printing, a sprung, stainless-steel blade pressed against

the printing cylinder. This scrapes away excess ink before the image is transferred to the paper. The pressure of the blade is finely judged; too much, and the doctor could scrape away the surface of the cylinder – a costly error. Too little, and the surplus ink could smudge the printed image.

Dolly   Film, TV, Video:
A trolley for a film or TV camera, used in studios and on location. The dolly is equipped with devices to ensure smooth action and prevent shake and shudder during operation.

Dot   Platemaking, Print, Production:
The smallest reproducible element in a halftone.
   See Definition, Pixel, Resolution.

Dot for dot   Platemaking, Print, Production:
Reproducing a halftone illustration from an image which has already been screened. For example, a picture of your chairman is needed for an advertisement. You have lost the most recent negative and prints, and the only suitable pic you have is one already published in your house magazine. You can't organise another photoshoot, because the chairman is on holiday in the Caribbean, and uncontactable.

   Nil desperandum. You cut out the chairman's picture from your house magazine, and have it reproduced on film, dot for dot, by your platemaker. Each dot on the magazine halftone is individually reproduced on film. Usually, little quality is lost by this method. However, don't enlarge or reduce the image by more than ten per cent, or serious loss of quality, as well as some bizarre distortions, may result.
   See Halftone.

Dot gain   Print:
A printer's nightmare. In printing halftones (qv), dots may increase in size once deposited on paper. This can produce a result different from the one planned by the creative team and artworker.

   The printed dot is absorbed into the paper and dries, or is 'cured', as a crust on the surface. The thickness of the crust, though microscopic, casts a minute shadow on the paper. The portion of the printed dot below the surface will usually spread, giving a further increase in dot size. Multiplied up by the screen density, with up to 6400 dots to the square centimetre, the printed result is in different tones and colours from the ones planned for. Pre-press techniques should therefore take the effect of dot gain into account.

Dot gain can be controlled. In theory, FM screening (qv) should increase the problems of dot gain. The dots are smaller than those obtained by conventional screening. However, although distributed at random on the plate, all the FM dots have the same surface area. This means that the level of gain is the same throughout the range of tones. Corrections can be fed back to the scanner and the settings adjusted to compensate for dot gain.

See FM, Halftone.

Double crown   Outdoor advertising:
An ancient, but still-used, name for the basic size of paper used for posters. Crown is 381 cm high × 254 cm wide (15 in high × 10 in wide), and double crown 762 mm high × 508 mm wide (30 in × 20 in).

Double-page spread   Print, Publishing:
Two facing pages in the centre of a publication, magazine or brochure, usually printed on a single sheet.

See Spread.

Download   Computing:
The transfer of electronic data from one computer to another, or from a computer to a storage medium such as diskette or tape. A technique used in Internet activities.

Down-stroke   TYP:
In a type character, a heavy downward stroke. This is equivalent to the downward stroke of your pen when producing characters by hand.

Draft   Art, Creative, DTP, EP, Publishing, WP:
Verb – to prepare a piece of copy, usually in the form of a typescript. Noun – a piece of raw copy, which may be amended, modified, added to; possibly even mutilated. Draft also applies to illustrations, usually line drawings. A final draft is one on which all the possible modifications and mutilations have been made, and is now ready for setting.

Dragging   Computing, DTP, WP:
Highlighting characters, words, and blocks of type. You can then move them, copy them, or change their style, eg from roman to italic.

Dragging is usually done by using your mouse to place the cursor at the start of the drag, holding down one of the buttons, then dragging up or down. Releasing the button stops the dragging. Many DTP and WP programs allow you to drag via the keyboard. Mouse dragging is simplest.

Dry mounting   Art:
Mounting a photoprint or illustration on to mounting board, using a heat-set adhesive. The technique is one of sandwiching an adhesive membrane between the print and the mounting board, and applying an electric iron to melt the adhesive. This then sets like concrete, and the only way to de-mount the print is to use a sharp knife. You may damage the print in the process. Given time, the adhesive will probably crack.

This technique, I am glad to report, is not much used any more in the marketing communications industry. The favourites at the moment are:

Cow Gum rubber solution, a brilliant invention which allows you to reposition a print on the mounting board once you have laid it down. You can usually do this safely up to 10 minutes later. You can de-mount a print without damaging it, even years later by applying, sparingly and progressively, a solvent such as lighter fuel. You dampen the edges and back of the print, and lift it off gently.

Tack-adhesive, a method of coating the back of a print with small dots of light adhesive. As with Cow Gum, you can reposition the print for quite a while after mounting it. I am not sure if you can as easily de-mount with a solvent; as always, read the instructions on the pack.

Dry proofing   Print, Production:
Proofing a print job without using printing plates or a printing press. Wet proofing – using a press for proofing – is slow, wasteful, expensive and unnecessary. It means shutting down a press for

setting up the proofing. There are several equally good methods available, all faster and more economical than wet proofing. Besides, printers earn their living when their presses are rolling, and lose money when they are idle.

See Cromalin, Progressive proofs, Proof, Wet proof.

Dry offset   Print, Printing processes:
Also known as indirect letterpress (qv). A letterpress (qv) process which uses the offset (qv) technique. The image is first transferred to a rubber blanket cylinder, which in turn transfers it to the paper. Unlike litho, no water is used; hence 'dry'.

See Litho.

Dry transfer lettering   Art, TYP:
A lettering system for the studio drawing board. In the absence of DTP, quite good for headlining. It uses characters pre-printed on a sheet of translucent, coated paper. The individual characters are self-adhering. You position each character wherever you want it on the page – with some precision – then rub it down with the blunt end of a pen, the back of a spoon, or a special instrument. Personally, I have never had much success with the special instrument, and prefer the spoon.

The main disadvantage with this system is that you can't reposition the character once you have rubbed it down. If you have messed up the positioning, all you can do is lift the letter off with self-adhesive tape and start again. Better still, give the job to a professional.

Dubbing   Film, TV, Video:
Adding sound to mute film or videotape. Sound includes voices, music and sound effects, and mixtures of these techniques.

Duplicate   Art, Film, Video:
An exact copy of an original print, illustration, drawing, transparency, film, video and other production material. Dupe is the usual abbreviation.

DVE   Video: Digital video effects.

Ears, earpieces   Advertising, Publishing:

Small advertising spaces on the front page of a newspaper, positioned either side of the main masthead.

ECU   Film, TV, Video:
Extreme close-up. When you can see the individual hairs of an actor's eyebrows, or when a human eye fills the screen, it's an ECU.

Electro   Print, Production:
A duplicate printing plate used in hot-metal letterpress printing. The dupe is produced by electrolysis from the original. The printing surface is grown as a copper skin, with the body of the plate added in base metal. Old-fashioned letterpress is either dead or on its last legs; I haven't seen any for years. However, it may still be in use in developing countries. If you know any printers actively using this kind of printing, please send me their names and addresses; I'd like to interview them.

Elite   TYP:
A unit in the measurement of type size.
   See Pica.

Em   Copywriting, Design, TYP:
A unit of measurement based on the space occupied by a capital M in 12pt. The length of a line of type is often indicated by the number of ems it takes up. Line length is now also measured in millimetres.

Embossing   Print:
Impressing an image into paper or board from the back, to raise the image's surface. The raised image is then printed.
   See Blind embossing, Copperplate, Die-stamping, Relief printing, Thermography.

Em dash   Copywriting, Design, TYP:
A long dash, the width of an em. Do not confuse with the hyphen, which is shorter and has a different semantic function.

En   Copywriting, Design, TYP:
Half the width of an em.

En dash   Copywriting, Design, TYP:
A short dash, the width of an en.

Estimate   Creative, Print, Production:
The costing of a job, prepared in advance, by a printer, production house, advertising agency, photographer or other supplier. Estimates are not normally binding; quotations are, so be careful.
See Origination.

Exploded view   Art, CAD, Design, DTP, EP:
An illustration of an object, such as a piece of equipment, showing how its components relate to each other. The illustration is complete in itself, and in proper perspective, usually with sections cut away to show what's underneath.

Extended   TYP, Typesetting:
A wider version of a roman or standard typeface. Also called expanded, or ultra.
See Condensed.

Face   TYP, Typesetting:
Shorthand term for typeface or character; the name given to the design of a particular typeface. Times roman, for example, is a typeface. Sometimes the term face is used to refer to a family to which a typeface belongs.

Fade   Film, TV, Video:
Gradually fading out a picture, to end up with a black or blank screen.
See Dissolve, Wipe.

Family   TYP:
A typeface (qv) with specific, identifiable characteristics running throughout its range. The members of the family are related to the base design. These include regular, medium, light, extra light, hairline, thin, bold, semi-bold, demi-bold, extra bold, heavy, ultra, roman, italic, condensed, expanded, shadow, outline, relief.

Fat   TYP, Typesetting:
Also, fat face. A typeface with wide contrast in the visual weight of its thick and thin strokes. Sometimes used instead of the term ultra.
   See Face, Font.

File   Computing, DTP, WP:
The name given to a unit or compilation of data stored under a single name.

Filler
1   DTP, EP, Print:
A piece of copy or an illustration inserted on a page to fill up a column. Most often used before the days of DTP and computer typesetting. Nowadays, you can usually juggle page elements on your screen so that fillers are unnecessary. However, a filler often makes a page easier on the eye than it would be with a strictly clinical layout. To enjoy some really delightful fillers, read the *New Yorker*.

2   Paper, Papermaking:
A material, usually a white mineral substance such as china clay or calcium carbonate. Added to the raw material from which the paper is made, it increases its opacity, improves its flatness and allows a smoother finish to the surface of the finished paper.

Film make-up   Art, Print:
Assembling the elements of an editorial page, or an advertisement, ready for film-making.

Film master   Art, Print:
A complete, made-up positive of an editorial page or advertisement.

Film-setting   *See* Photosetting.

Film speed   Photography:
The sensitivity of photographic film to light, usually known as speed rating. The rating scale, which has been adopted internationally, is set by the American Standards Association. Film speed

is usually designated by the initials ASA and ISO. The higher the ASA rating, the higher the film 'speed', and therefore the 'faster' the film stock. It follows that the faster the film speed, the shorter the exposure needed. Not to be confused with shutter speed (qv).

See ASA, ISO.

Filter   Art, Photography, Production:
A transparent coloured glass or plastic sheet placed in front of a camera lens. This has the effect of changing the colour and quality of the light reaching the film. Thus, in four-colour process film-making:

| *Blue filter* | *Green filter* | *Red filter* | *Yellow filter* |

Gives colour values for making the plate to print

| *Yellow* | *Magenta* | *Cyan* | *Black* |

Finished artwork, finished art   *See* Artwork.

Finished rough   *See* Visual.

Fisheye lens   Film, Photography, Video:
A camera lens with a wide angle of view, usually more than 60°. Distortion produced by such a lens is extreme, curving straight lines and exaggerating curved ones. Strictly for special effects.

Fixed pitch   DTP, TYP, WP:
A typeface with characters of equal width, and where the spaces between the characters are also of equal width.

Flatbed   Print:
A printing press in which the printing surface is flat. This is a bed called a forme, which contains the metal type and illustrations. The forme passes to and fro under an impression cylinder, the paper being compressed between the two. You won't find many flatbed presses use in Britain today; most print shops use offset litho. You may find some in developing countries.

See Cylinder press, Forme, Letterpress, Plate, Pull.

Flexography   Print:
See the Print chapter of this book.

Flip chart Presentations:
A large layout pad, fixed or ring-bound at the top. The presentation material is pre-mounted on the pages and flipped over during presentation. Flip charts are popularly used during presentation of film and video storyboard material. Also used during lectures and other presentations as live material. Often used in addition to, or instead of, whiteboards.

Floating accent DTP, TYP, WP:
An accent sign which does not require its own space. It combines with a type character and prints with it as a single unit.

Flush left Copywriting, DTP, TYP, WP:
A form of text alignment. Copy arranged in a straight vertical line on the left of a typescript or block of copy. The right-hand edge is unaligned, uneven.

Flush right Copywriting, DTP, TYP, WP:
In this case, the right-hand edge is vertically aligned, the left-hand edge uneven.

FM
1   Media planning, Production: Facing matter.
An advertisement inserted facing editorial material in a magazine or newspaper. FM is indicated in the space order, and usually costs more than run-of-paper insertions.

2   Radio transmission: Frequency modulation.

3   Print, Production: Frequency modulation.
Also called stochastic screening. A form of halftone screening in which the distribution of dots is random. The effect is rather like the sand on sandpaper. The familiar rosette effect of conventional halftone screens is avoided.

Advocates of FM screening claim that the printed results are sharper than the conventional method. However, I have not found this to be the case; or rather, I haven't detected any difference on certain types of stock. In one case, the result was, if anything, slightly fuzzier than an image printed on identical paper using conventional halftone. FM screening techniques will undoubtedly improve, and may overtake the conventional. Watch this space. In the meantime, continue to exercise intellectual honesty in evaluating production techniques, as I have done here.

See Dot gain, Halftone.

Folio   Print, Publishing:
A page number.

Font   TYP:
The complete range of one size and visual weight of a type face. This includes upper and lower case characters, small caps, accents and accented characters, punctuation, numerals, fractions and symbols. Also known as a fount. Both names reflect the history of printing, much of which was carried out in churches or on church property. The real origin of font is probably French: *fonte*, from *fondre*, meaning found; or old French, *fondre*, meaning to use a foundry.

See Face, Typeface.

Foot   Print:
The unprinted margin at the foot of a page.

Footage   Filming, Photography:
The running length of a piece of film – 35 mm film runs at 24 frames a second. Be careful: television pictures are transmitted at 25 frames a second, which can get out of phase with the running speed of film footage. That's why the wheels of a moving car, at certain speeds, look as though they are rolling backwards.

See FPS, Frame.

Format
1   Art direction:
The size, shape and appearance of a design page, and its subsequent printed version.

2   Computing, DTP, WP:
Instructions to your computer for determining the size, shape and appearance of material on screen. This affects what is subsequently reproduced.

Forme Print:
In letterpress printing, a metal frame containing type, illustrations or both. The material would be made up into pages, ready for printing.
See Cylinder press, Flatbed, Letterpress, Plate, Pull.

Forty-eight sheet Outdoor advertising, Print, Production:
A poster size, 20 ft high × 10 ft wide.

Fount *See* Face, Font, Typeface.

Four-colour process Print:
An economical printing system using only four colours to represent the whole visible colour spectrum. Using only yellow, cyan, magenta and black, you can print virtually any colour. It is economical because the printing inks are standard throughout the industry, and manufactured and sold in vast quantities.

Four-colour scan Print:
A set of film positives, made from a full-colour transparency or photoprint by electronic scanning.

FPS Film, TV, Video: Frames per second.
In the UK, television images are screened at 25 frames per second; 35 mm film runs at 24 frames per second, worldwide.
See Footage, Frame.

Frame Film, TV, Video:
An individual picture in a sequence. In filming, each picture is shot as an individual frame, at 24 frames a second. The sequence is projected on to a screen at 24 frames a second, giving the illusion of movement.

Film used for television is scanned at 25 frames a second. This difference is virtually undetectable on the screen. However, if you are running conventional film on television, this needs some adjustment, otherwise the frames appear to creep slowly up the screen, one after another.

One oddity of the 25 fps technique can be seen on screen, when the wheels of cars seem to revolve backwards while the car is moving forwards. This happens when the projection speed and the speed of the wheels are out of phase. While the wheels are revolving at under 25 revolutions per second, they appear to move in the same direction as the car. At exactly 25 rps, the wheels appear stationary. At more than 25 rps, the wheels appear to revolve backwards. Bizarre. No one has yet succeeded in curing the effect, though someone is probably working on it right now.

See FPS, Freeze-frame, Opticals, Shot, Still.

Free-phone   Direct marketing response technique:
A free telephone service used in press, outdoor and broadcast advertising, and direct mail. It is a facility offered by advertisers, to encourage consumers to respond or order by telephone. The customer's call is paid for by the advertiser. The customer dials 100, and asks for the advertiser's Free-phone 'number'. Actually, this is not usually a number, but a word, which can be the advertiser's company name, brand name or any word he chooses.

This response technique is certainly better than trying to get consumers to remember a telephone *number*. Today, telephone numbers can be 12 digits or longer. Imagine trying to grasp such a number when watching television, or sitting in your car listening to the radio. The Free-phone word, when carefully selected, can be recalled hours later, when you are at home or in your office. Mobile telephones make the response process much easier and faster. Caution: do not use your mobile phone while driving; you could wind up on a marble slab.

Freepost   Direct marketing response technique:
A free address used by advertisers to encourage consumers to respond or order by post. The return postage is paid for by the advertiser. Used in press, outdoor and broadcast advertising and direct mail campaigns.

Freeze-frame   Film, TV, Video:
Holding the same frame on screen, producing the effect of a still image. In filming, this is done by printing the same frame for as many seconds as required to hold the image, at the rate of 24 frames per second. In television, the same frame is scanned for the required time, at 25 fps.
See Shot.

Front matter   Publishing, Print:
Pages at the front of a printed document, containing the title, contents and introduction material.

Full out   DTP, Print, Production, TYP, WP:
An instruction to the DTP operator or compositor, to set the copy without indents, across the full measure.
   See Justified, Measure, Ragged, Range.

FVO
Film, TV, Video: Female voice-over.
   See Voice-over.

Galley   Print:
The proofs of typeset matter before it is made up as artwork; usually set in columns or blocks of type. Historically, a metal tray in which columns of metal type were stored before making up into pages.

Galley proof   DTP, Print, TYP:
The popular name for one form in which typeset copy is presented for proof-reading.

Giveaway   Sales promotion:
A gift or premium, given free of charge to customers as an incentive. Usually a low-cost item, sometimes of practical value.

Gravure   Print:
   See the Print chapter of this book.

Grant projector   Art, Production, TYP:
Studio equipment. A large camera-like enlarger, used by art directors, visualisers, typographers and artworkers to reduce and enlarge illustrations.

Grid   Art, DTP, Print, TYP:
A guide used by designers, visualisers, typographers and paste-up artists, for creating layouts. The grid consists of vertical and horizontal lines, usually printed faint blue, either on opaque or translucent paper.

The grid sets out the complete format of the page or spread. This enables the designer to work accurately, and conform to the format of the pages throughout the publication.

The grid includes the overall page size, the top, bottom and side margins; the trim; the width of the columns; the spaces between the columns; and the areas earmarked for illustrations.

See Gutter.

GSM   Paper, Print: Grams per square metre.
The unit of weight of paper stock. Also appears as gm^2.

Gutter   Design, Print, Publishing:
The column of white space between two facing pages.
See Grid.

Halftone   Art, Photography, Print, Production:
Technically, the representation of tonal gradation by an image composed of dots of varying sizes, the centres of which are equidistant. But don't worry, it gets much more interesting as you read on.

To understand halftones, you must first know something about photography.

Most objects you see are made visible by reflected light. Light hits the object you are photographing, and reflects the image to your eyes.

Using a camera, you capture the reflected image on film with a light-sensitive coating. When you release the shutter, an instant of light from the object is projected on to the film. This creates a latent image on the film, which will need to be 'developed' with chemicals before you can see it.

Negative image
The film is processed chemically, producing a negative image of the object you have photographed. On negative film, the tones are reversed. Areas that will print white are black on the negative; black areas on the negative will print white. The tonal areas between these extremes are called mid-tones.

To make a photographic print, you must expose the negative on to another negative, usually made of paper. You project the nega-tive film image through an enlarger on to a sheet of photographic paper with a light-sensitive coating. In the marketing communications studio this is usually called a bromide (qv).

The bromide needs to be developed chemically. The image latent in the photographic coating then becomes visible.

Range of continuous tones

The picture you have produced will have a wide range of tones, from black to white. The bromide shows all the tonal values of the object captured by the camera.

In black-and-white photographs, the colours of the object will show up as shades of grey. In colour photographs, the colours of the object will be more or less true to the original.

When correctly exposed and printed, the light areas (highlights), dark areas (shadows), and the mid-tones, should give a balanced picture.

This is called a continuous-tone print. The tones are contiguous – that is, they flow into each other, with no line showing where one tone ends and another begins.

Obviously, it is impractical to print newspapers, magazines and brochures using continuous-tone prints. After a few copies had been run, the results would be muddy splodges on the paper, rather than clear, sharp images.

Recognisable image

The solution is to convert the continuous-tone image into dots. Each dot becomes a spot of ink on the printed page, and together they become a recognisable image of the original you started with.

To create the dotted image, the bromide is rephotographed on to film, using a grid of fine, opaque lines. The grid – called a screen – breaks up the continuous tone into dots. Effectively, this gets rid of about half the continuous tones in the image, leaving the remaining half on the film. Hence the term halftone.

The effect on your brain of a halftone screen is interesting. When your eyes scan the screened image on the page, your brain cannot separate them out. The dots are so small and so densely packed together that your eye and brain cannot resolve the dot pattern into its individual elements. The screen creates the optical illusion of a continuous-tone image, and the picture becomes recognisable.

Dot screens vary widely in size, shape and density. There are other types of screen, such as line screens and random screens.

But the result is the same: a recognisable image on the printed page.

Measuring halftone screens
Halftone screens are measured by the number of lines per centimetre. The more lines per centimetre, the finer the quality of the halftone printing. A 22-line screen has 484 dots per centimetre; an 80-line screen has 6400. In the USA, dot screens are given in lines per inch.

If you are to achieve the best results, the halftone screen must be matched to the paper stock, board or other surface to be printed.

When printing on newsprint, or other coarse, absorbent paper, you should specify a coarse screen; for example 22 to 34 screen. Otherwise, the spaces between the dots will fill with a mixture of ink and tiny fragments of paper fibre, producing a muddy image.

With smoother paper surfaces, you can employ finer screens, and get sharper images. Coated art paper is among the smoothest you can get, and the printed images can be spectacularly sharp and bright. Take a look at the latest Jaguar, Rover, BMW or Porsche brochures, and judge the quality for yourself.

Remember, the smoother the paper, the finer the screen you should use. As always, consult your photographer, art director and printer before spending your budget.

See Keyline, Paper, Paste-up, Screen, Tint.

Hard copy   DTP, EP, WP:
The printed version of a document created with a computer. Also called a printout (qv).

Hardware   Computing:
The main electro-mechanical parts of a computing system; usually the computer itself and its monitor. The printer, external disk drive, modem, etc, are usually called peripherals, but are nevertheless hardware. If you can drop it on your foot and it breaks a bone, it's definitely hardware.
See Software.

Head-on site   Outdoor advertising:
A poster site facing approaching road traffic.

Heavy DTP, EP, TYP:
An alternative term for bold (qv).

Highlight Art, DTP, Photography, Platemaking:
The lightest tones of a photographic illustration or drawing. Extreme highlights can be achieved by eliminating tones altogether, letting the whiteness of the paper form the highlight.
See Halftone.

Hoarding Outdoor advertising:
A poster, or group of posters, facing the road, parallel to a pavement.

Hologram Art, Creative:
An illustration or flat image giving the illusion of three dimensions. This effect is created with the use of lasers and specialised lighting.

House style Art, Creative, DTP, EP, Publishing, TYP, WP:
A specific and distinctive style used by a company in its advertisements, sales and technical literature and other publications. It can extend to its stationery, livery, the design of its retail outlets and showrooms; and to staff uniforms.

Icon Computing, DTP, WP:
A graphic image or symbol on a computer screen. Each symbol represents an application (qv) or a file already in the system; you use the icon to access it.

IFC DTP, Print: Inside front cover.

Illustration Art, Creative, DTP, Print:
Any drawing, painting, photograph, or other graphic used in art or print. Sometimes used to distinguish a drawn image from a photographic one.

Imposition Art, DTP, Print, Production:
The arrangement of pages in artwork and on printing plates. This must ensure that all pages will be printed in the correct order when the sheets are folded and trimmed.

Incentive Advertising, Sales promotion:
A gift or service offered by an advertiser, to get customers to carry out a particular task. Its main application is to get retailers, resellers and wholesalers to sell more product. In the best example I know, the salespeople had a choice of holidays, furs or jewellery. The sales director got a car. The product in this case was financial investment.

Indent Copywriting, DTP, TYP, WP:
Starting a paragraph or line of text with a blank space, one or more characters in width. Experience suggests that three characters are enough blank space for an indent. Any fewer would not show up well; any more would look eccentric, and possibly render the copy less easy to read.

The whole point of using indents is to guide the eye easily and smoothly from the end of one paragraph into the next. In advertising copy, which consumers generally don't really want to read, you have to seduce them into doing so.

Making your copy easy to read and understand helps readers to get to the point where you are asking them to take action. Typographers should ponder this well. Advertising is not an art form – it is an essential part of marketing. And marketing pays your salaries.

Ink-jet printer Computing, DTP, WP:
A printer with a printing head which does not make contact with the paper. Instead, it squirts tiny droplets of ink to form the image. The dot density of many inexpensive printers is 300 dpi (dots per inch, qv). Some printers deliver a density of 600 dpi or higher, which increases the quality of the printed image.

In-pack Sales promotion:
A free item of low-cost merchandise, such as a toy or a household gadget, placed inside a product pack. In-pack giveaways are used as an inducement to consumers to keep them buying the product. Sometimes the giveaways are collectable, which offers the advertiser a degree of brand loyalty.

In pro Art, DTP, Print, Production, TYP:
In proportion. When photoprints or line drawings are used as

illustrations, enlargements and reductions are two-dimensional. If you wish to enlarge or reduce one of a group of illustrations, to fit a layout for example, you may want the others to follow them in the same degree of enlargement or reduction. You then specify that the others are to be enlarged or reduced in proportion to it – in pro.

Inserts   Print, Production, Publishing:
Leaflets, catalogues or printed cards inserted into a publication, either loose or glued. This process takes place after the publication itself has been printed and bound. Often a catalogue insert is bound into the publication.

Intaglio   Print:
Printing from a recessed image. That is to say, the image is engraved into the printing surface. Gravure is the only intaglio printing process in use today.
   See Gravure, Photogravure.

Interline spacing   DTP, TYP, WP:
A term used in many word-processing packages. In printing, it is called leading (qv); pronounced ledding.

IPA   The Institute of Practitioners in Advertising.
The organisation representing the interests of UK advertising agencies. It helps its members through the minefield of legislation affecting agency business and activities. Since the volume of legislation coming out of Brussels is growing at a frightening rate, the IPA's specialist advice is becoming more and more valuable.
   Among the activities and services offered to its members, the IPA's specialist departments guide and advise members on problems relating to government action. It helps them negotiate with their clients and the media, and advises on marketing research and other specialised activities.
   The IPA has close connections with similar organisations throughout the world, and is therefore able to help its members on international advertising matters.
   See BARB, ISBA, ITC, ITVA, JICTAR.

ISBA   The Incorporated Society of British Advertisers.
Founded in 1900, the ISBA is the only organisation in Britain dedicated entirely to caring for the needs of advertisers. It represents its members, as a body, on all aspects of advertising, and defends their interests: to government, the media, advertising agencies, key opinion-formers and the general public. Any advertiser can belong to the ISBA, with the exception of advertising agencies and media owners.
   See BARB, IPA, ITC, ITVA, JICTAR.

Island site   Press advertising, Production:
A press advertisement surrounded on three or four sides by editorial material. If the ad is the only one on a page, its position is called solus (qv).

ISP   The Institute of Sales Promotion.
The organisation representing the interests of companies in the sales promotion business.

ISO   Photography: International Standards Organisation.
A measure of light-sensitivity of photographic film; the 'speed' rating of film stock. The higher the ISO figure, the 'faster' the film-speed, and the greater its sensitivity to light.
   The speed of film stock determines the aperture of the lens and exposure time. For example, in bright light, a fast film will need less exposure; a slow film will need more.

Issue date   Publishing:
Sometimes called cover date. The publication date of a newspaper, magazine or directory. This date usually appears on the cover, but in reality may not be the actual date on which the publication hits the street. With national daily newspapers, the issue date is always the date of publication.
   Some full-colour consumer, business and technical magazines appear a month or more ahead of the issue date. *Amateur Photographer*, *Ideal Home* and *Personal Computer World* are examples of this phenomenon. It is based on every publisher's compulsive desire to get on the bookstalls first, before the competition. It was probably a good idea when it started. However, since a lot of publishers are doing the same thing, the advantage is lost. Why do

they continue to do it? As John Wayne used to say: 'It sure beats the hell out of me.'

Italics Copywriting, DTP, TYP, WP:
Type characters which slope to the right. *The Oxford Dictionary* indicates that it was introduced to Europe about 1500 by Aldus Manutius of Venice. Upright characters are called 'roman' (qv), spelled without a capital r.

ITC The Independent Television Commission.
A government body controlling the activities and conduct of television in the United Kingdom.
See BARB, IPA, ISBA, ITVA, JICTAR.

ITV Media:
The generic name for independent commercial television; so called to differentiate it from the British Broadcasting Corporation. ITV's income comes from advertising and other commercial activities; the BBC's is from licence money, a form of taxation, extorted from the television-viewing public.

ITVA The Independent Television Association.
The organisation representing the interests of UK commercial television companies and contractors.
See BARB, IPA, ISBA, ITC, JICTAR.

JICTAR Audience research: Joint Industry Committee for Television Audience Research.
Now obsolete. Replaced by BARB, the Broadcasters Audience Research Board.
See BARB, IPA, ISBA, ITC, ITVA.

Junior page Publishing:
See Mini-page.

Justification Copywriting, DTP, Typesetting, TYP, WP:
Arranging copy so that it is set in columns with one or both edges perpendicular.
See Full out, Justified, Measure, Ragged, Range.

Justified   Copywriting, DTP, Typesetting, TYP, WP:
Type set in a block or a column, in which the edges are either evenly aligned – straight up and down – or ragged.

Justified left, the copy has a straight, vertical left-hand edge.

Justified right, the right-hand edge is straight and vertical.

Fully justified, both edges are straight and vertical; warning ... this usually looks like a wall of words.

See Full out, Measure, Ragged, Range.

Kerning   DTP, TYP, WP:
The tightening up of letterspacing between characters in a typeset word.

Key   Creative, Print, Production, Research:
A code-word or number within a coupon in an advertisement. This should indicate the name and issue date of the publication in which it appears. Unless you key an advertisement, you may have no idea where the replies are actually coming from.

The only other way to identify an un-keyed coupon is to turn it over and see what's on the back. This cannot be counted as a professional research technique. What's more, it is tedious and time-consuming; especially when the volume of coupons from an advertisement is heavy.

Key codes should always be computer-compatible. You can then break out all the information you need for improving on your highest response so far. Unfortunately, not all advertisers do this – even some of the most marketing-aware ones. I always have to nag my clients for research data on response, and often fail because they haven't bothered to do it.

Key codes are equally essential on reply cards included in mail-shots.

Keyboarding   Computing, DTP, TYP, WP:
Inputting or entering data into a computer's memory through its keyboard.

Keyline   Art, Production:
A rectangle or outline drawing of an element of finished artwork, included on a paste-up (qv). This shows the exact position, shape and size of the element in the layout. Keylined elements can include halftones (qv), line drawings and transparencies.

Kodatrace   Art, Production:
Kodak's brand of translucent film, used for overlays in finished artwork. It is used for positioning additional material, and for carrying instructions to printers and platemakers. With the rise and rise of computerised artwork production, flat artwork and overlay techniques are disappearing.

Laminate   Print, Production:
A laminate is an ultra-thin film applied to the surface of a printed item. Mostly used for covers of expensive brochures, and for point-of-sale material. Its function is to protect against damage, deterioration and beery thumbmarks.

LAN   Computing: Local area network.
A system for linking computers and other equipment into a single, operational network. This is done both with software and hardware, and a lot of extra wiring. A local area can be a single office, a building or a campus.

Landscape   Art direction, DTP, WP:
A horizontal page format. The orientation of a printed page, where the short sides are on the left and right of the page. In other words, a shape wider than it is high. Some DTP software packages call this wide format.

Some brochures work well in this format, and the copy can be made to look easy on the eye. Caution: landscape does not adapt readily from the other format, portrait.

As always, liaise closely with your art director and typographer when considering a landscape format for your next advertisement or brochure.

See Portrait.

Layout   Art, Creative, DTP, EP, Production, WP:
A sketch or drawing of a printed page, advertisement, brochure or other printed material. The graphic interpretation of editorial or advertising ideas, laid out on the drawing board or computer screen, showing how they will look when printed.

Leader
1   Creative, DTP, TYP, WP:

A group of full-points or dashes at the beginning of a sentence, or between two words or sentences. A leader is used to link two sentences, usually where the ideas expressed in them are similar.

2 Publishing:
The leading article in a newspaper, magazine or house journal.

Leading
DTP, TYP, WP:
Pronounced 'ledding'. Also known as line-spacing or inter-line spacing. Space between lines of type. So called because in former times, when hot metal typesetting was used, strips of lead alloy were inserted between lines of type to open them up and create more white space. Hot-metal typesetting has now virtually disappeared in Europe and the USA.
See Letterspacing.

Letraset   Art, Creative, Production, TYP:
The name of a company, and its brand of dry-transfer lettering used in drawing-board layouts and artwork.

Letraset sheets are of translucent paper, on which are mounted type characters. The backs of the characters are sticky. To transfer a character on to your layout, you position it accurately over the chosen spot, then rub it down with an instrument – usually the tip of a ballpoint pen. You can then burnish it with the blunt end of the pen.

A bit low-tech, when you compare it to desktop computer typesetting. But brilliant for headlining, especially in the event of a power cut or a computer crash.

Letterpress   Print:
See the Print chapter of this book

Letterspacing   DTP, TYP, WP:
The spacing between individual characters and numbers.
See Leading.

Library shot   Art, Creative, Photography, Production:
A picture or illustration provided by a library specialising in this kind of material. Today, most large libraries provide

photo images and line illustrations on CD-ROM. Some libraries issue catalogues, classified into general or specialised photo subjects.

Many newspapers and magazines have photo libraries. The main advantage in using libraries is that it's more economical buying from them than taking your own shots. The best libraries carry up-to-date material, and the quality is first-class. Newspapers carry newsworthy photographs, adding to their collections on a day-to-day basis.

Light-pen Computing:
An electronic tool, used rather like a mouse. Its function is to move a cursor around a computer screen, move data and images from place to place. Given the right software, you can use it to draw; and also remove, insert and retrieve images and bits of images. Like a mouse, it can carry out much of the work done by a keyboard.

You can install an alphanumeric pad on which your light-pen can input alphabetical characters and numbers. This is slow and tedious; a keyboard is faster and less frustrating.

Life stages Advertising research:
A research tool used for determining the lifestyle and disposable income of consumers at different stages in their lives.

Life stage	Situation
Single, living with parents	Few financial commitments. Fashion-following and 'trendy'.
Single living in rented or shared accommodation	Basic household goods; car; fashion; concentration on leisure and entertainment; convenience and takeaway foods. If in well-paid job, good supply of cash available.
Married couple, or living together; no children	If both working, double income and high spending on fashion, personal products and services, household items. Cars, foreign holidays. Plenty of cash available.

Full nest 1; first child under 6 years	Dynamic house-purchasing period; child takes up much cash and product purchase; not much spare cash available.
Full nest 2; other children	Food and household products bought in bulk; many purchases made for children and their needs; school fees, music lessons and sports equipment; teenage fashions, usually expensive.
Empty nest; children no longer at home, living independently or at higher education establishments	Replacement expenditure on house and household products, eg brown and white goods, bedrooms, bathrooms, kitchens. Better and longer holidays and breaks; larger sums invested. Desire for better lifestyle now this is possible with more money available.
Retirement	Lower disposable income; often moving to smaller house or to apartment; less furniture. Higher spend on medical products and services.
Solitary survivor	Simpler life altogether; more medical and physical attention needed.

Ligature   TYP:
Two or more characters joined together to make a single unit. For example ae, ct, sp, ts.

Line and tone   Art, Platemaking, Print, Production:
A film and platemaking technique for combining line art and halftone material in the same illustration. In the days of hot metal printing, line and tone negatives were combined, and printing plates made from this.

Line artwork   Art, Platemaking, Print, Production:
Artwork in black and white only, with no middle tones. This can be printed without halftone screening. Pen and ink drawings are an example of line art.

Linefeed   Computing, Production, Print:
A term used in photosetting, otherwise called inter-line spacing or leading (qv).

Line spacing
See Leading.

Lip-synch   Film, Video:
Lip synchronisation. The synchronisation of an actor's lip movements on screen with the soundtrack. When they get out of synch, the results can be hilarious; in a commercial, they can be damaging. Electronic editing makes poor lip-synch less common than it was in the days of cut and splice.

List   Direct marketing:
Common shorthand for a mailing list.
   See List broker, List cleaning.

List broker   Direct marketing:
A specialist individual or company that markets mailing lists. The most competent broker scrutinises, analyses and evaluates a list offered by the company that owns it, and matches it to the needs of advertisers who want to use it. He prices each list, usually offering it for hire, with the aim of making a profit.
   See List cleaning.

List cleaning   Direct marketing:
Correcting mailing lists and bringing them up to date. In the proper professional hands, the cleanest lists are those in frequent use. People whose names are on mailing lists have the irritating habit of dying, moving house, changing jobs and dropping out of sight. Frequent use of a mailing list will reveal the gone-aways and not-knowns, so that the list operator can eliminate them. A clean list is usually more valuable than a dirty one, and may cost more to hire or buy.
   See List broker.

Literal   Art, Copywriting, Creative, DTP, Print, Production, TYP, WP:
An uncorrected spelling or typing error in a typescript, typeset copy or printed text.

Litho Print:
See the Print chapter of this book.

Lithography
See Litho, Offset.

Litho negatives and positives Platemaking, Print, Production:
Screened film, ready for platemaking. Negs and positives
supplied to printers by production houses are based on creative
material and artwork generated by advertisers and their
agencies.

Logo Art, Creative, DTP, Print:
Shorthand for logotype. The trademark of an organisation or
company, in the form of a distinguishing symbol, by which it is
known to its public. In book publishing, this is known as a
colophon or imprint.

   In the world of business and marketing, a company's logo is
usually part of its branding and corporate identity scheme. Or
should be. Some products and services carry the company's logo,
as well as that of the product itself. Among the best-known logos
in the world are Coca-Cola and Mickey Mouse. There can't be
many people who have not seen them and don't understand what
they stand for.

   It goes even deeper than that. If you see the Rolls Royce logo,
even out of context, you do not need to be told that it represents
the best car in the world.

   See Brand, Branding, Brand loyalty.

Log on Computing, DTP, WP:
Entering certain identification details on a computer or terminal
before starting work. A personal password, for example.

Log off Computing, DTP, WP:
Signing off when you have finished with the computer or terminal.
This has to be done, as with all computing procedures, in a pre-
determined, orderly manner.

Lower case DTP, TYP, WP:
The small letters in a typesetting alphabet. The capital letters are
called upper case (qv), capitals and caps (qv).

The origin of this, like many terms used in printing, is both historical and fascinating. Printing techniques have been in use for hundreds of years. It is said the Chinese started it, together with papermaking, before the Common Era.

Printing, in the form we recognise today, came to Europe in the 14th and 15th centuries. The process was accelerated by the invention of movable type by Johann Gutenberg of Mainz, a small town on the Rhine. He and his partners tried to keep it secret; but you can't publish and not risk being found out – and copied.

The secret of Gutenberg's movable type was this: you cast individual type characters in individual moulds. You set up the type for articles and books, print them, then break up the pages and use the type again. Before Gutenberg, this was virtually impossible, because the technology was unknown or undeveloped. Gutenberg developed movable type technology, so that books could be produced in *commercial quantities!* A goldmine for those who possessed the secret.

Gutenberg's Mazarin Bible came out about 1450. By 1470, the secret had hit the street, with Nicholas Jensen, a Venetian printer, starting to design and cast movable type. By 1475, William Caxton was producing his first books in London.

The type characters were of three types: capital letters, small letters, and numerals and symbols. In the composing-room, type was kept in chests of drawers, called 'cases'. The capitals were housed in one case, the small letters and numerals in another. The drawers were organised into compartments. Usually, the cases were stacked, the capitals case on top of the case containing the small letters.

The compositor assembled lines of type by hand, and needed easy access to capitals and small letters. Following the author's manuscript, the comp would dip into the upper case for the capitals, and into the lower one for the small letters. In time, capitals came to be known as upper case, and small letters lower case.

See Capitals, Caps.

Machine proof   Print, Production:
A wet proof taken off a printing machine, using inks to be used in the forthcoming print run. If this kind of proofing is done on a production press, the cost can be prohibitive. You will probably

need no more than a dozen proofs in all – for you, your agency, the printer and possibly one for your chairman's wife. Some printers keep a special proofing press for short-run proofs, but the cost is still likely to be high. Better try another method; for example, Cromalin or other branded dry-proofing technique.

See Cromalin, Proof.

Magenta   Art, Design, Print:
One of the subtractive primaries used in four-colour printing. This one is a kind of bluish-pink. Used with cyan, yellow and black, it enables you to print virtually any colour at reasonable cost. The range of four-colour inks is manufactured in huge quantities worldwide, which helps to keep costs down.

See Process colours, Black, Cyan, Pantone, Yellow.

Make-ready   Print:
Setting up a printing press so that the paper receives the highest-quality image. On letterpress machines, this is a painstaking and expensive activity – one reason why litho printing has become the widest-used process.

See Cylinder press, Flatbed, Forme, Letterpress, Plate, Pull.

Make-up   Art, DTP, TYP, Print, Production, WP:
The arrangement of type and illustrations into sections and pages, so that everything fits perfectly. Making up is a technique for assembling the various elements of a page, prior to producing artwork, film and printing plates.

Make-up is also applied to the physical arrangement of the pages of a newspaper, magazine or book.

See Composition, Mark-up.

Manuscript   Copywriting, Creative:
A handwritten or typed text, submitted for or awaiting publication.

See Copy, Hard copy.

Margin   Art, Copywriting, Creative, DTP, Print, Production, WP:
On a printed page, this is the blank area outside the printed matter. Margins can be top, bottom, left, right, all round; and also the

gutter, the column of white space between two facing pages.
See Grid.

Marked proof   Copywriting, Art. Creative, DTP, Print,
                   Production, TYP, WP:
A proof supplied specifically for proof-reading. Corrections will be
marked on this proof by those qualified to handle it. This includes
copywriter, proof-reader, approver and printer.

To distinguish who has done each check, copywriters usually
mark their corrections in red, account-handlers in black, printers in
green. Caution: this is simply a convention, not a hard rule.

Another caution: you may be asked to sign a marked proof you
have checked, even though you have found no errors or omissions
on it. This means that you have to be thorough in your proof-
checking, and also stand by your decisions. Apart from any other
considerations, accurate proof-checking saves money.

Mark-up   Art, TYP:
Carefully worked-out instructions on how a piece of copy should
be typeset. Computerised word-processing, artworking and typesetting has made this much easier; in many cases, eliminated it
altogether.
See Make-up.

Married print   TV and Video post-production:
Film or videotape on which picture and sound have been synchronised in the editing suite. Also called a combined print.

Masking   Art, Production:
1   When part of an illustration or photoprint is to be air-brushed
    or painted over, the rest of the artwork is usually protected
    from unintentional spraying or splashes. This protection is
    called masking. It is usually done with special masking tape
    and transparent film.
2   Where part of an image itself needs to be painted out with
    opaque medium, so that it will not reproduce, this is called
    masking. Also called blocking out.

Master proof   Production, Print:
A definitive proof, containing all corrections and remarks, held by
the printer for current and future reference. And to protect his rear.

Masthead   Publishing:
The title of a newspaper or magazine, which runs across its front page, title page, contents and leader pages. Sometimes also used to denote the section giving details of the publisher and his staff.

Matter   Creative, DTP, Editorial, Production, Print, TYP, WP:
Generally used to denote copy in any form – manuscript, typescript or printed text and illustrations. Hence the term facing matter used in media planning; meaning an advertisement directly facing editorial material on a spread. Or next matter, meaning right next to a piece of editorial on the same page.

Advertisements facing or next to matter usually cost more than those which are run-of-paper; ie anywhere the publisher fancies.
See Mini-page, Run-of-paper, Solus.

MEAL   Research: Media Expenditure Analysis Ltd.
The research organisation specialising in monitoring and reporting advertising spend.

Measure   Art, Creative, DTP, TYP, WP:
The length of a line of type; the width of the column it makes.
See Full out, Justified, Make-up, Mark-up, Margin, Measure, Ragged, Range.

Mechanical   Art, Production:
A mechanical is the complete version of layout, artwork and copy, ready for reproduction, with all instructions in place.
See Make-up, Mark-up.

Media
1   Advertising, Media planning and buying, Public relations:
A term usually denoting the range of communication channels used for entertainment, news, advertising and public relations activities. Colleges and universities now offer courses in media studies, and before long you can probably take a degree in it.

Media, in a marketing communications connotation, are tools by which we are able to reach specific target audiences. Media publishers offer a staggering volume of research information on their readers, viewers and listeners. They give you the opportunity, and the means, to reach virtually every target audience your campaigns need – from accountants to zoologists. They are capable of doing this *accurately, and with minimum waste.*

Creatives working on advertising campaigns need to study media research, as much as does account management. The data can give you illumination on the targets your campaign is designed to influence. You can gain valuable insight into their lifestyles and buying behaviour. And how they are likely to react to advertising.

2 Computing:
The means by which you store material generated by computer. Magnetic media include hard, floppy and zip disks. CD-ROM disks also store computer material, but are not magnetic.

Media schedule   Media planning and buying:
The document compiled by media planners, showing the range of media booked for an advertising campaign. This should include dates, times, insertion sizes, spots, packages, discounts and costs. In Britain, the EU and the USA, today's media schedules are usually computerised.

Merchandising   Retailing:
A wide range of marketing activities conducted at the point of sale. The idea is to move as much product as possible in the shortest possible time.

The point of sale is the final opportunity for influencing your customers and prospectives. You want them to make buying decisions in favour of your brand, and to take action immediately. It follows that, having spent money on other marketing communications tools, such as advertising and public relations, you would want to go the whole way. Not so in many cases. Astute advertisers put money into merchandising. Others do not, and wonder where their brand leadership has gone.

Merchandising activities include special packaging, special displays, banners, showcards, posters and mobiles; live demonstrations and interactive videos; and pricing offers and deals.

Merchandising tools are usually designed, produced and offered to retailers by advertisers for their own products. For the best examples, look round your local supermarkets. Other retailers, Marks & Spencer and IKEA for example, produce their own; their goods carry their own branded labels. Dixons, the electrical product retailers, also produce their own, even though they sell many different brands.

Mini-page   Media planning and buying:
A newspaper and magazine advertising space, about three-quarters of a page. Usually solus, with editorial on two sides. This format gives you the chance to dominate the whole page without actually paying for the whole of it. Naturally, this special position may cost more than the same space run-of-paper; but it's worth it if you can also specify which page as well.
See Matter, Run-of-paper, Solus.

Minus leading   DTP, TYP, WP:
See Negative leading.

Mix
Film, TV, Video:
1   A dissolve (qv)
2   Combining sound tracks on to a single track, and adjusting each track to optimum level.

Mock-up   Art, Creative, DTP, Production, TYP, WP:
A rough-design rendering of a leaflet, brochure, booklet, show-card, poster, pack, and any other two- or three-dimensional promotional tool.
See Origination, Visual.

Moiré pattern   Art, Creative, Photography, Platemaking, Print, Production:
An unwelcome pattern of dots, produced when two or more halftone screens clash on the printed page.
   This effect is produced when halftone screens are incorrectly angled during filming, platemaking or printing. You sometimes see it on television, when an actor is inappropriately dressed; say, wearing a chequered jacket.
   One of the finest examples I know is John McCririck, Channel 4's racing correspondent. He is a great showman, often resplendent in sideburns, wearing deerstalker, check or chintz waistcoat, carnation buttonhole, pince-nez, and other Victoriana. John is a

truly original English eccentric, and his copy is truly magnificent journalism. His waistcoats, however, sometimes produce bizarre effects on my television screen, including moiré patterns.

Television screen lines are horizontal; John's waistcoat stripes, checks, polka dots and wiggles clash with them. The resultant myriad multicoloured sparks, flashes and whorls are a visual delight – unless you are a TV producer.

Unless you are determined to get these effects on your printed page – and sometimes you need to incorporate them into your brand imaging – they are best avoided. If they are definitely not what you want, you may be entitled to get your money back from the supplier who cocked it up.

See Halftone.

Mono   Art, Photography, Print:
Jargon shorthand for monochrome; ie printing in black and white only.

Monotype   Art, Production, TYP:
An American company, formerly specialising in hot-metal type-setting machines for setting type in single characters. The alternative system was Linotype, which set hot-metal type in slugs – whole lines.

Monotype now do hardware and software for computer type-setting. They may still make hot-metal machines for use in developing countries; but not, I think for Europe, the USA, Australia, Japan and other developed economies where the computer rules.

See Character, Nought, Null, Proof, Proof-reader, Proof-reader's marks, Quote, Zero.

MPS   Direct marketing: Mailing Preference Service.
The British Direct Marketing Association's service to consumers. You can have your name added to or deleted from an advertiser's database, by invoking the MPS and contacting its operator.

Multiple exposure   Photography, Platemaking, Production:
A visual technique which involves printing an image several times, to form a single image. The images can be laid down on top of one another, superimposed, slightly offset; or alongside one another in columns or rows. Multiple exposure can also be made using several different images.

MVO Film and Video: Male voice-over.
See Voice-over.

Narrowcast TV, Video:
All forms of television and video activity not actually put out on air by terrestrial or satellite transmitter. The opposite of broadcast.

Examples of narrowcast include cable TV, videos and video games. The term may now may include multimedia and Internet activities. However, the Internet is now so huge that it might as well qualify as broadcast. According to Global Internet Business Services, more than 2.2 million business people in Britain alone currently have access to the Internet in their places of work. By the year 2010, over a billion people worldwide may be connected to the Net.

Negative Art, Creative, Photography, Platemaking, Production:
In black-and-white photography, for example, a negative is a photographic image in which the colours are reversed. Black is represented by clear film; white represented by dense black. Intermediate tones are also there, but in reversed form. Thus, light grey is shown as dark grey, and vice versa.

The negative is an intermediate stage, between the object being photographed and the flat printed image it eventually turns into.

The secret is this: the film in the camera is *negative*. After development, it is itself exposed on to another *negative*, such as photographic paper or a printing plate. Since two negatives make a positive (in photography as in many other aspects of life), the final result is a positive image of your pack-shot or your Auntie Mary on the beach.

In colour photography, much the same principle applies. The difference is that the colours in the negative are the *complementaries* of those in the final print. Thus, a yellowish greeny-blue in the negative represents flesh tones in the positive.

Some photographic films produce positive images without an intermediate negative. These are called reversal films. They are used for the high-quality transparency photography used for printing, as well as holiday slides. The quality of reversal film is much better than prints taken with negative film. For evidence, look at brochures produced for expensive cars; or look through the glossy magazines, such as *Vogue*.

Better still, read some of the huge literature on modern photography. Also, see the reading list at the back of this book.
See Photograph, Positive.

Negative leading   DTP, TYP, WP:
Type set with less space from baseline to baseline than the height of the characters themselves. This can be done in computer setting, but not in hot metal. For example, when 16pt type is set with 14pt leading, the ascenders and descenders overlap. Useful for achieving special typographic effects.
See Minus leading.

Newsprint   Art, Creative, Paper, Print, Production:
A coarse, absorbent paper made mostly from wood pulp and small amounts of chemical pulp. Usually used for printing newspapers; hence the name.

Take care when preparing artwork for reproduction on newsprint; consult your photographer, art studio and pre-press house. Printing on newsprint from artwork prepared for any other paper, and you may find the results different from your expectations. The absorptive quality of the paper alone should give you pause for thought. Also, you should take care of the halftone screen you are specifying.
See Halftones, Paper.

News proof   Print, Production:
A proof taken on newsprint (qv). This should be capable of reproducing the image, ink density and colour quality expected from the actual print run. Always consult your printer before specifying news proofs; they can be expensive. There are special proofing presses for this job, but not every printer has them.
See Newsprint, Wet proof.

Normal lens   Film, TV, Video:
A lens which gives a normal angle of view and natural perspective.

Nought   Creative, DTP, TYP, WP:
A word used to differentiate between the characters 'o' and '0'. On screen, a nought is usually represented by a dot in the centre of the character, or an oblique stroke running through it.

In proof-reading, the distinction is not easy to make, and can cause confusion and errors. Many typesetters refer to zero as null (qv) or zero (qv). Always say 'nought', 'null' or 'zero' when proof-reading and reading out copy, especially over the telephone.

See Character, Monotype, Null, Proof, Proof-reader, Proof-reader's marks, Quote, Zero.

NTSC   TV, Video: National Television System Committee.
The broadcast system used in the United States of America. Also known in Europe, rather cruelly, as 'Never The Same Colour'. This was coined after British and other European TV engineers had rejected the US system on grounds of unpredictable colour results during test transmissions.

If it has been made in NTSC, you cannot use a videotape on your European PAL video-player. Likewise, you should not export video material made in PAL to a country using another TV standard. You can get tapes converted, but you risk loss of quality in the conversion. Some video-players have built-in converters.

See PAL, SECAM, VCR, VTR, TV standards (World).

Null   DTP, EP, TYP, WP:
A word used to differentiate between the character 'o' and '0'.

See Character, Monotype, Nought, Proof, Proof-reader, Proof-reader's marks, Quote. Zero.

OBC   Advertising, Publishing: Outside back cover.
The outside back cover of a newspaper, magazine, brochure or book.

Oblique   Creative, DTP, TYP, WP:
Type slanted at an angle from the vertical. This looks like italic, but is more usually a leaning roman. Some software uses the word slanted to describe this effect. Usually, the software offers you degrees of slant, as a percentage from the vertical, more or less infinitely variable.

OCR   Computing, DTP, WP: Optical character recognition.
The electronic scanning of typescript and typeset copy. The characters read by the OCR scanner are converted to digital equivalents, then converted into normal word-processing file forms. They are

then readable on your computer screen. Also, optical character reader, the hardware for carrying out OCR.

Off-line
See On-line.

Offset   Print:
In litho printing (qv), a blanket cylinder picks up the image from the printing plate and deposits it on the paper. There is no contact between the printing plate and the paper; the blanket offsets it, and allows the printing plate a longer working life.
   See Dry offset, Litho, Set-off.

One-inch   TV, Video:
One of the main videotape standards used for originating and editing TV commercials.

On-line   Computing:
When a network of computers is connected up, under the control of a central server computer, they are said to be on-line. They can be remote from one another, connected by a telephone line. In this case, the operator pays for the time it takes to stay on the line.
   The opposite of this is off-line, which is a lot cheaper. You carry out the computing function and compile all the data *before* you go on-line. Only then do you go on-line, sending the results down the telephone. This is considerably cheaper, because it takes up less telephone time. Internet activities, e-mail for example, allow you to do this.

On-pack   Advertising, Sales promotion:
A giveaway goodie attached to a retail product pack.

On-sale date   Publishing:
The actual date on which a magazine hits the bookstalls. This date may be different from the cover-date, the date printed on the cover of the magazine.
   For many years publishers have been trying to out-do each other, by bringing their on-sale dates forward more and more. This can cause ludicrous anomalies, such as November issues appearing in September or October. Naturally, publishers would

not consider reverting to matching on-sale dates with cover dates. That would be too sensible and logical. But it would make for sensible copy dates.

Opticals   Film, TV, Video:
A wide range of effects added to film and video during the post-production stage. These include an ever-growing variety of transition effects, such as fades, dissolves, wipes, explosions, implosions, fragmentations, superimpositions (supers) and page-turns; also titles and other typographical effects. These effects used to be achieved mechanically, using an optical printer, and sets of duplicate negatives and inter-negatives. They are now done by computer.
See Frame, Freeze-frame, Pan, Tilt, Shot.

Orientation   DTP, WP:
A page either in landscape (horizontal) or portrait (vertical) form.
See Landscape and Portrait.

Original   Art, Creative, Platemaking, Print:
Original material intended for reproduction. This includes text and illustrations.

Origination   Copywriting, Creative, Design, Art:
The preparatory stages of an advertising or print job. This includes copywriting, visualising, flimsies, scamps, roughs, finished roughs and presentation visuals (qv all of these). What follows, after approval, is proofing and production.
See Estimate.

Outdoor   Advertising, Media:
All forms of advertising appearing in the open air. Some indoor advertising is referred to as outdoor. Confused? Read on.
Posters, billboards, Adshels (qv), bus and taxi-cab sides and rears, signs, fascias, and banners dragged by aircraft, are forms of outdoor advertising. However, bus interiors, car-cards on underground and main-line trains, also come within the outdoor definition. They are more accurately termed transport advertising. Posters within underground and railway stations also come under outdoor; they too are transport advertising, but treated by media planners as outdoor. Yes, it is confusing, but you can get used to it.
See Adshel.

Out-take Film, Video:
A filmed sequence shot during production, but taken out during editing. Usually ends up on the cutting-room floor – another piece of filmic jargon.

Overlay Art:
1 A transparent cover on copy where instructions, key-lines, corrections or colour-breaks are marked.
2 Transparent or translucent prints. When in position on each other, they form a composite picture.

See Key-line, Register marks, Registration.

Overmatter Art, Copywriting, Creative, DTP, Print, Production, TYP, WP:
Typeset copy which does not fit a predetermined area. If you have planned to fill a specific space with copy, but your writer has written more than will fit into it, the overspill is dubbed over-matter.

Overprinted Print, Production:
Type or illustrations printed on top of another printed area. A retailer may have his name, address and telephone number printed on a leaflet provided by a manufacturer. The retailer's details may be printed in an unprinted, white area, and not actually on top of some other image. This however is still called over-printed.

Page make-up Art, Creative, DTP, Production, Print:
See Composition, Make-up, Mechanical.

Page proofs Production, Print, Publishing:
Proof of a piece of print, arranged as pages assembled in the correct order.

In former times, before computerisation, copy would be typeset in hot metal and proofed in galleys, single columns (qv). After checking and approval, the columns would be assembled into pages, and proofed again. These were page proofs.

A third stage of proofing could then be undertaken. These were made on a proofing machine. These were called machine proofs.

Pagination   Production, Print, Publishing:
Organising and arranging the pages of a newspaper, magazine, brochure or other publication in page sequence. This term also applies to the numbering of the pages.

Page scrolling   Computing, DTP, WP:
Displaying on a computer screen the pages of a document, a bit at a time; or one complete screen page at a time. You can scroll backwards as well as forwards, and from side to side.
   See Scrolling.

PAL   TV, Video: Phase Alternating Line.
The TV system used in the UK and several European countries. There are now various technical up-dates on PAL.
   Unfortunately, the three main systems used in the TV world are incompatible. You need to convert PAL videos to the SECAM system used in, say France and Russia, or NTSC used in North America, before they can be viewed on their VCRs (qv). A PAL TV set or monitor cannot be used in countries with incompatible systems unless it has built-in conversion capability.
   See NTSC, SECAM, Television standards, VCR.

Pan   Film, TV, Video:
To swing a camera on its mounting in an arc to the left or right, following the action during a shoot.
   See Shot, Tilt.

Pantone   Art, Creative, Print, Production:
A range of designer's colours, matched accurately in printing inks.
   This system enables you to produce designs in the range of colours you have selected; then proof them and print them in exactly the same colours. In the designer's terms, what you see is what you get. It is also a control system, linking advertiser, designer and printer.

Paper sizes
See 'A' Paper Sizes.

Paper-set   Advertising, Publishing:
Advertisements typeset by the publications they are to appear in

are termed paper-set. The layouts may be supplied by the advertisers or their agencies. Some publications also offer design services.

Password Computing, DTP, WP:
A security measure. You enter your password into your computer's keyboard before you can access the material you want. It protects against unauthorised access.

You can 'lock' documents, so that they cannot be retrieved except by entering the password. When you want to retrieve a locked document, the computer asks you to enter the correct password on the keyboard. You had better do it right because some systems lock you out permanently if you get it wrong three times.

There are several problems with this kind of security. For example, you may forget the password. Some software has no method of letting you retrieve your documents if you forget the password.

The temptation to devise an unforgettable password is hard to resist. If you use your forename or family name, practically anybody can breach your security in about 25 seconds. If you write your password down, anyone can get hold of it and use it against you. You can try using numbers, but a lot of computer software is specifically designed to crack numeric passwords; there are also many alphanumeric password-crackers on the market.

Paste-ups Art, Studio work:
The organisation of a piece of finished artwork, where all the elements are mounted in place with precision. The elements include copy, display headlines, line drawings and other illustrations, and keylines (qv). Most paste-ups, especially for newspapers and magazines, are now done by computer without a drawing-board in sight. Even small studios now do it this way.

The advantages are in the saving of time and effort; flexibility; accuracy; and the ability to save the results on disk.

See Halftone, Keylines.

Penetration Media planning and buying, Research:
Penetration is calculated on the basis of the proportion of the total population represented by a readership, a viewing or listening audience.

See Circulation, Controlled circulation, Profile, Rate card, Reader, Readership, Television rating points, VFD.

Perfect binding   Print, Production:
A technique for binding magazines, brochures and booklets. After folding, the pages are trimmed and glued at the spine. The cover is drawn on and held in place by glue. No stapling is used. The effect is a flat, squared-up spine, rather than a rounded one. The main promotional advantage is that the spine is available for printing.
See Binding, Finishing.

Photocomposition   TYP, Typesetting:
A method of typesetting using photographic techniques. This involves using a photographic matrix containing font. The typesetting machine moves the matrix over photographic paper, one character at a time. It also keeps track of the matrix, and each individual character, as it proceeds. As the matrix moves over the paper, each character is exposed to the paper by a light-source. In this way, the matrix is manipulated so that it sets lines of display and body copy.
  In a way, this exposure method is rather like the way you take pictures in a camera. You wind the film on and press the shutter. The light coming through the lens exposes the film. You wind on again and repeat the process to the end of the film.
  In the UK, the EU and the USA, photocomposition has largely given way to computer setting. This is because photo-typesetting is less flexible than the computer method. For example, you have to develop the photographic paper before you can see the image. You may find photocomposition in less developed countries, or in places where the computer is not king.
  Tip: always find out what production methods are in place when entrusting artwork and typesetting to overseas suppliers.

Photograph   Art, Creative, Platemaking, Print, Production:
This term is so well known, there's really no need to define it. But somebody will no doubt write to me complaining that I haven't covered it.
  A photograph is a pictorial image, usually made in a camera, by the chemical action of light on light-sensitive film. The image produced is latent, until developed by chemical processing. The

resulting image is either positive or negative. If negative, the image needs to be exposed again on to another negative, light-sensitive surface, and again developed chemically so that it becomes positive.

Where the final image is made on photographic paper, this is called a print, the abbreviated form of photoprint. This is still sometimes called a bromide (qv).

Photogravure   Print, Production:
A printing process using printing cylinders rather than printing plates. This is intaglio (qv) printing, with dots, or cells, etched or engraved into copper-plated steel cylinders. The sunken cells, representing the printing image, hold the ink. The cylinder rotates in a bath of ink, with the excess scraped away by a doctor blade (qv). In some gravure techniques, wrap-around plates are used.

See the Print chapter in this book.

Photolitho   Print, Production:
Another name for litho (qv). All commercial litho is produced photographically. The image to be printed is photographically transferred to the printing plate, either direct or via film.

Photomontage   Art, Photography:
Different photographic images brought together and mounted in position on artwork. This produces a combined image which contains all the different photo elements.

In former times, this was done by hand on the drawing board; today, it is done electronically, on the computer screen. The computer technique allows editing on screen, and no messing about with Cow Gum or glue. Personally, I miss Cow Gum; it used to be the greatest asset a studio could ever have, with the possible exception of process white (qv). It used to be said that the more Cow Gum and process white a studio used, the more successful it was.

Photoprint   *See* Photograph.

Photosetting   Art, Creative, Platemaking, Print, Production:
Display and body copy typeset photographically. Otherwise known as film-setting (qv).

Photostat   Graphic reproduction
A photocopy. An original document copied electrostatically by a machine dedicated to this technique. The quality of a photostat made by a new machine is almost indistinguishable from the original. Sometimes called a Xerox, after one of the manufacturers who developed the process and made it popular.

Pica   DTP, WP, TYP:
A unit in the measurement of type size; 6 picas = 72 points = 1 inch. This term is not much used in the UK or the EU, but is still popular in the USA. Type composed on computers is usually capable of enlargement or reduction on an infinite scale, or the size denoted in millimetres. With some software packages, you have a choice.

Manual typewriters usually have two type sizes: either pica, 10 characters to the inch; or elite, 12 characters to the inch. I first learned to type on a portable Remington Rand, which I still use.

The type is Courier pica, 12 characters per inch. My first newspaper feature article was typed on it, and earned me my first fee. Why do I keep it? Not entirely for sentimental reasons. In the event of a power cut, which has sometimes happened, I am the only person in the office who can do any work.
See Elite, Pitch, Typography.

Pin register   Art:
Pins on a scanner frame, corresponding to holes in artwork mounting boards. The objective is accurate positioning and registration.
See Registration.

Pitch   DTP, TYP, WP:
The number of typescript or typeset characters to the linear inch. With 10-pitch, there are 10 characters to the inch, the same as pica size; 12-pitch is 12 characters to the inch, elite size.

This is not the same as *point size* (qv) – 12-point typewriter type has 10 characters to the inch; 10pt has 12. Confused? Don't worry; modern computerised typesetting and DTP systems work it all out for you.
See Point size, Typography.

Pixel Computing: *PIC*ture ELement.
The smallest addressable element of a bit-mapped screen. In simpler language: a dot on a computer screen. The smaller the dot, and the tighter the dots are packed together, the higher the definition, the sharper the picture you see.
See Definition, Dot, Resolution.

Planographic Print:
A technique for printing from a flat surface. The best-known method of planographic printing is litho (qv).

Plate Print:
A sheet of metal or other material carrying a printing image. The plate is mounted on the impression cylinder of a printing press. When the press rolls, the image on the plate is inked, then transferred to paper or whatever material is being printed. Litho, flexography and letterpress presses use plates.
See Cylinder press, Flatbed, Flexography, Forme, Letterpress, Litho, Pull.

PMT
1 Art, Production: Photo-mechanical transfer.
A very superior form of photoprint, produced on a PMT camera. The sizing of the prints is very accurate, and the results very sharp and dense, to finished-artwork standard. The camera is precision-engineered, with very accurate controls.

2 DTP, EP: Page make-up terminal.
A terminal at the sharp end of electronic publishing, used for laying out and making up pages of a publication, fitting type and illustrations.
The PMT is used for originating text and graphics, and retouching illustrations to an extremely high order of accuracy.

Point size DTP, TYP, WP:
The basic unit in the measurement of type. The size of a typeface is measured from the top of the ascender to the foot of the descender (qv both these).
The British–American system is based on 72 points to the inch. This has served the printing industry well for more than a century.

With the arrival of word processing and desktop publishing, metric sizes have begun to take over. Don't worry: type is usually scalable. This means that you can increase or reduce the size on a more-or-less infinite scale. And the computer works it all out for you.

See Ascender, Descender.

Portrait   Art, Creative, DTP, WP:
The orientation of a printed page, where the short sides are top and bottom of the page. As an example, A4 letterheads are portrait orientation.

POS   Advertising, Marketing, Media: Point-of-Sale Display.
Advertising display material on show at the point of sale. It is usually designed to call attention to the product, and often reminds the customer of the message used in an associated advertising campaign.

This is the last chance to influence the customer into making a decision about trying or buying a product. Yet POS is the Cinderella of the marketing communications business, and under-rated as an advertising medium. You don't believe it? Look around you.

Positioning
See the Branding chapter in this book.

Positive   Art, Creative, Photography, Platemaking, Production:
A photographic image on film, paper or metal, usually obtained from a negative (qv).

See Photograph.

Poster   Outdoor advertising, Media:
An advertising sign, usually displayed in a public place. The size of a poster is usually linked to the viewing distance. On a London underground platform, the size is modest, since the viewing distance is a few feet. Across the track, a poster may be up to 16 times larger.

Poster sites are found in, opposite or near to shopping centres, where customers' money is exchanged for products and services. The promotional messages are designed to influence consumer decision-making.

Often, messages displayed on posters bear no relation to products on sale nearby. Some of the posters displayed near where I live seem to bear no relation to any product, person or thing, living, dead or inanimate. This is not the fault of the site owners. It is the result of creativity gone absolutely loony, with little marketing input involved. The marketing message is hidden by the creativity. Read what David Ogilvy says about posters, in his brilliant book *Ogilvy on Advertising*. To say he doesn't like them is a gross understatement.

Premium   Sales promotion:
A piece of merchandise, offered by an advertiser, to induce customers to try or buy a product or service. Premiums are usually free to the customer, or offered for a small sum of money; sometimes just for the cost of the postage.

Some years ago, you could have heard a neat bit of doggerel among vociferous consumer groups: 'Have you heard the latest premium racket? A mouldy old duster in a half-empty packet.'

Today, most premiums are good value, and customers actually want them. Not long ago, Rice Crispies came up with an offer of model vintage cars and public transport vehicles. I know a family that went for the whole collection, and of course consumed vast quantities of Crispies. They came to no discernible harm, and now have a collection which will be quite valuable in a few years. Well done, Kellogg marketeers!

Presentation visual   Art, Creative:
A highly finished visual, suitable for presenting to your board of directors; or, if you are an advertising agency, to your client. It is designed to give the closest possible representation of the finished product. Also called a finished rough (qv).

In pre-computer times, these visuals were usually mounted on board and covered with transparent acetate. The acetates served two purposes: to prevent accidental damage from coffee, beery thumbmarks and other contaminants; and to deter clients from making alterations during a presentation. This was a wise precaution, since presentation visuals were expensive to produce, and there was only one of each. Today, visuals of all kinds can be computer generated, and you can have as many as you like – or can afford.

Press date   Print, Production, Publishing:
The date on which a newspaper or magazine is published. Do not confuse this with the cover date, which is the date on the cover of the publication.

You need to exercise some caution here. Some magazines, of the glossy and housekeeping kind for example, hit the bookstalls a month or more ahead of their cover dates. The objective seems to be to steal a march on their competitors. However, since many publications which compete with each other adopt the same strategy, it defeats itself, and serves only to confuse media buyers. Creatives and agency production managers also suffer from this bogus timescale, since it is completely out of step with the reality of working life. It probably has the same effect on the reading public.

Press proof
1   Print, Production, Publishing:
The final proof submitted by the publisher before going to press. This proof needs to be signed off by the advertiser, who takes responsibility for it, this being the final authorisation.

2   Print:
A proof made on a printing press before a production run. This is unacceptably expensive because it means devoting an entire press to pulling off a few proofs; no printer dare do it and hope to survive in business. Therefore, specially scaled-down versions of production presses are used instead. The production value of proofs taken from such mini-presses can usually be relied on to resemble the real thing.

See Cromalin, Forme, Letterpress, Plate, Proof, Proof-reader, Proof-reader's marks, Pull, Quote, Zero.

Press run   Print, Production, Publishing:
The number of copies produced in a print run.
See Print run.

Primary colours   Art, Creative, Photography, Print, Production:
The primary colours of light, known as the additive colours, are red, blue and green.

The colours used in four-colour process printing are cyan,

magenta, yellow and black. Most other colours can be made up by combining these four. This is usually termed subtractive colour mixing.

Four-colour process printing has a number of limitations. Your eye is a brilliant visual instrument, capable of detecting millions of colours. But four-colour process printing can reproduce only a small percentage of them.

Hues produced by four-colour process printing are made up of dots – a combination of cyan, magenta, yellow and black. It is difficult, however, to reproduce some shades of colour; for example, deep blues, violets, greens and oranges.

In colour science, colour is measured by three basic criteria: hue, saturation and luminance. In ordinary language, these are the colour itself, its depth and brightness.

In colour proofing, the four primary colours are designated CMYK, a useful shorthand. The K stands for black, to distinguish it from blue and brown.

Prime time   Media, Radio, TV:
Periods during the day when the highest number of people are viewing or listening. On TV, this is between 9 pm and 10.30 pm. TV advertising rates vary with the size of the audience. Prime-time rates are the highest. Other times are called off-peak.

Radio has two distinct peak times, commonly called drive time. This refers to the captive audience sitting in their cars during the morning and evening travel peaks. The hours are 7–9 am and 4.30–6 pm.

Print
1   Art, Print, Production:
The professional term for printing. The person who buys printing services is called a print buyer, not printing buyer.
   See Copy.

2   Art, Creative, Photography, Production:
Professional jargon for a photograph (qv). An abbreviation of photoprint.

Print run   Print, Production, Publishing:
The number of copies of a publication required from a printer. This

is usually specified in the print briefing and the subsequent printer's quotation. The actual printing of the copies is also referred to as a print run.

See Cromalin, Press proof.

Printout   Computing, DTP, WP:
The recording on paper of a computer, DTP or WP file. Also called hard copy (qv).

Process colours   Print, Production:
The subtractive primary colours, cyan, magenta, yellow and black. Combinations and blends of these four can produce most colours in the spectrum. This is, of course, cheaper than using special colours to achieve the same results. The process colours are designated CMYK.

See Primary colours.

Process white   Art, Studio
A very white, opaque, water-based paint used for whiting-out errors and removing unwanted spots on artwork. Also used for re-shaping photographic images and illustrations.

Profile   Media research:
The difference between penetration and profile is this: a magazine read by half the women in Britain has 50 per cent penetration, but its profile is 100 per cent women. This calculation is theoretical, and also an over-simplification. In practice, the profile might be 85 per cent women and 15 per cent men, since women's magazines have male readership. Other profiles could be based on age bands, socio-economic groups, geographical areas or product usage. Bear in mind that however many sub-groups are included, profiles always add up to 100per cent.

See Circulation, Controlled circulation, Penetration, Rate card, Reader, Readership, VFD, Viewer, Television rating points, VFD.

Progressive proofs   Art, Platemaking, Print, Production:
Also called progressives; in the USA, progs. Proofs taken from individual plates or cylinders in colour process printing. They are made in an order which shows the sequence of printing, and the result after each succeeding colour has been laid down.

This is a complicated way of saying that each colour is proofed separately, and also imposed upon one another, in this order:

Y   Yellow
M   Yellow + magenta
C   Yellow + magenta + cyan
K   Yellow + magenta + cyan + black.

Doing it this way enables the printer, designer and advertiser to judge the hue, saturation and luminance of each colour, and evaluate the end result. They see how the result compares with the original.

See CMYK, Proof, Press proof, Process colours.

Promotion   Marketing:
Advertising and other forms of sales presentations, designed to encourage the consumer or trade up-take of a product or service.

The form of any promotion depends on its objectives, and also on the imagination of the team producing it. It can vary from a simple in-store demonstration of a range of cosmetics, or a sampling of Jaffa oranges, to a tie-in with a cinema blockbuster.

A promotion for travel insurance, for example, might be appropriate during a local screening of the film *Titanic*. A promotion for kitchen knives, for example, could have been mounted during the national release of the film *Fatal Attraction*. These are extreme examples, possibly in bad taste, but you see what I mean.

Proof   Art, Creative, Platemaking, Print, Production:
An impression taken from an inked printing plate, cylinder or other printing surface, ahead of a production run. Proofing is done so that the pages of a print job can be checked for image, accuracy, colour and so on. When proofing is carried out on a printing machine, using printing inks, it's called wet proofing (qv).

Today, other techniques for evaluating printed material ahead of a run are available. This is done by computer; and by techniques such as Cromalin (qv), in which case it is called dry proofing (qv).

See Proof-reader, Proof-reader's marks, Reader, Quote, Zero.

Proof-reader Copywriting, Creative, Production, Print:
A person whose job it is to read proofs, correct inaccuracies and revise copy. Copywriters and other creatives also routinely read proofs of the jobs they create. Management often does the same.

Ideally, the way to read proofs is to have two people doing it. One reads aloud from the proof; the other, the copy-holder, holds the typescript or other original copy, and checks it against what is being read out. The reader calls out every word and all punctuation, and spells out names in full. Where numbers are part of the copy, the reader calls out each individual figure, including decimal points, commas, subscripts and superscripts.

If you have to read proofs without the help of a copy-holder, life can be difficult, especially if you have written the copy yourself. One way of overcoming this problem is to turn the proof upside down and read it that way. It's not ideal, but you soon get used to it.

There is a convention that copywriters make their corrections in red and blue ink; printers' proof-readers use green. This clearly shows who has made the corrections, and generally indicates who is to pay for them. If a printer has made an error, he is obliged to correct it free of charge. Where an advertiser or his agent has made a mistake in original copy, and the printer sets it as it stands, the advertiser usually pays. The advertiser is then charged for author's corrections.

Because it can cost £50 or more to change a comma on a proof, it naturally pays to take pains over the accuracy of original copy sent to printers.

See Proof-reader's marks, Quote, Zero.

Proof-readers' marks Art, Creative, DTP, Print, Production, WP:
A series of marks and symbols used by proof-readers for correcting and revising proofs. These are accepted and used by the printing industry in the UK and Europe, and in other parts of the world. They are, of course, essential for correcting typescripts. Using them helps to reduce the risk of errors caused by ambiguous instructions, and avoid unnecessary expense and delay.

Because of the international trade in print, proof-correcting marks need to be international in character. This means that it is unwise to use words in the correction procedure. In the days before much of the English-speaking world went mad with decimalisation, words and symbols were used together very effectively for proof correcting. I am glad to observe that the American printing industry has sensibly retained the combination of words, marks and symbols for correcting its proofs.

The British Standards Institution has published a booklet which recommends to writers and printers the standardisation of proof-reading marks and symbols. You can get it at Her Majesty's Stationery Office. Ask for BSI 5261 Part 2 1976. Check: there may now be a later version.

See Proof, Quote, Zero.

Proportional scan   Art, CAD, Creative, DTP, Production:
Reduction or enlargement of a shape, where the height and width remain in proportion to each other.

Pull   Print:
A proof taken off a letterpress printing block or type forme. In hand-proofing, the block is inked with an inking roller, and the paper gently laid on top of it. Pressure is applied to the paper, then released. The paper, carefully pulled off the block, will have the inked image transferred to it.

See Cylinder press, Flatbed, Forme, Letterpress, Plate.

Pull-out section   Print, Publishing:
A complete, self-contained set of pages in a newspaper or magazine. This is usually designed so that it can be detached and read separately. The editorial and advertising are usually closely related, but in the UK do not normally corrupt each other.

Quarter-tone   Art, Production:
A dot-based method of reproducing continuous-tone images. Similar to the halftone (qv), but retouched in the studio so that some of the tones are eliminated. This produces a sharp, dramatic, high-contrast effect.

See Halftone.

Quotation   Creative, Print, Production:
Also known as a quote. The costing of a job, prepared in advance, by a printer, production house, advertising agency or other supplier. Estimates are not, as far as I know, binding. However, quotations are, so be careful.

See Estimate.

Quote   News, PR, Propaganda, Publishing:
A quotation or a statement. Spoken or written words, reproduced exactly as they were spoken or written by the person who originated them, and placed inside single or double quotation marks.

See Proof, Proof-reader, Proof-reader's marks, Reader, Zero.

Radio Authority   Media controls:
A body which licenses and regulates the independent radio industry in accordance with the statutory requirements of the Broadcasting Act 1990 (qv).

It plans frequencies, awards licences, regulates programming and radio advertising. It plays an active role in the discussion and formulation of policies affecting the independent radio industry and its listeners.

The Authority takes a firm and objective stance in support of the development and growth of a successful UK independent radio network that offers a wide listening choice.

The Broadcasting Act requires the Authority to draw up, periodically review, and enforce a code which sets standards and practice in advertising. The Authority advises its licence-holders on interpretation of the code, and monitors compliance by investigating complaints.

By laying down clear, precise rules, the Authority encourages self-regulation. It believes that the ultimate responsibility for checking advertisements for compliance with its Code of Practice and the general law, lies with the broadcaster.

It is a condition of a Radio Authority licence that radio stations comply with the Authority's Advertising Code, and that they employ trained staff to check all advertising carefully before accepting it for broadcasting.

In practice, local and regional advertisements are normally approved for broadcasting by station staff. National advertisements, and those which fall into certain categories, have the additional safety net of being checked by the Copy Clearance Secretariat of the ITV Association (qv), in an arrangement with the Broadcast Advertising Clearance Centre.

Ragged   Creative, DTP, Typesetting, TYP, WP:
A block or column of type with a vertically uneven edge.
   See Full out, Justified, Measure, Range.

RAJAR   Research: Radio Joint Audience Research Ltd.
See AIRC.

Range   Creative, Production, Typesetting:
Instruction by a typographer to a typesetter on how a piece of copy
should be set in type.
   Range left asks for a straight, vertical left-hand edge. By implica-
tion, the right-hand edge will not be so.
   Range right asks for the right-hand edge to be set straight and
vertical. The left-hand edge will not be.
   See Full out, Justified, Measure, Ragged.

Rate card   Media, Media planning, Publishing:
A document produced by a newspaper or magazine publisher, TV
or radio station owner, giving advertising rates. A rate card will
also give production details and deadlines, and much other information. It is usually presented as a media pack, with advertising
rates accompanied by research information on circulation and
readership; or viewing and listening audience.
   Among the information found in the *Hendon Times* rate card:

■ the newspapers in the group
■ a brief description of each paper
■ run-of-paper advertising rates for each paper, expressed in £
   per single-column centimetre
■ advertising rates for individual sections of the newspaper; for
   example entertainments, situations vacant, motors, property,
   sales & services, holidays, public notices and church notices
■ circulation and readership data; whether this is ABC or VFD
■ circulation area and map
■ advertising agency commission
■ mechanical data; precise information on:
   – page type area
   – no of columns
   – column length and width
   – halftone screen

- image resolution
- film required
■ representatives' names and addresses, telephone and fax numbers
■ cross-references to other publications in the group.

See Circulation, Controlled circulation, Penetration, Profile, Rate card, Reader, Readership, Viewer, VFD, Television rating points.

Reader
1   Art, Creative, DTP, Print, Production, Publishing:
The person who reads and corrects DTP hard copy and printer's proofs. Also called a proof-reader (qv). Ideally, he is one half of a team of two; the other half is a person who holds the original copy and checks the reader's reading-out of the proofed text.
See Proof, Proof-reader, Proof-reader's marks, Quote, Zero.

2   Media planning and buying, Media research, Press media:
Average Issue Readership (AIR) is defined as the number of people claiming to have read or looked at one or more copies of a publication for at least two minutes during the issue period – the publication frequency. A reader is therefore a participant in a press media research sample.

In press terms, 'reading and looking' covers anything from reading a publication thoroughly, to a casual flip through it. The actual issue of the publication does not seem to matter; any issue will do for the purpose of this research.

Question: would you buy advertising space on this basis? Is it precise enough?
See ABC, Circulation, Controlled circulation, Penetration, Profile, Rate card, Television rating points, VFD, Viewer.

Readership   Media planning and buying, Publishing:
The number of people reading each issue of a publication. Do not confuse with circulation (qv).
See ABC, Circulation, Controlled circulation, Penetration, Profile, Rate card, Reader, Television rating points, VFD, Viewer.

Recto   Publishing:
A right-hand page.
See Verso.

Register marks   Art, Platemaking, Print, Production:
Small cross-hair marks on artwork or negatives. Hairline crosses or
other symbols are drawn on or applied to original artwork before
photography. These are vital for:

■ accurately positioning overlays on artwork
■ keeping negatives and overlays in exactly correct positions; and
  for
■ overlays where they are used on artwork
■ the accurate positioning of two or more colours in proofing and
  printing.

See Colour bars, Overlay, Registration.

Registration
1   Print:
The precise superimposition of one colour upon another.

2   Art:
The precise alignment of any artwork element with another.

See Colour bars, Overlay, Register.

Register   Art, Platemaking, Print, Production:

■ the precise fitting of two or more images on to a printing
  surface, in exact alignment with each other
■ in colour printing, the accurate positioning of one colour on
  another
■ in printing, the correct alignment of pages, together with their
  margins accurately positioned.

See Colour bars, Register marks, Registration.

Relief printing   Print, Production:
A printing technique in which the image is produced by raising the
surface of the stock from the back.
  See Blind embossing, Copperplate, Die stamping, Embossing,
Relief printing, Thermography.

Resolution   Computing, Photography, Print:
The density of dots or grain, and the ability of various systems to discriminate, register, resolve and reproduce them. This term also applies to the human eye.

1   Computing:
On a computer screen, the capability of a screen to reproduce images. A lot depends on the size of the pixels (qv). A high- resolution screen produces finer and sharper images than a low-resolution one. The higher the resolution, the higher the quality of the image, the sharper the picture.

2   Photography:
The fineness of detail which a lens, prism system or photographic film can discriminate.

3   Print:
The number of dots per inch or per centimetre of a halftone screen. The greater the number of dots, the higher the reproduction quality, and the sharper the results.
   See Definition, Dot, Pixel.

Reversed   DTP, EP, Print:
Copy appearing as white on a solid black or colour background.

Reversal film   Photography:
Photographic film that produces a positive image, rather than a negative one. Usually applied to film used for colour transparencies or slides.

Roman   DTP, TYP, WP:
Type that stands perpendicular, as distinct from slanted, oblique or italic. In the middle of a sentence, roman is correctly spelled with a lower case r.
   See Italics, Oblique.

Runaround   DTP, TYP, WP:
Type set to follow the contour of an illustration. The type literally runs round the shape.

Run-of-paper Media, Media planning and buying:
An advertisement inserted into a newspaper or magazine wherever the advertisement director chooses; and at the standard cost. If you want more control over where your advertisement appears, you have to opt for solus, facing matter, next matter, or one of the other special positions. This of course costs more. Consult the advertisement rate card.
See Matter, Mini-page, Solus.

Sans Serif DTP, TYP, WP:
Type without serifs.
See Serif.

Scaling Art, Production:
Working out the proportions of an artwork element, so that it can be enlarged or reduced to fit a given area on a page.

Screen angle Print, Production:
The angle of rotation of a halftone screen (qv). When making colour separations, the screens need to be laid down at specific angles to avoid image distortion, disturbing patterns and other unwanted effects on the negatives.
See Colour separation.

Screen printing Print:
See the Print chapter of this book.

Scrolling Computer jargon:
Moving up and down a computer screen; or, rather, making the image on the screen move up, down and sideways. When there is more to a document than can be displayed on the screen, you are obliged to use the screen as a window. You therefore have to treat the material on screen like a scroll, scrolling up and down it, or scrolling side to side. You can then see only the bits of the document that fit into the window.
See Page scrolling.

SECAM TV, Video: Systeme en Couleurs a Memoire.
The broadcast TV system used in France, Russia and countries of the former Soviet bloc.
See NTSC, PAL, World TV standards.

Separations Print:
See Colour separations, Screen angle.

Serif DTP, TYP, WP:
A small terminal cross-stroke at the end of a main stroke of a character. Serifs come in various shapes, sizes and angles.

Set-off Print:
An effect which occurs when the ink of one printed sheet marks the next sheet being delivered.

This used to be a printer's nightmare in the days before wet-on-wet printing. To some extent, it still is. Before the perfection of modern inks and drying techniques, you had to let one colour dry on the page before printing another on top of it.

With many modern printing presses, drying is not an actual drying process. This is now achieved as curing, by ultra-violet light. Some of the credit has to be given to the environmental lobbies, who campaign for the elimination of volatile liquids from printing inks. Most of the marks, of course, go to the printing industry itself, who recognised the economies to be gained from using less-volatile inks. It is possible to recover the volatile substances from the inks during printing, and to recycle them. But it's expensive, and probably not cost-effective except in the very long run.
See Set-off, Show-through.

Sheet-fed Print:
A printing press which uses individual sheets of paper.
See Paper, Web.

Shot Film, Photography, TV, Video:
The content of a photographed scene or screen, complete with action, sound, camera movement and so on.
See Frame, Freeze frame, Opticals, Pan, Still, Tilt, Voice-over.

Show-through Print:
Occurs when the printed side of a sheet shows through the paper to its reverse side, and interferes with the copy. This is usually the result either of a bad choice of ink, or of over-inking; or a bad choice of stock (qv), which is too thin or not opaque enough.
See Paper, Stock.

Shutter speed   Photography:
The speed of the shutter in a camera.
   See Film speed.

Small caps   DTP, TYP, WP:
Small capital letters with the x-height of a particular font, as distinct from full-size caps.
   See X-height.

Software   Computing:
Programs and applications for a computer.
   See Hardware.

Solus   Media, Media planning and buying:
A newspaper or magazine advertisement space, on a page with no other advertising matter on it. The advertiser usually specifies which page. The cost is therefore higher than the same space would be if inserted run-of-paper.
   See Matter, Mini-page, Run-of-paper.

Speed rating   Film:
See film speed.

Spine   Print:
The edge of a brochure, booklet or other publication which supports the binding. The back of a bound book connecting the covers.

Spot   Media, Media planning and buying, TV:
The airtime duration of a television commercial; also its date and transmission time.

Spot colour   Print:
A small area of colour in a black-and-white advertisement or item of print.

Spread   Advertising, Print:
Two contiguous, facing pages. Do not confuse with double-page spread (qv).

Still
1   Film, TV, Video:
A non-moving picture or illustration on the screen.

2   Photography:
A photograph taken during film or video production, sometimes on the set, and used for publicity purposes.
  See Commercial, Frame, Freeze-frame, Shot, Titling, Voice-over.

Stock
1   Photography:
Film to be used for photography.

2   Print:
Paper or other material used for printing.

Storyboard   Creative, Film, TV, Video:
A sequential series of illustrations showing the highlights of a script. It is the basic document advertising agencies present to their clients for discussion and approval. Film-makers plan their production work using storyboards, sometimes modifying them during a shoot.
  See Animatic.

Sub-head   Copywriting, Creative, DTP, EP, TYP, WP:
The heading above a paragraph. The main heading of a piece of advertising copy is called the headline. In news-release copy it is called a heading. Subsidiary headings are called sub-heads. Where a sub-head sits on a line in a central position above a paragraph, it is called a cross-head.
  Either way, the sub-head indicates a main division in your copy. In copywriting, it should be written as a benefit. In news releases, particularly long ones, the sub-head should be as bland as possible, conveying only the information essential to divide the copy. Editors usually prefer to create their own.

Super   Film, Video, TV:
Titling superimposed on to a picture.

Tab   Copywriting, DTP, WP: Tabulation.
A jump in spacing to a position decided in advance. Horizontal tabs are sideways jumps; vertical tabs jump up and down.

Tabloid Print:
Page size used in newspaper and magazine printing. The trimmed page size is approximately 425 mm high × 300 mm wide, depending on the printing house. Tabloid is about half the trimmed size of broadsheet. *The Daily Express*, *The Mirror*, *The Sun* and the *Harrow Observer* are tabloids.
See Broadsheet.

Teleciné Film, TV, Video:
A machine which transfers film to videotape.

Television rating points Media planning and buying, Media research:
Usually called TVRs. The value of television to advertisers is calculated in TVRs – television rating points. Each TVR represents one per cent of the potential TV audience. This is expressed in terms of individuals or homes with TV sets.

A viewer is defined as a person in a room with a TV set switched on for at least 15 consecutive seconds.

In television terms, in the room means anything from watching attentively to casually glancing at the screen while doing something else.

Question: would you buy TV airtime on this basis? Does it need tightening up?

See ABC, Circulation, Controlled circulation, Penetration, Profile, Rate card, Reader, Readership, VFD, Viewer.

Television standards TV, Video:
There are three basic broadcasting standards available in international TV:

PAL   Phase Alternating Line
NTSC   National Television System Committee
SECAM   Systeme en Couleurs a Memoire.

Unfortunately, these standards are incompatible. Worse, there are variations of PAL and SECAM.

The following list is up-to-date at the time of writing, given the speed of change now taking place in broadcasting. When digital audio and TV are introduced, there will be further changes. It will help you to watch this space in future editions of this book.

Country	Standard	Country	Standard
Afghanistan	PAL-B	Czech Rep	SECAM-DK
Albania	PAL-BG	Denmark	PAL-BG
Algeria	PAL-B	Djibouti	SECAM-K
Angola	PAL-I	Dominican Rep	NTSC
Antigua	NTSC	Ecuador	NTSC
Antilles	NTSC	Egypt	SECAM-B
Argentina	PAL-N	El Salvador	NTSC
Australia	PAL-BG	Ethiopia	PAL-B
Austria	PAL-BG	Finland	PAL-BG
Bahamas	NTSC	France	SECAM-L
Bahrain	PAL-B	Gabon	SECAM-K
Bangladesh	PAL-B	Germany	SECAM-BG
Barbados	NTSC	(Former Dem)	
Belgium	PAL-BG	Germany	PAL-BG
Benin	SECAM-K	(Former Fed)	
Bermuda	NTSC	Ghana	PAL-B
Bolivia	NTSC	Gibraltar	PAL-B
Botswana	PAL-I	Greece	SECAM-B
Brazil	PAL-M	Guam	NTSC
Brunei	PAL-B	Guatamala	NTSC
Bulgaria	SECAM-D	Guinea	SECAM-K
Burkina Faso	SECAM-K	Haiti	NTSC
Burma	NTSC	Hawaii	NTSC
Burundi	SECAM-K	Honduras	NTSC
Cameroun	PAL-BG	Hong Kong	PAL-I
Canada	NTSC	Hungary	SECAM-DK
Cayman Islands	NTSC	Iceland	PAL-B
Central Af Rep	SECAM-K	India	PAL-B
Chad	SECAM-K	Indonesia	PAL-B
Chile	NTSC	Iran	SECAM-B
China	PAL-D	Iraq	SECAM-B
Colombia	NTSC	Israel	PAL
Congo	SECAM-K	Italy	PAL-BG
Costa Rica	NTSC	Ivory Coast	SECAM-K
Cuba	NTSC	Jordan	PAL-B
Cyprus	SECAM-BG	Kenya	PAL-B

Country	Standard	Country	Standard
Kuwait	PAL-B	Singapore	PAL-B
Lebanon	SECAM-B	South Africa	PAL-I
Lesotho	PAL-I	Spain	PAL-BG
Liberia	PAL-B	Sri Lanka	PAL-B
Libya	SECAM-B	Sudan	PAL-B
Luxembourg	PAL-BG +	Surinam	NTSC
	SECAM-BG/L	Swaziland	PAL-BG
Madagascar	SECAM-K	Sweden	PAL-BG
Malaysia	PAL-B	Switzerland	PAL-BG
Maldives	PAL-B	Syria	SECAM-B
Mali	SECAM-K	Tahiti	SECAM-DK
Malta	PAL-B	Taiwan	NTSC
Mauritania	SECAM-K	Tanzania	PAL-I
Mauritius	SECAM-B	Thailand	PAL-B
Mexico	NTSC	Togo	SECAM-K
Morocco	SECAM-B	Trin & Tob	NTSC
Mozambique	PAL-I	Tunisia	SECAM-B
Nepal	PAL-BG	Turkey	PAL-B
Netherlands	PAL-BG	UAE	PAL-BG
New Zealand	PAL-B	Uganda	PAL-B
Nicaragua	NTSC	UK	PAL-I
Niger	SECAM-K	Uruguay	PAL-N
Nigeria	PAL-B	USA	NTSC
Norway	PAL-BG	Russia*	SECAM-DK
Oman	PAL-BG	Venezuela	NTSC
Pakistan	PAL-B	Virgin Is, Br	NTSC
Panama	NTSC	Virgin Is, US	NTSC
Paraguay	PAL-N	Yemen	PAL-B
Peru	NTSC	Yugoslavia**	PAL-B
Philippines	NTSC	Zaire	SECAM-K
Poland	SECAM-DK	Zambia	PAL-B
Portugal	PAL-BG	Zanzibar	PAL-I
Puerto Rico	NTSC	Zimbabwe	PAL-B 90
Qatar	PAL-B		
Rumania	PAL-DK	Notes:	
Rwanda	SECAM-K	* Former USSR	
Saudi Arabia	SECAM-BG	** Now separate states	
Senegal	SECAM-K		
Sierra Leone	PAL-B		

Text type   DTP, TYP, WP:
See Body type.

Thermography   Print:
A method of producing a relief effect similar to embossing and die-stamping, but without the high set-up costs involved. The inked image is coated with a powdered resin compound, and passed under a heated grill. The heat causes the resin and the ink to fuse, to swell and rise up in relief.
   See Blind embossing, Copperplate, Die-stamping, Embossing.

Tilt   Film, TV, Video:
To move a camera on its mounting up or down in a vertical arc, following the action during a shoot.
   See Pan.

Tint   Art, DTP, EP, Print:
A tone area of a solid colour, usually achieved with dots or lines. The end result is an apparent shade or pastel of the solid colour. There are endless variations of tint, from regular dot patterns to random ones. In the computerised creation of art, the computer itself can generate a wide variety of dot shapes.
   See Dot gain, Halftone, Screen.

Titling   Film, TV, Video:
Words shown on the screen.

Typescript   Creative:
A typed copy of a text.
   See Copy, Hard copy.

TVR   Media, Media planning and buying, Television: Television rating points (qv).

Typeface   DTP, TYP, WP:
The design of a particular type style, with its own name. Univers, for example, is a typeface.
   See Face, Font.

U-Matic   TV, Video:
A video cassette tape format, using ¾ inch tape. This is high-band, near-broadcast quality, and therefore a very practical format for commercial material. It is excellent for creative presentations, being able to deliver higher quality than VHS (qv).

Upper case   DTP, TYP, Typesetting, WP:
Capital letters in an alphabet, as distinct from lower case (qv) which are small letters.
   See Font, Lower case, Roman.

Verso   Print, Publishing:
A left-hand page; the reverse side of recto (qv).

VFD   Media planning and buying, Media research: Verified Free
      Distribution.
A circulation-auditing service for free newspapers and magazines. Like ABC (qv), it offers publishers and advertisers independently researched, accurate data on the number of copies actually distributed.
   See Circulation, Controlled circulation, Penetration, Profile, Rate card, Reader, Readership, Television rating points, Viewer.

VCR   TV, Video: Video cassette recorder.

VDU   CAD, Computing, DTP, EP, WP: Visual display unit.
A fancy name for a computer screen.

VHS   TV, Video: Video Home System.
A video cassette tape format, using ½ inch tape. The quality is fine for domestic use, but can be a bit sub-standard for top-notch creative presentations. It is nowhere near good enough for use in broadcasting. VHS was conceived and developed by JVC. For some years, several systems competed for the commercial market, including Betamax and Philips 2000; these have long since gone to the graveyard.
   The quality of videotape reproduction depends on four factors: tape speed, head speed, the width of the tape and the quality of the coating material. U-matic uses tape wider than VHS, and has higher head and tape speeds; consequently, the quality of reproduction is higher.

I am not knocking VHS. It is intrinsically a good system, but is sometimes let down by the camcorders (qv) and playback machines used with the cassettes. Digital recording and playback systems will overtake and improve everything now in use.

See U-matic.

Viewer   Media research, Broadcast media:
A viewer is defined as a person in a room with a TV set switched on for at least 15 consecutive seconds. In television terms, in the room means anything from watching attentively, to casually glancing at the screen while doing something else.

See Television rating points.

Visual   Art, Creative, Print, Production:
A layout representing the design of an editorial page, advertisement or piece of print. There are several qualities of visual, from the cheapest, basic scribble to the highly polished version used for boardroom presentations.

Flimsy or scamp:
A pencil or marker rendering of first ideas. Flimsy is so called because the paper usually used for flimsies is itself flimsy; sometimes also called detail paper. I'll buy a drink for the first reader who can provide me with the true origin of the word scamp.

Rough:
A step up from flimsy, indicating that it has developed from the original basic visual. Usually done to a better standard, with readable headlining and recognisable illustrations. Roughs are usually used for internal discussion, and are not for the eyes of clients or directors.

Finished rough:
A good-looking visual of fair quality. Sometimes, clients are presented with visuals of this standard. Many design groups and agencies, however, are unwilling to go forward to client presentation stage with finished roughs, even though they are economical and show a prudent regard for clients' money.

Presentation visuals:
First-class visuals, with typeset headlines and sub-heads.

VO   Film, TV, Video: Voice-over (qv).
The instruction in a script for the voice-over to begin.

Voice-over   Film, TV, Video:
In scripts, this indicates where spoken words are to be heard while action is taking place on the screen. Voice-overs are usually not in synchronisation with an actor's lips, but sometimes linked to the action.

In commercials, voice-overs are used for delivering sales points, comments or thoughts. Widely used while a caption or a still picture is on screen, often accompanying titling (qv).

When the voice and titling are different, it can be very confusing to the viewer. In entertainment, voice-overs are the equivalent of speech bubbles in a printed cartoon.

There is a range of initials denoting who should be speaking the voice-over. MVO = male voice over; FVO = female voice over, and so on.

See Commercial, Still, Titling.

VTR   Video: Videotape recording.

Web
1   Print:
A reel or roll of paper used on rotary presses. The webs used to print national newspapers and magazines can be 9 to 12 miles long. There are also sheet-fed (qv) presses, which use individual sheets of paper.

2   Communications, Computing:
The current popular name for the Internet.

Weight   TYP:
The visual heaviness of a typeface, mainly the amount of ink it puts on the page when printed. Bold type is heavier than light type. Also, the relative thickness of the individual strokes of a type character.

See Bold, Boldface.

Wet on wet   Print:
In state-of-the art colour printing, one colour is printed on top of another before the first is dry.

See Cromalin.

Wet proof   Print, Production:
Using a printing press for proofing, ahead of a print run. This is slow, wasteful and expensive. There are better and more economical ways of doing it; using a special proofing press, or dry proofing.
  See Cromalin, Dry proof, Progressive proof, Proof.

Wipe   Film, TV, Video:
A technique for quitting one shot (qv) and bringing on the next, without cutting, dissolving or fading. This is usually done by reducing the existing shot in a movement from one side of the screen, with the next shot following it without a break. Sometimes done from top to bottom.
  Popular wipes include the implosion, explosions, fragmentation and flying rectangle. Iris, circular and square wipes were favourite techniques during the silent film era. You can sometimes see them in today's commercials, though rarely in entertainment productions.

Wordspacing   Copywriting, DTP, TYP, WP:
The space between individual words in typescript or typesetting.
  See Letterspacing.

WYSIWYG   Computing, DTP, WP: What you see is what you get. A vulgarism from America, meaning that what you see on your computer screen resembles what you will see printed after you hit the print button. Most word-processing packages have a view mode, where you can see how your copy will be printed.

X-height   TYP:
The height of a lower case x. The x is regarded as typical of the lower case characters in a font without ascenders or descenders (qv).

Yellow   Print:
One of the subtractive primary colours used in four-colour process printing.
  See Black, CMYK, Cyan, Magenta, Process colours.

Zero   Copywriting, DTP, TYP, WP:
A word used to differentiate between the characters 'o' or 'O', and the numeral '0'. On screen, a zero is usually differentiated by a dot in the centre of the character, or a slash running through it. In proof-reading, the difference is not easily made, and can cause confusion and errors. Many typesetters refer to zero as nought, null or nuller.

See Character, Monotype, Nought, Null, Proof, Proof-reader, Proof-reader's marks, Quote.

Zoom   Film, TV, Video:
An optical technique which makes an object seem to draw closer to the viewer – zoom in; or draw away – zoom out. This is achieved by using a variable-focus lens, or an optical printer. The zoom lens changes the magnification of the image.

21

Essential Contacts

Addresses, telephone numbers, e-mail addresses and URLs change frequently, sometimes without notice. Please feel free to suggest new entries or updates of existing ones; it will be very helpful for the next edition. All such contributions will be acknowledged and attributed. Please send updates to the author at Kogan Page.

ABC//electronic
Electronic Media Audits Ltd
Norman House, 207–09 High Street
Berkhamsted, Hertfordshire HP4 1AD
Contact: Richard Foan
Tel: (01442) 870 800
Fax: (01442) 877 409
e-mail: raf@abc.org.uk
Web: www.abc.org.uk
An associate company of the Audit Bureau of Circulations.

The Advertising Archives
45 Lyndale Avenue
London NW2 2QB
Tel: (020) 7435 6540
Fax: (020) 7794 6584

The Advertising Association
Abford House, 15 Wilton Road
London SW1V 1NJ
Tel: (020) 7828 4831
Fax: (020) 7931 0376
Web: www.adassoc.org.uk

The Advertising Creative Circle
22 Poland Street
London W1V 3DD
Tel: (020) 7734 9334

The Advertising Standards Authority (ASA)
Brook House, 2–16 Torrington Place
London WC1E 7HN
Tel: (020) 7580 5555
Web: www.asa.org.uk

The Adwomen
18–24 Westbourne Grove
London W2 5RH
Tel: (020) 7221 1819
Fax: (020) 7221 2707

Agfa-Gevaert Ltd
Business Group and Graphic Systems
27 Great West Road
Brentford, Middlesex TW8 9AX
Tel: (020) 8231 4922
Fax: (020) 8231 4957
Chromapress and IntelliStream digital printing systems.

Association of Business Advertising Agencies
Hammer Business Communications
23–28 Great Russell Street
London WC1B 3PX
Tel: (020) 7753 0005
Fax: (020) 7753 0036

The Audit Bureau of Circulations Ltd (ABC)
Black Prince Yard, 207–09 High Street
Berkhamsted, Herts HP4 1AD
Tel: (01442) 870 800
Fax: (01442) 877 407
e-mail: abcpost@abc.org.uk
Web: www.abc.org.uk

BARB
Broadcasters' Audience Research Board
18 Dering Street
London W1R 9AF
Tel: (020) 8741 9110
Web: www.barb.co.uk

BMRA
British Market Research Association
16 Creighton Avenue
London N10 1NU
Tel: (020) 8374 4095
Fax: (020) 8883 9953
e-mail: admin@bmra.org.uk
Web: www.bmra.org.uk

The British Association of Industrial Editors
3 Locks Yard, High Street
Sevenoaks, Kent YN13 1LT
Tel: (01732) 459331
Membership: editors of house journals. Entry by examination.
Journal: *BAIE News*.

British Library Business Information Service
25 Southampton Buildings
London WC2A 1AW
Tel: (020) 7412 7454
Fax: (020) 7412 7453
Web: www.bl.uk

Broadcast Advertising Clearance Centre (BACC)
200 Grays Inn Road
London WC1X 8HF
Tel: (020) 7843 8000
Fax: (020) 7843 8158
Checking and clearance of radio and TV commercials.

Broadcasting Standards Commission
7 The Sanctuary
London SW1P 3JS
Tel: (020) 7233 0544
Fax: (020) 7233 0397
e-mail: bsc@bsc.org.uk
Web: www.bsc.org.uk

CACI
CACI House, Kensington Village, Avonmore Road
London W14 8TS
Tel: (020) 7602 6000
Fax: (020) 7603 5862
e-mail: marketing@caci.co.uk
Web: www.caci.co.uk

CAM
The Communication, Advertising and Marketing Education
Foundation
Abford House, 15 Wilton Road
London SW1V 1NJ
Tel: (020) 7828 7506
Fax: (020) 7976 5140
Web: www.cam.co.uk
Certificate and diploma examinations. Vocational examination for
those working in British communications industry. Holders of
CIM Diploma exempt from Certificate, except PR, if they wish to
take CAM Diploma in PR.

CAM Graduates Association
Abford House, 15 Wilton Road
London SW1V 1NJ
Tel: (020) 7828 7506
Fax: (020) 7976 5140

The Chartered Institute of Marketing (CIM)
Moor Hall, Cookham
Maidenhead, Berkshire SL6 9QH
Tel: (01628) 427 500
Fax: (01628) 427 499
Web: www.cim.co.uk
Publications: *Marketing Business, Solutions*
Professional body for 65,000 members worldwide. Professional
and vocational qualifications. Activities include legal and other
advisory services; library, information and research services;
training in marketing, sales, strategy and associated techniques.

The Chartered Institute of Marketing
CIM Central London
Web: www.cim-central-london.org
Publications: *CIM Central London News*, e-newsletter
The flagship branch of the CIM; over 4000 members. Activities
include branch events with key speakers on professional issues
and topics, CPD training events, social events, student support
(CIM, MBA etc), "Marketing 101" Web-based professional discus-
sion and information forum, business and career networking.

Commercial Radio Companies Association Ltd
77 Shaftsbury Avenue
London W1V 7AD
Tel: (020) 7306 2603
Fax: (020) 7470 0062

Cinema Advertising Association
12 Golden Square
London W1R 3AF
Publications: CAVIAR Cinema and Video Industry Audience
Research, UK Advertising Admissions Monitor, Cinema Coverage
and Frequency Guide.

Committee of Advertising Practice (CAP)
2 Torrington Place
London WC1E 7HW
Tel: (020) 7580 5555
Fax: (020) 7631 3051

Web: www.asa.org.uk
Publications: The British Codes of Advertising and Sales Promotion.

Confederation of British Industry
Centre Point, 103 New Oxford Street
London WC1A 1DU
Tel: (020) 7397 7400
Fax: (020) 7240 0988
e-mail: enquiry.desk@cbi.org.uk
Web: www.cbi.org.uk

Council of Outdoor Specialists (COS)
Posterscope
55 North Wharf Road
London W2 1LA
Tel: (020) 7724 7244
Fax: (020) 7724 7620

Data Protection Registrar (DPR)
Wycliffe House, Water Lane
Wilmslow, Cheshire SK9 5AF
Tel: (01625) 545 745
Fax: (01625) 524 510
e-mail: data@wycliffe.demon.co.uk
Web: www.dpr.gov.uk

The Debating Group
196 Verulam Court, Woolmead Avenue
London NW9 7AZ
Tel & fax: (020) 8202 5854

Department of Trade & Industry (DTI)
151 Buckingham Palace Road
London SW1W 9SS
Tel: (020) 7215 5000
Fax: (020) 7222 0612
e-mail: dti.enquiries@imsv.dti.gov.uk
Web: www.dti.gov.uk

Direct Mail Accreditation & Recognition Centre (DMARC)
Haymarket House, 1 Oxendon Street
London SW1Y 4EE
Tel: (020) 7766 4430
Fax: (020) 7976 1886

Direct Mail Information Service
5 Carlisle Street
London W1V 6JX
Tel: (020) 7494 0483
Fax: (020) 7494 0455
Web: www.dmis.co.uk

Direct Marketing Association (UK) Ltd (DMA)
5th floor, Haymarket House, 1 Oxendon Street
London SW1Y 4EE
Tel: (020) 7321 2525
Fax: (020) 7321 0191
e-mail: dma@dma.org.uk
Web: www.dma.org.uk

DuPont (UK) Ltd
Imaging Systems Department
Wedgwood Way
Stevenage, Herts SG1 4QN
Tel: (01438) 734523
Fax: (01483) 734522

Enterprise Identity Group
6 Mercer Street
London WC2H 9QA
Tel: (020) 7574 4000
Fax: (020) 7574 4100

European Marketing Association
18 St Peters Steps
Brixham, Devon TQ5 9TE
Tel: (01803) 859 575

Independent Television Commission (ITC)
33 Foley Street
London W1P 7LB
Tel: (020) 7255 3000
Fax: (020) 7306 7800
e-mail: publicaffairs@itc.org.uk
Web: www.itc.org.uk
Journal: *Spectrum*

Independent Television Network Centre
200 Grays Inn Road
London WC1X 8HF
Tel: (020) 7843 8000
Fax: (020) 7843 8158

Indigo UK
Suite 1, Awberry Court, Croxley Business Park
Watford, Herts , WD1 8YJ
Tel: (01923) 242 402
Fax: (01923) 242 412
Web: www.indigonet.com
Digital printing presses and equipment

Institute of Direct Marketing
1 Park Road
Teddington, Middlesex TW11 0AR
Tel: (020) 8977 5705
Fax: (020) 8943 2535
Web: http://tendou.corpex.com/users/idm

Institute of Practitioners in Advertising
44 Belgrave Square
London SW1X 8QS
Tel: (020) 7235 7020
Fax: (020) 7245 9904
e-mail: mark@ipa.co.uk
Web: www.ipa.co.uk
The professional representative body for advertising agencies.

Institute of Public Relations
The Old Trading House, 15 Northburgh Street
London EC1V 0PR
Tel: (020) 7253 5151
Membership by age and experience plus CAM Diploma or its
equivalent. Journal: *Public Relations*. Annual Sword of Excellence
awards.

Institute of Sales Promotion
Arena House, 66–68 Pentonville Road
London N1 9HS
Tel: (020) 7837 5340
Fax: (020) 7837 5326
Web: www.isp.org.uk

IPSOS-RSL Ltd
Media research specialists
Kings House, Kymberley Road
Harrow, Middlesex HA1 1PT
Tel: (020) 8861 8000
Fax: (020) 8861 5515
Web: www.ipsos.com

ISBA
Incorporated Society of British Advertisers
44 Hertford Street
London W1Y 8AE
Tel: (020) 7499 7502
Fax: (020) 7629 5355
Web: www.isba.org.uk

The Independent Television Commission
33 Foley Street
London W1P 7LB
Tel: (020) 7255 3000
Fax: (020) 7306 7800
Web: www.itc.org.uk

ISDesign
14 The Squirrels
Pinner, Middx HA5 3BD
Tel: (020) 8866 0856
Fax: (020) 8866 2634
e-mail: ivan@isdesign.co.uk
Contact: Ivan Svetlik MCSD
Graphic design, corporate identity, packaging, print and production.

JICREG
Joint Industry Committee for Regional Press Research
Bloomsbury House, 74–77 Gt Russell Street
London WC1B 3DA
Tel: (020) 7636 7014
Web: www.jicreg.co.uk

Letraset UK
195–203 Waterloo Road
London SE1 8XJ
Tel: (020) 7928 7551

LCCI
The London Chamber of Commerce and Industry
Examinations Board
Athena House, Station Road
Sidcup, Kent DA15 7BJ
Tel: (020) 8302 0261
Fax: (020) 8302 4169
Web: www.lccieb.org.uk
Third Level Certificate Examinations in Advertising, Marketing, Public Relations, Selling and Sales Management (with Diplomas for passes in three or four subjects taken at the same time). Diploma in Management Studies if three subjects passed at different times.

The London College of Printing
Elephant & Castle
London SE1
Tel: (020) 7735 8484
A constituent college of the London Institute.

London Management Training Centre
166 Upper Richmond Road
London SW15 2SH
Tel: (01342) 326704
Specialises in business training for overseas management, including business, marketing, advertising, PR, finance and human resources.

Maiden Outdoor
128 Buckingham Palace Road
London SW1W 9SA
Tel: (020) 7838 4000 and 7838 4040
Fax: (020) 7838 4002
Web: www.maiden.co.uk

The Mailing Preference Service
5 Reef House, Plantation Wharf
London SW11 3UF
Tel: (020) 7738 1625
Fax: (020) 7978 4918

The Mail Order Protection Scheme (MOPS)
16 Tooks Court
London EC4A 1LB
Operated by publishers of the national press.

The Market Research Society
15 Northburgh Street
London EC1V 0AH
Tel: (020) 7490 4911
Fax: (020) 7490 0608
e-mail: info@marketresearch.org.uk
Web: www.marketresearch.org.uk

The Marketing Society
St George's House, 3–5 Pepys Road
London SW20 8NJ.
Tel: (020) 8879 3464
Fax: (020) 8879 0362
e-mail: info@marketing-society.org.uk
Web: www.marketing-society.org.uk

Mintel International Group
18–19 Long Acre
London EC1A 9HE
Tel: (020) 7606 4533
Fax: (020) 7606 5932
e-mail: enquiries@mintel.co.uk
Web: www.mintel.co.uk

National Readership Surveys Ltd
42 Drury Lane
London WC2B 5RT
Tel: (020) 7632 2915
Fax: (020) 7632 2916
e-mail: anyname@nrs.co.uk
Web: www.nrs.co.uk

NOP Research Group
Ludgate House, 245 Blackfriars Road
London SE1 9UL
Tel: (020) 7890 9099
Fax: (020) 7890 9744
Web: www.nopres.co.uk

Office of Telecommunications (OFTEL)
50 Ludgate Hill
London EC4M 7JJ
Tel: (020) 7634 8700
Fax: (020) 7634 8943
e-mail: crs.oftel@gtnet.gov.uk

ONdigital
PO Box 4, Plymouth, PL1 3XU
Tel: (0808) 100 0101
Web: www.ondigital.co.uk

The Outdoor Advertising Association (OAA)
Summit House, 27 Sale Place
London W2 1YR
Tel: (020) 7973 0315
Fax: (020) 7973 0318
e-mail: mcarrington@oaa.org.uk
Web: www.oaa.org.uk

The Oxford University Press
Walton Street
Oxford OX2 6DP
www.oup.co.uk

POSTAR
Summit House
27 Sale Place
London W2 1YR
Tel: (020) 7479 9700
Fax: (020) 7298 8034
e-mail: info@postar.co.uk
Web: www.postar.co.uk

PR Newswire Europe
Communications House, 210 Old Street
London EC1V 9UN
Tel: (020) 7490 8111
Fax: (020) 7454 5322
e-mail: research@prnewswire.co.uk
Website: www.prnewswire.co.uk

Public Relations Consultants Association (PRCA)
Willow House, Willow Place
London SW1P 1JH
Tel: (020) 7233 6026
Fax: (020) 7828 4797
Web: www.martex.co.uk/prca
Corporate membership. Overseas Associates.
Publications: *Public Relations Year Book, What's Happening at the PRCA* (newsletters), Guidance Papers (training), Briefing Papers (legal).

The Radio Advertising Bureau
77 Shaftesbury Avenue
London W1V 7AD
Tel: (020) 7306 2500
Fax: (020) 7306 2505
e-mail: rab@rab.co.uk
Web: www.rab.co.uk
Marketing arm of the commercial radio industry. Provides independent information to advertisers.

Radio Advertising Clearance Centre
Radio House, 46 Westbourne Grove
London W2 5SH
Tel: (020) 7727 2646
Fax: (020) 7229 0352
e-mail: adclear@racc.co.uk

The Radio Authority
Holbrook House, 14 Great Queen Street
London WC2B 5DG
Tel: (020) 7430 2724
Fax: (020) 7405 7062
e-mail: info@radioauthority.org.uk
Web: www.radioauthority.org.uk

RAJAR
Radio Joint Audience Research Ltd
81 Oxford Street
London W1D 2EU
Tel: (020) 7903 5350
Fax: (020) 7903 5351
e-mail: info@rajar.co.uk
Web: www.rajar.co.uk

Royal Mail Direct Marketing Department
Room 221, Royal Mail House, 148/166 Old Street
London EC1V 9HQ
Tel: (020) 7250 2346
Fax: (020) 7250 2366
Publications include: *The Complete Guide to Advertising Your Business by Post, The Direct Mail Guide, Postal Services for Business.*

Standard Rate & Data Service (SRDS)
1700 Higgins Road
Des Plaines, Illinois 60018–5605
United States of America
Tel: (847) 375 5183
Fax: (847) 375 5009
Monthly media directories, covering US newspapers, consumer magazines and business publications.

Telephone Preference Service (TPS)
5th Floor, Haymarket House, 1 Oxendon Street
London SW1Y 4EE
Tel: (020) 7766 4422
Fax: (020) 7976 1886
e-mail: tps@dma.org.uk
Web: www.dma.org.uk

Training Resources & Courses
63 Cheyneys Avenue, Edgware , HA8 6SD
Tel: (020) 8951 3732
e-mail: danyad@cwcom.net
A faculty of professional trainers, consultants and practitioners,
providing training across the whole range of marketing, management media and business disciplines.

VFD
Verified Free Distribution
Black Prince Yard, 207 High Street
Berkhamsted, Herts HP4 1AD
Tel: (01442) 870 800
Fax: (01442) 877 409
Web: www.abc.org.uk
Part of the Audit Bureau of Circulations.

Winmark
15 Berghem Mews, Blythe Road
London W14 0HN
Tel: (020) 7603 8890
Fax: (020) 7603 8226
e-mail: research@winmark.co.uk
Web: www.winmark.co.uk
Market research and business analysis.

Women in Advertising & Communications
Guardian Newspapers, 119 Farringdon Road
London EC1R 3GR
Tel: (020) 7278 2332
Fax: (020) 7837 0651

22

Essential Reading

Note: Marketing communications, and its design, production and print technology, is in a state of constant change. Much of that change works for the benefit and greater profitability of the industry and its customers.

To keep in touch with the movements in the business, check if there have been up-dates since this book went to press. Infrequent publications most likely to have been up-dated are marked with an asterisk.

Language
The Concise Oxford English Dictionary, Oxford University Press.
Hart's Rules for Compositors and Readers, Oxford University Press.

Design, layout and typography
Campbell, Alastair *The Designer's Handbook*, Macdonald Orbis, London.*
White, Jan V (1988) *Graphic Design for the Electronic Age*, Watson-Guptill Publications, New York.*
The Creative Handbook (annual), Cahners Publishing Co, London.

Production and typography:
Bann, David *The Print Production Handbook*, Macdonald, London.*
Pocket Pal, International Paper Co, Memphis TN 38197, USA.*
The DuPont Series on Print Production and Reprographics (1998), DuPont (UK) Ltd, Stevenage, Herts.
Evans, Robin B (1988) *Production and Creativity in Advertising*, Pitman, London.*

Marketing

Oliver, Gordon *Marketing Today*, Prentice Hall, New York and London.

Marketing Handbook (annual), Hollis Directories, Teddington, Middlesex.

Advertising

Davis, Martyn P (1997) *Successful Advertising: Key Alternative Approaches*, Cassell, London.

Hopkins, Claude *Scientific Advertising*, MacGibbon & Kee, London.

Jefkins, F and Yadin, D (2000) *Advertising*, Pearson Education, Harlow

Ogilvy, David *Ogilvy on Advertising*, Pan Books, London.

Ogilvy, David *Confessions of an Advertising Man*, Atheneum, New York.

Public relations

Jefkins, Frank and Yadin, Daniel (1997) *Public Relations*, Pitman.

Media

British Rate & Data (Monthly), Maclean Hunter Ltd, Barnet, Herts.

Davis, Martyn P (1997) *The Effective Use of Advertising Media*, Century Business, London.

Proof correcting

British Standard BS 5261: Part 2 1976.

Copy Preparation and Proof Correction – Specification of Typographic Requirements, Marks for Copy Preparation and Proof Correction, Proofing Procedure, The British Standards Institution.

Codes of practice

The British Codes of Advertising and Sales Promotion, The Advertising Standards Authority.

The ITC Code of Advertising Standards and Practice, Independent Television Commission.

The Radio Authority Code of Advertising Standards and Practice and Programme Sponsorship, The Radio Authority.

Index

NB: numbers in *italics* indicate charts, figures or tables